The Campus History Series

WORCESTER STATE UNIVERSITY

On the Cover: Students are pictured in the Great Hall of the Worcester Normal School. Used for assemblies, announcements, and lessons, the Great Hall was the main room of the school where all students and faculty members could meet. This view is of what speakers might have seen looking out into the audience. (Worcester State University [WSU] Archives and Special Collections.)

Cover Background: Worcester Normal School students enjoy the weather as they sit on the campus grounds behind the main building at the turn of the 20th century. (WSU Archives and Special Collections.)

The Campus History Series

WORCESTER STATE UNIVERSITY

THOMAS E. CONROY
FOREWORD BY PRES. BARRY M. MALONEY

ARCADIA PUBLISHING

ISBN 978-1-4671-2844-5

Published by Arcadia Publishing
Charleston, South Carolina

Printed in the United States of America

Library of Congress Control Number: 2017958935

For all general information, please contact Arcadia Publishing:
Telephone 843-853-2070
Fax 843-853-0044
E-mail sales@arcadiapublishing.com
For customer service and orders:
Toll-Free 1-888-313-2665

Visit us on the Internet at www.arcadiapublishing.com

To all members of the
Worcester State University community,
past, present, and future,
especially to its students and faculty

Contents

FOREWORD

In 1874, Worcester State University's foundation was laid when the Worcester Normal School arose on St. Anne's Hill. At the time, Bay Stater Horace Mann's public school movement converged with an influx of immigrant children, whose parents worked in the mills and machine shops that transformed Worcester from a rural town into an industrial-era powerhouse. Those public schools needed well-educated teachers, and we provided them.

From the outset, our doors were open to the many, not just the few; we offered excellent academic preparation; and we strove to fill a regional workforce need. These founding principles remain a central part of who we are today as a public, full-scale liberal arts and sciences university with more than 6,000 students in the city of Worcester.

Then and now, we enrolled both women and men from a variety of backgrounds. Two early graduates, Jennie Clough (1878) and Sarah Wilson (1894), were African Americans who went on to teach in Worcester's public schools. Wilson taught 49 years at Belmont Street School and was a community leader on social justice issues.

In the intervening decades, as academic programs expanded, our alumni impacted fields as diverse as municipal and state government, the financial industry, the arts, photography, and medicine, even as our teachers, police officers, and health-care professionals helped communities thrive.

I am humbled by their achievements and those of the ten presidents who served before me. My predecessors led the way as we changed to meet the needs of the region, from the normal school to a teachers' college, to a liberal arts state college, to a university with both arts and sciences.

In many ways, we are still a teachers' college—in fact, close to half of Worcester Public School educators are alumni—and we are so much more, the fortunate result of the gains we have made these past 144 years.

Yet we remain rooted in the region. About 85 percent of our graduates remain in Massachusetts. Even as Worcester State expands their horizons, so many of them ultimately determine that the best horizon is the one that's rimmed by Worcester's hills.

I am pleased that a book chronicling the history of Worcester State has come to fruition under my tenure, and that it is author, professor, and chair of our Urban Studies Department Thomas E. Conroy, PhD, who has brought that history to the printed page.

—Pres. Barry M. Maloney

ACKNOWLEDGMENTS

Works of this nature frequently require the assistance and expertise of many people. As such, I would like to thank them here for their efforts, all of which have made this a richer enterprise.

Pres. Barry M. Maloney has been a strong supporter of this project from the beginning as has the Worcester State Foundation. Other institutional supporters include Thomas McNamara, the vice president of university advancement, and Dr. Lois Wims, provost and vice president of academic affairs. Members of the board of trustees—especially George Albro and Maryanne Hammond—have also contributed images and provided contextual information.

Many Worcester State University offices and departments have been especially helpful in locating materials and generous in sharing them for this project. To that end, I need to recognize Karen Sharpe, assistant vice president of development and university advancement; Sandra Olson, director of facilities; Nikki Narducci, sports information director in the athletic department; Tim Sullivan, associate dean of student affairs and director of the office of student involvement and leadership development (retired); Nathan Herrera, marketing coordinator; Joanne Jaber Gauvin, Urban Action Institute; Mary Flibbert, Department of Urban Studies; and Renae Lias Claffey, assistant to the president for campus communications.

Deserving of special recognition is university archivist Ross Griffiths. Ross lent freely of his knowledge, inquisitive spirit, and growing collection that he oversees. Readers can help preserve Worcester State history by donating their WSU-related materials to the archives. For more information please contact the archivist at 508-929-8391.

Unless otherwise noted, all images in this book appear courtesy of WSU Archives and Special Collections.

My faculty colleagues, particularly those in my department—Shiko Gathuo, Madeline Campbell, Timothy Murphy, and Adam Saltsman—are supportive and collaborative academics with whom I am privileged to work. So, too, are my students, in particular, Peter Peloquin, who served as my research assistant for the project.

Finally, I thank my family: Robyn, whose help on the project amounted to much more than letting me spend extra time at work; Thomas, who has long been a close conspirator in life and learning; and Evelyn, new on the scene but unconsciously determined to remind me what is most important.

INTRODUCTION

What is today known as Worcester State University has had four different names in its evolution from a predominantly teacher-training school to a comprehensive liberal arts and sciences university. That evolution, approaching 150 years in the making, is still taking place.

In its first incarnation, it was founded as the State Normal School at Worcester in 1874. The first classes numbered fewer than 100 students and there were five faculty members including E. Harlow Russell, the principal. That was downtown, slightly east of the urban core at the time, high atop a hill that looked down at the city center. However, as that city center sprawled east and the original buildings aged, leaders from the school, city, and community began to explore moving the normal school to a less densely populated area of the city.

By the early 1930s, plans were in place for a fundamental shift in the school's destiny. Curricular changes had already been made that expanded degree options. A new building was erected on the west side of the city. Accordingly, school operations, classroom materials, books, and personnel moved to the new campus during the winter break of 1931. The next year, the school was opened, dedicated, and rechristened Worcester State Teachers College (WSTC).

For the next three decades, the school expanded its physical plant and enhanced its academic program at the new site. Although it retained its teacher-training functions, it had become more of a liberal arts and sciences school. Consequently, another name change occurred that was illustrative of the evolution. In 1963, the word "teachers" was dropped from the institutional name, leaving it as Worcester State College.

During the half century after that name change, Worcester State College continued to grow as it added new academic and student spaces, enhanced academic programs, and conferred graduate degrees. Dormitories, two new science buildings, a Student Center, and a library were erected while existing facilities were renovated. By 2010, the Massachusetts Legislature made all the state colleges into universities, recognizing a shift that had actually been underway for decades. As such, the fourth iteration of the school occurred as the onetime teacher-training institution, the Worcester Normal School, became Worcester State University, a comprehensive public liberal arts and sciences university.

One

The Evolving Campus

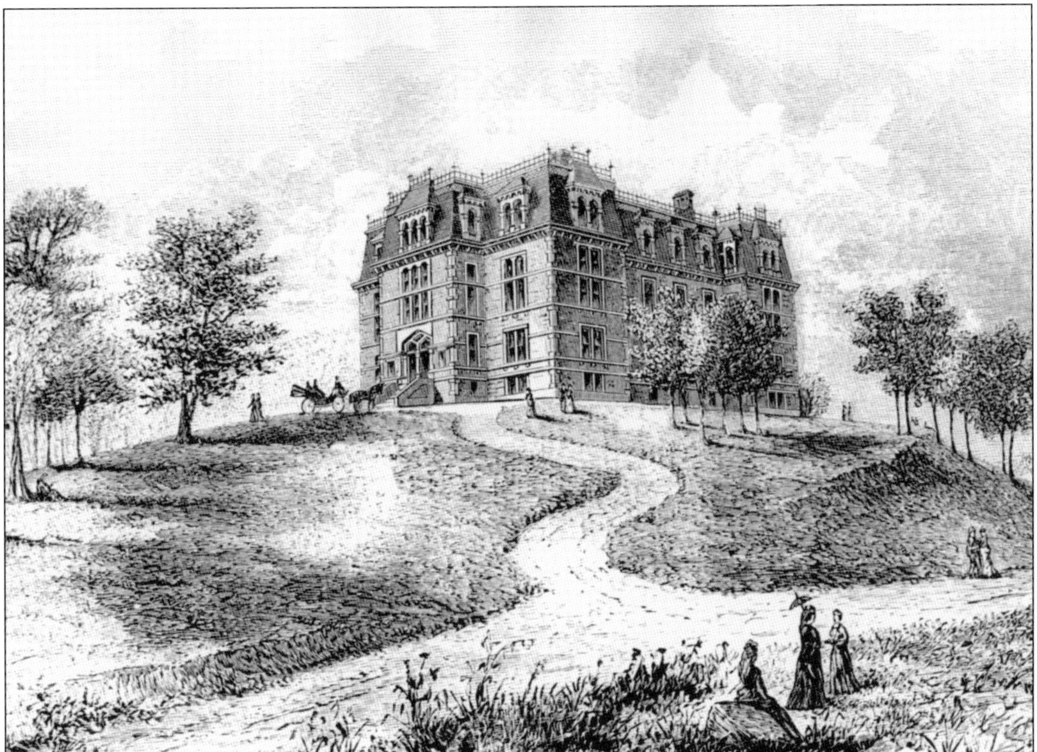

The Worcester Normal School opened in 1874, four years after the idea began to gain traction among area educators and local and state politicians. Worcester school officials favored its creation because the state-funded school would replace a city-run teacher-training program operating out of the Dix Street School. What would become Worcester State University more than a century later was born.

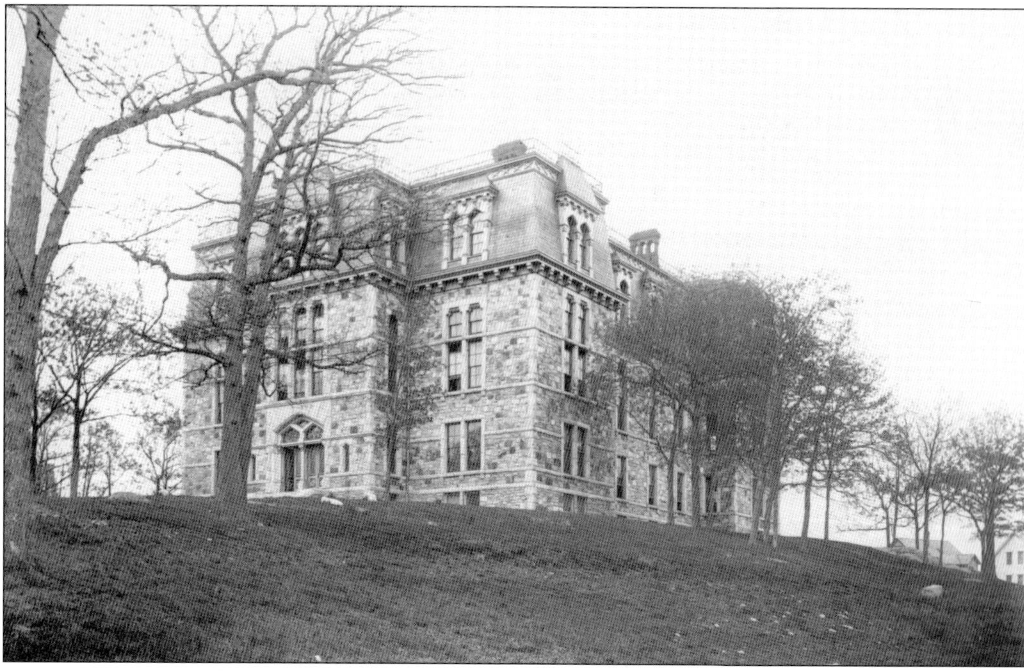

In 1871, the Massachusetts Legislature appropriated $60,000 for the school building, granted the endeavor five acres of state hospital land, and required the city to contribute $15,000 to the project. Built to accommodate 200 students, the school opened in this four-story structure with classrooms, labs, a library, common spaces, and a meeting hall. The accomplished faculty taught classes here; apprentice teachers worked in city schools under faculty supervision.

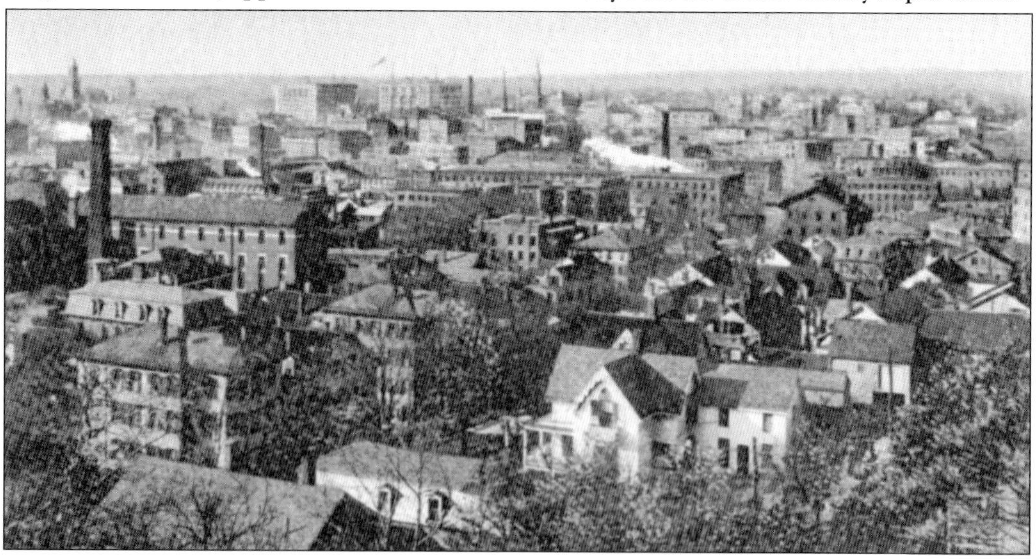

Nearly all of the previous normal schools—Framingham (1839), Westfield (1839), Bridgewater (1840), and Salem (1854)—were built in urban areas because their growing populations had greater need for well-trained teachers than rural counterparts did. While the Normal School at Worcester sat at what was then the suburban edge of the rapidly expanding city center, those on Normal Hill gazed down at a bustling urban core. (WSU CityLab, Vincent "Jake" Powers Archives.)

The area on which the original campus was built went by many names over time, including Hospital Hill (it was once Worcester State Hospital land), Normal Hill (the location of the normal school), and St. Anne's Hill (named after the neighboring Catholic Church, St. Anne's). The church's spires are seen dominating the skyline in this image taken from the bricked path that connected the academic building to the normal school's dormitory.

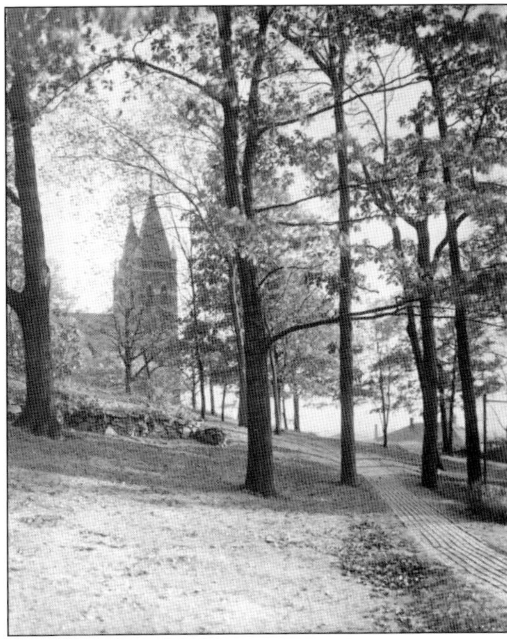

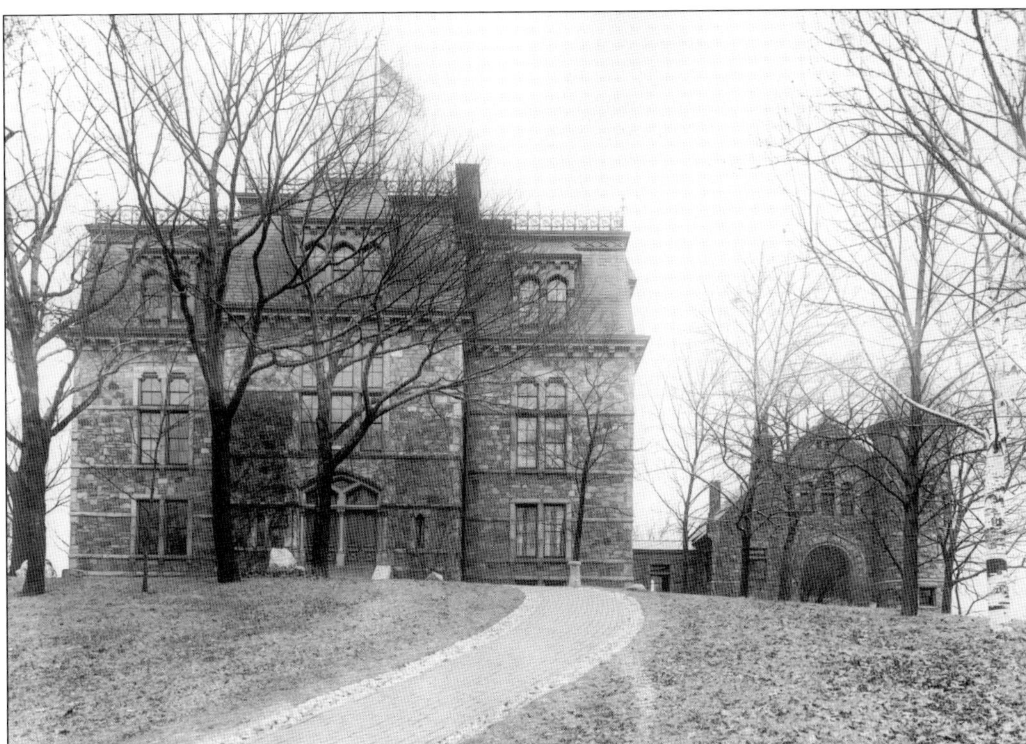

By the 1890s, increasing enrollments and continuing developments in elementary and secondary education required an expansion of the normal school's physical plant. A series of new structures were erected in a relatively short period, including a new gym in 1894. Attached to the main building by a short passageway, the new building was equipped to train students in physical education coursework as well as to provide them with recreational outlets.

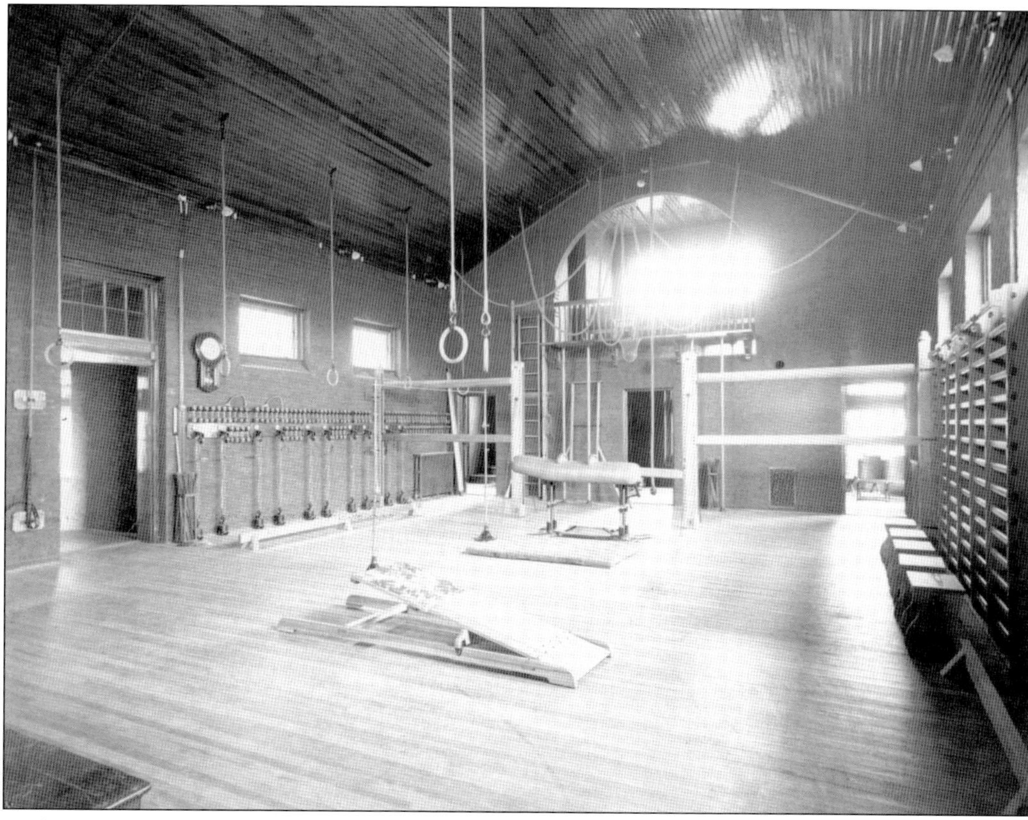

In the late 19th century, notions of physical education, group exercise, and organized recreation were being transformed. Inherited ideas emphasized repetitive calisthenic-based exercise occasionally with apparatus. YMCAs in the Pioneer Valley challenged that in 1891 and 1895 with the creation of basketball and volleyball—faster-paced team-based recreations. The normal school gym, built for the former, was made to accommodate the latter over time.

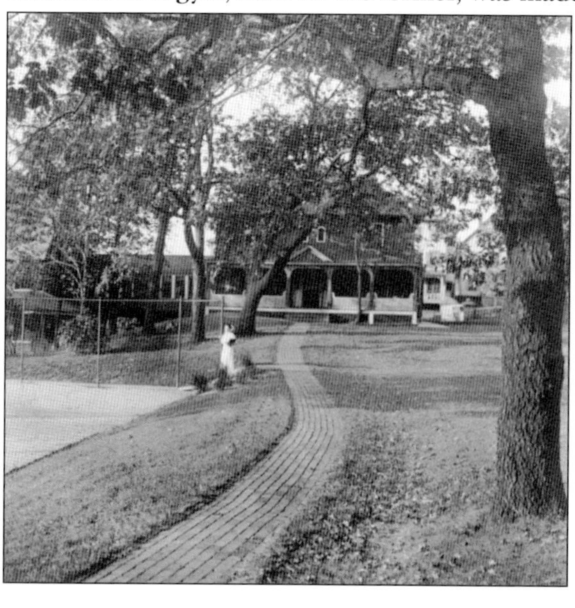

This image shows Worcester State University's first dormitory, Stoddard Terrace, as built in 1891. Named for Elijah Benjamin Stoddard, a lawyer, politician, and longtime supporter of the school, the building housed 20 female students and faculty members. Attached to the principal's house to the west, Stoddard Terrace did not offer regular "table board" (meals), which residents obtained from nearby families. The annual cost to stay in the dorm was $38 in 1901.

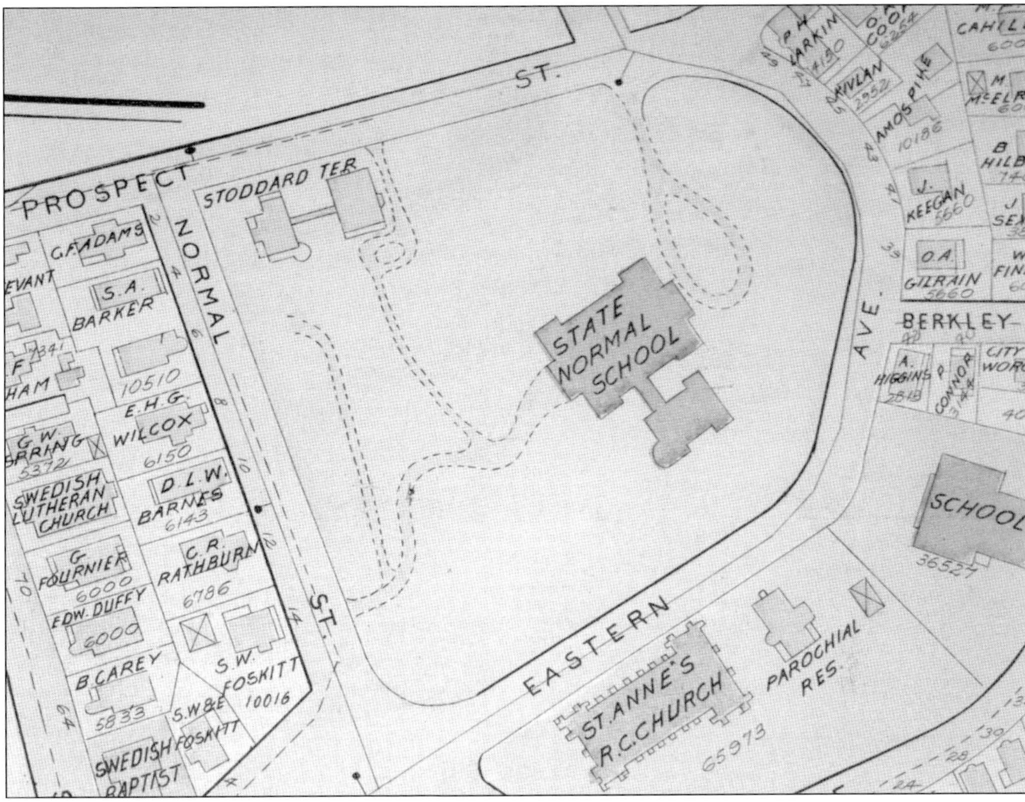

When Worcester's normal school was created, there was little development in the Hospital Hill area. By 1900, the city core was sprawling down Shrewsbury Street on the south and Belmont Street on the north, creating an increasingly populated area urban landscape around the school. To the west was the county jail, and to the southwest stood the city's central train depot, the first Union Station. Factories and worker housing lay throughout. (WSU CityLab, Vincent "Jake" Powers Archives.)

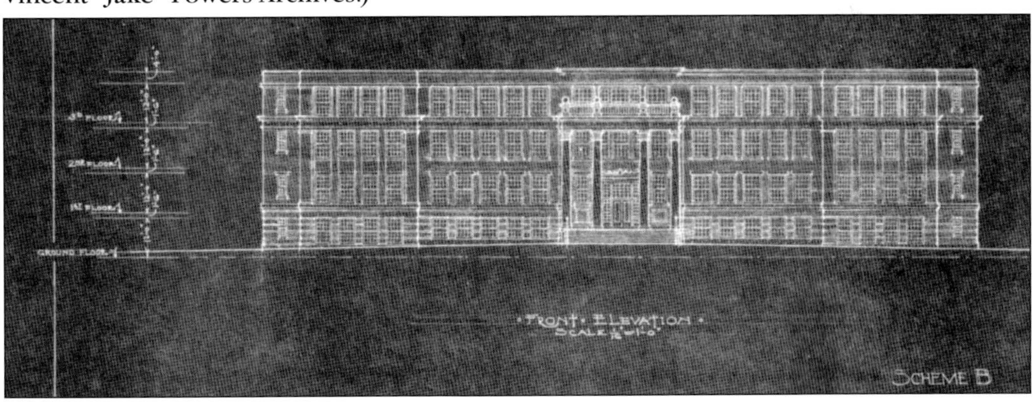

Although achieved in 1932, the move to the school's current location had been under way for years. In 1912, Pres. Francis Lane thought the school needed to expand. By 1930, the state was assessing whether the farmhouse on the new site could be converted to student dormitories. When it proved infeasible, plans to destroy the farmhouse and replace it with a grand school structure moved forward, but even these plans were not entirely realized; note that the blueprints call for a full fourth floor. (WSU Office of University Advancement.)

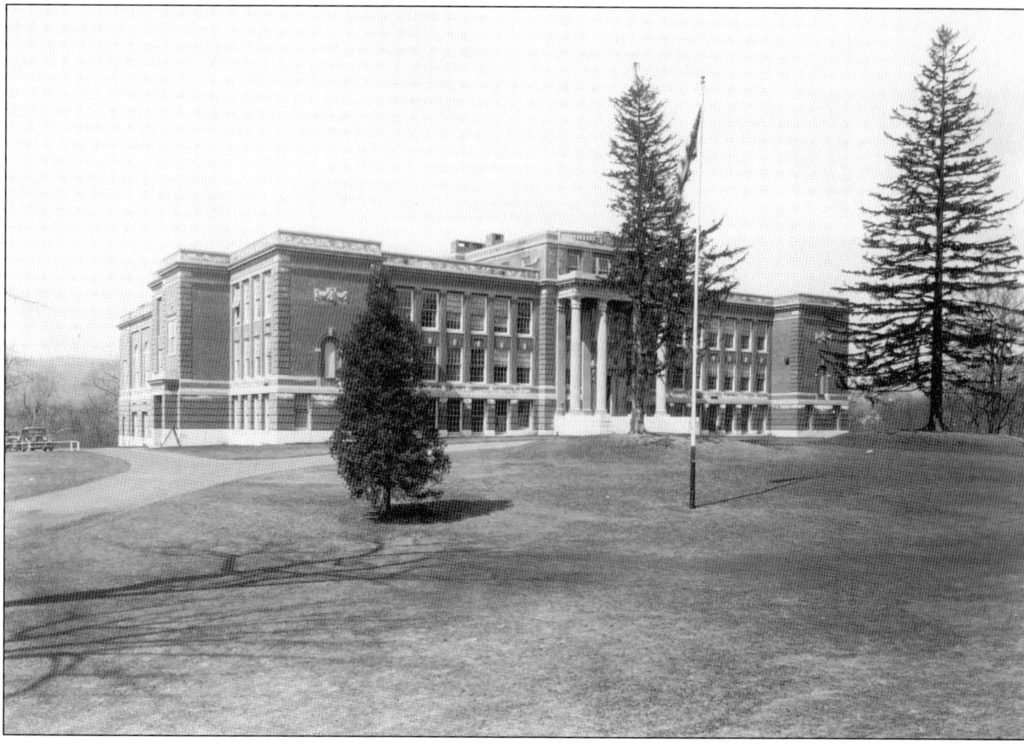

The new building was a three-story structure with all it needed except dormitories. Academic spaces and administrative offices occupied the main building, the library was atop of the structure, and two wings—one with a gym and another with a main assembly hall and stage—protruded from the building's rear facade. Another significant change was to drop "normal school" from the name and become what it had already moved toward: Worcester State Teachers College.

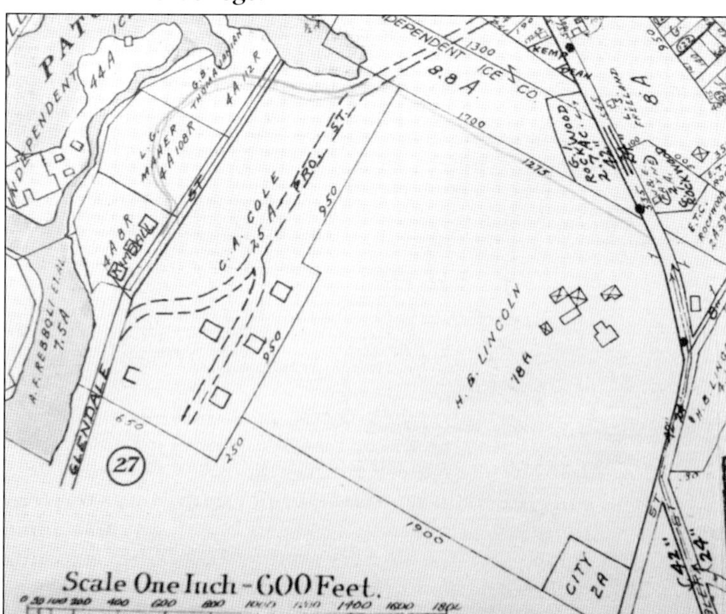

The land Worcester State University occupies today began with a 20-acre parcel on Chandler Street called, in part, Willow Farm. George Rockwood sold it to the city, which in turn transferred it to the state to relocate the normal school. Rockwood, a supporter of the school, donated more land in 1942, comprising all of Willow Farm and more, which has allowed the university to expand over time. (Worcester Public Library.)

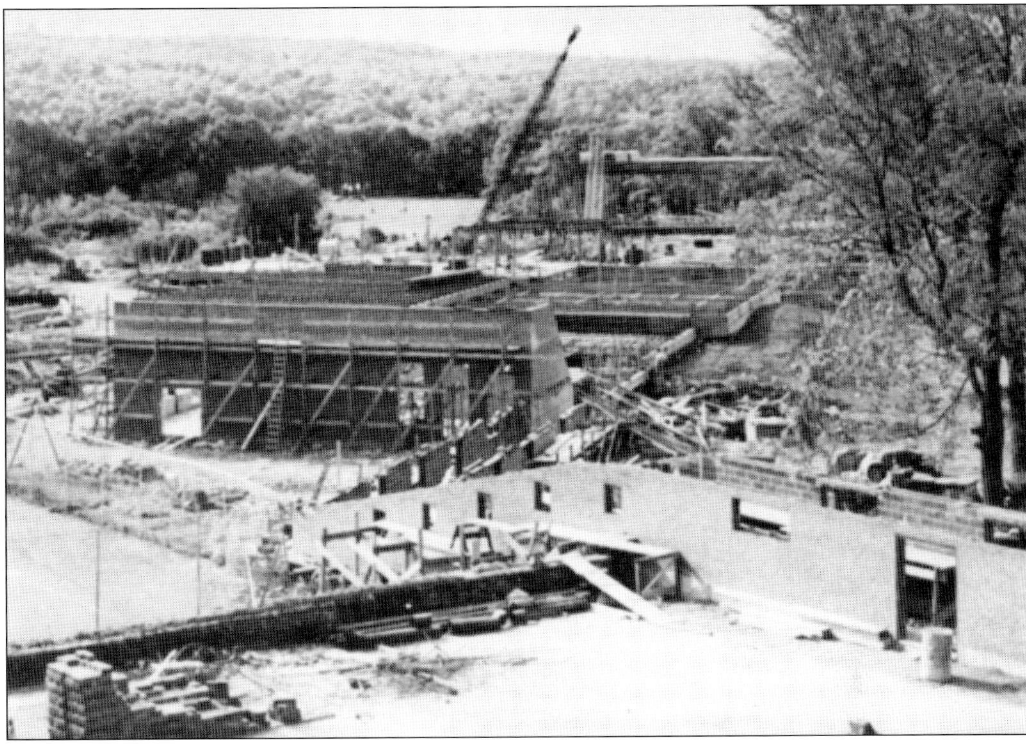

The first major building added since the school moved onto its new main building and campus was a multipurpose structure that contained a gymnasium and athletic facilities, a cafeteria, library, student spaces, faculty offices, and classrooms. When it was built, there were only two main varsity sports: basketball and baseball. But plenty of recreational sports and physical education classes promised to keep the building busy.

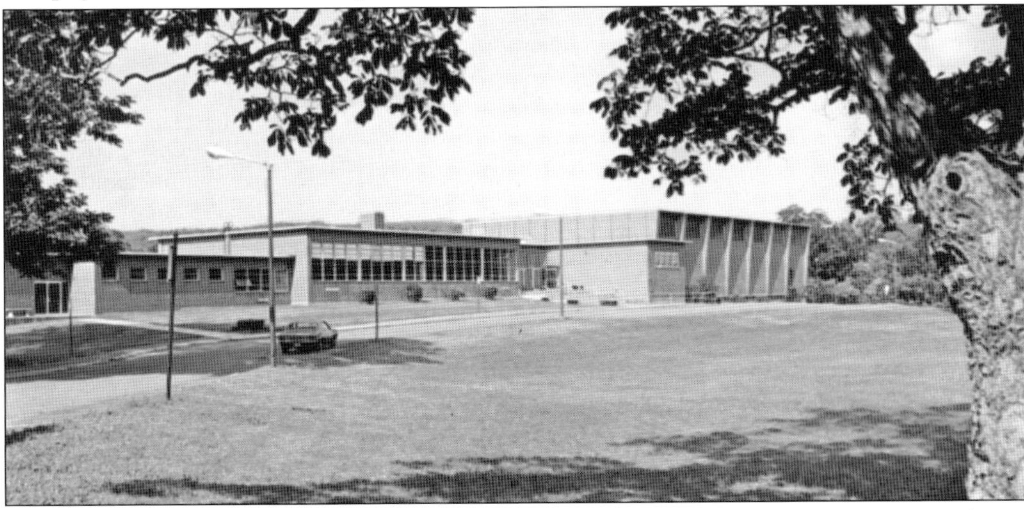

The gym was completed in 1958. Replacing the main building's gymnasium, it was referred to as the "new gym" by students at the time. It served many functions over the years. Home to athletic and academic departments, it also provided library services before the Learning Resource Center (LRC) and fed students before the Student Center. By 2014, when it was removed to make way for a new sports complex, it had become the "old gym."

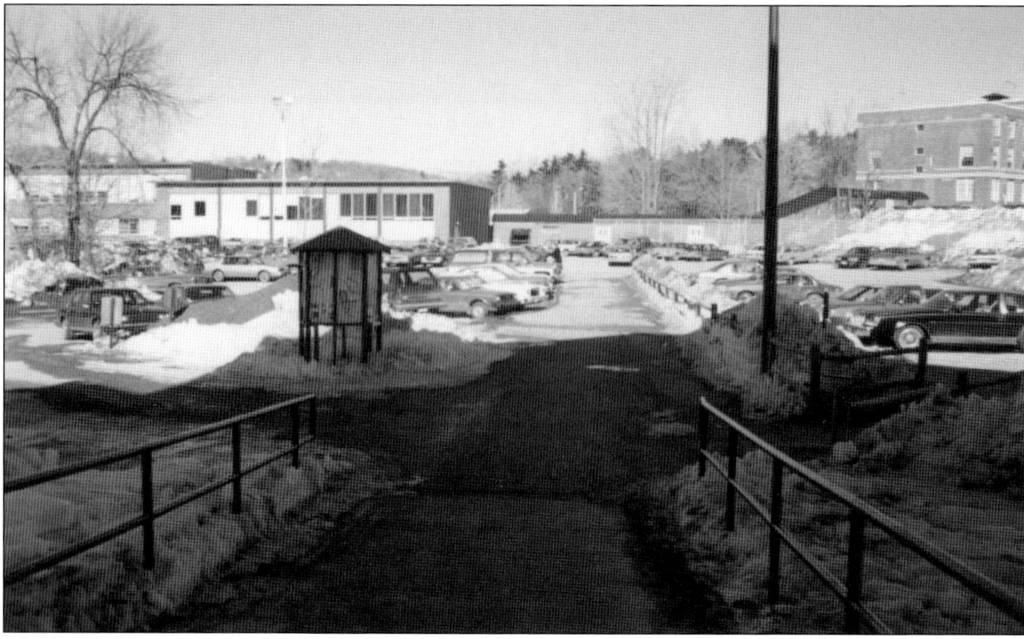

An enclosed passageway, colloquially called the tunnel, once connected the main building to the gym. It can be seen here in the distance and in the previous image during construction. The tunnel was removed as the campus expanded west. Evidence of the tunnel can still be seen in the built environment behind the administration building and on the wall from the wing that once contained the gym.

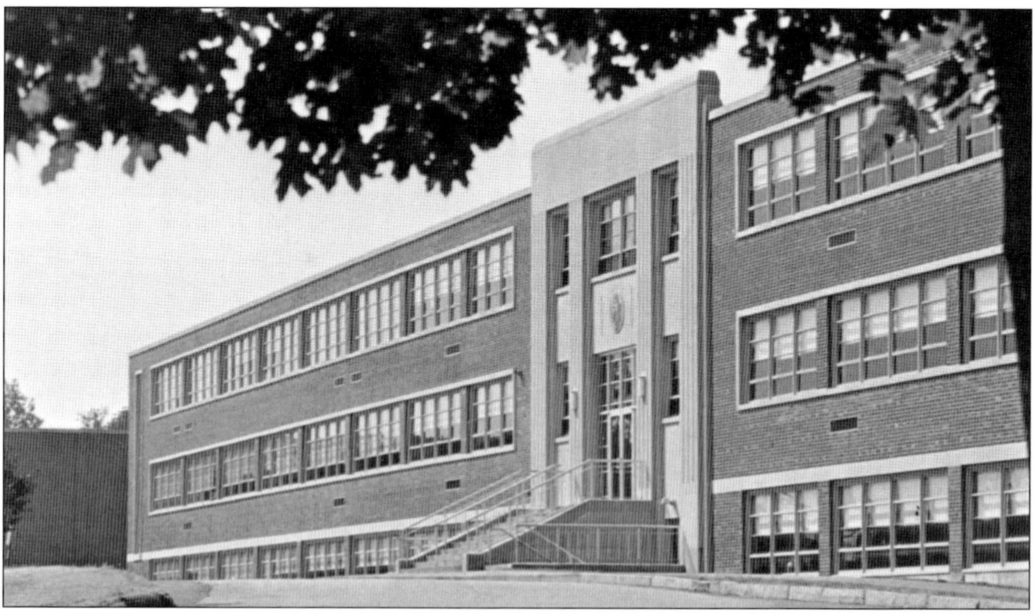

What is now the Sullivan Academic Center was opened in 1965 as the campus's science building. The three-story 110,000-plus-square-foot facility contained classrooms, laboratories, a lecture hall, a faculty lounge, and a greenhouse. The primary science departments relocated there from the main building, which was increasingly given to administrative functions over time. (WSU CityLab, Vincent "Jake" Powers Archives.)

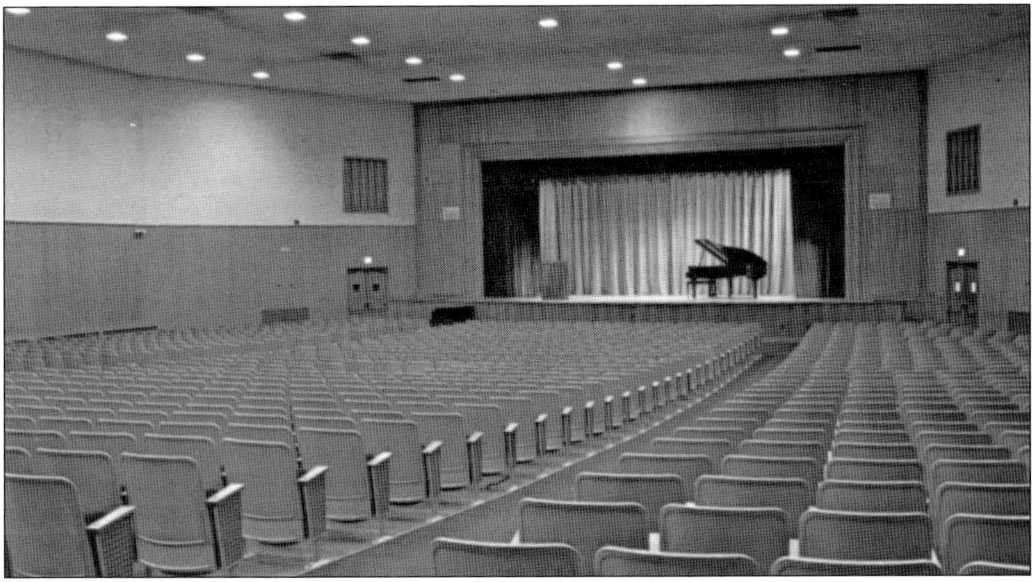

The Sullivan Auditorium was built at the same time as the new science building. A 1,100-seat raked theater with a stage and proscenium arch, it is used for productions, music rehearsals and college-wide assemblies as well as academic events including convocation and graduate commencement more recently.

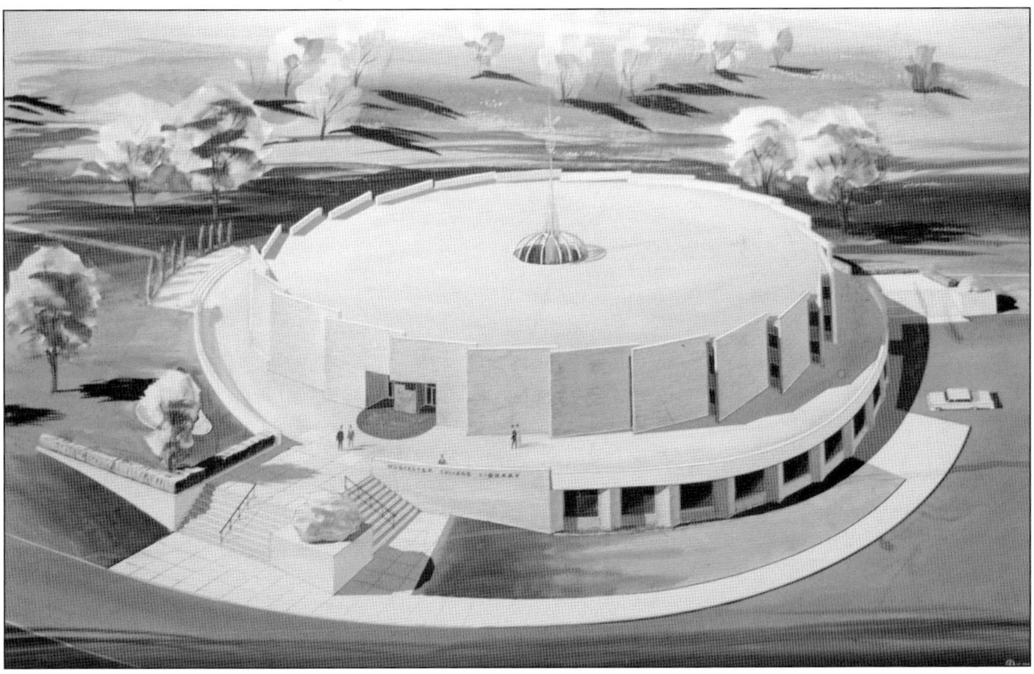

The Learning Resource Center (LRC) is a three-story, 113,000-square-foot structure opened in 1971. Some features in this conceptual rendering did not make it into the finished product, notably the central atrium, and the executed entrance configuration is different from the initial draft. In addition to being the university's library, the LRC contained academic departments, classrooms, lecture halls, television production studios, photography labs, the university archives, information technologies, and administrative offices.

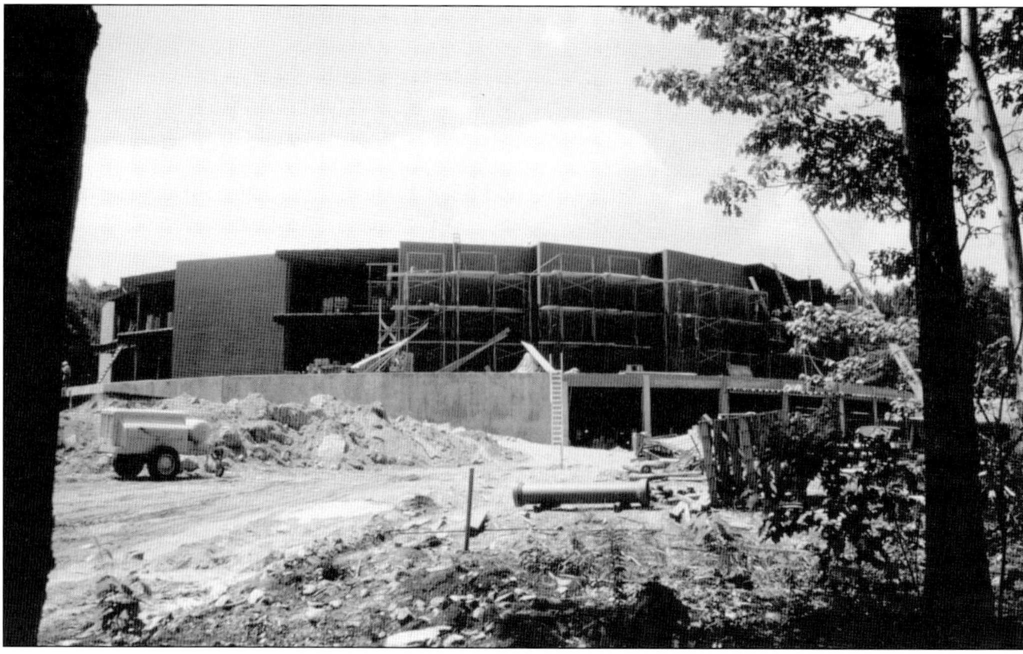

This picture shows the construction of the LRC, the first building to be placed deeply off Chandler Street. At the time, the structure marked the southernmost and westernmost points of the physical campus. The reason for such a setting had to do with campus access—parking lots occupied the spaces immediately behind the Sullivan Building and main building—and the desire to develop more of the campus's land.

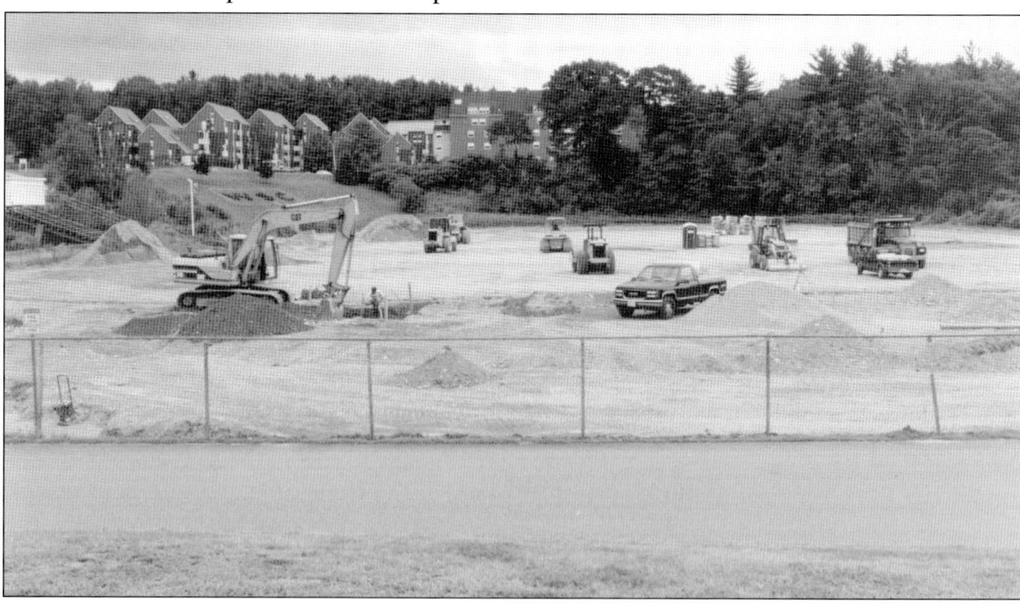

The John Coughlin Memorial Field was built to provide a more modern and standardized playing surface for Worcester State's football, soccer, field hockey, and, eventually, women's lacrosse teams. Its development also involved the creation of 2,500 seats to replace the field's small bleacher section and, over time, has seen significant lighting and sound-system improvements. (WSU Athletics Office.)

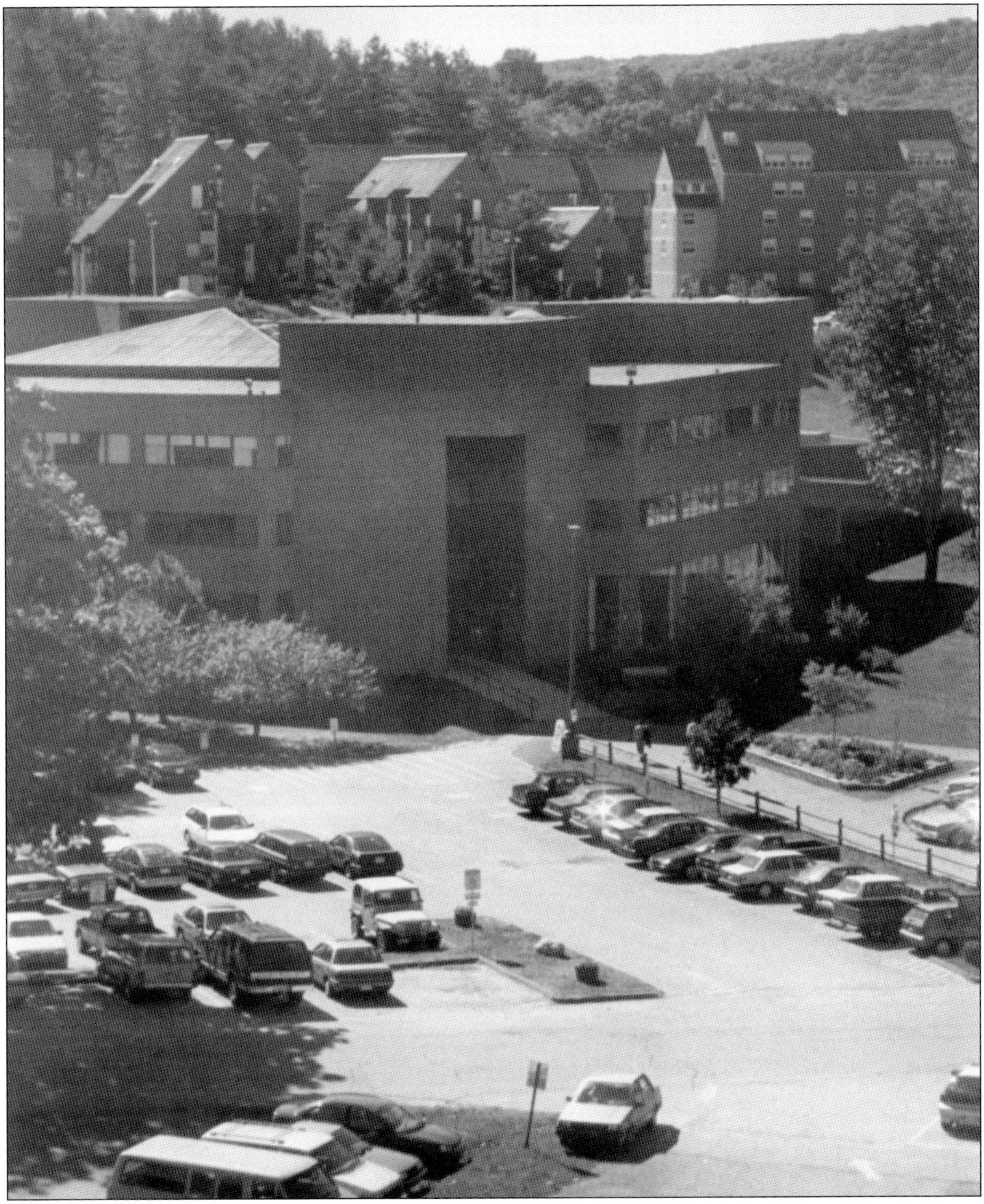

Opened in 1978, the 71,000-plus-square-foot Student Center is called the "student union" in the 1978 yearbook. Over its 40-year history, it has housed student affairs offices, a radio station, student lounges and clubs, and hosted many events, some of which can be seen in the following pages. Perhaps the greatest physical changes it has endured are the addition of a central staircase allowing for easier access to its three floors and the removal of the cafeteria. (WSU Student Involvement and Leadership Development Collection.)

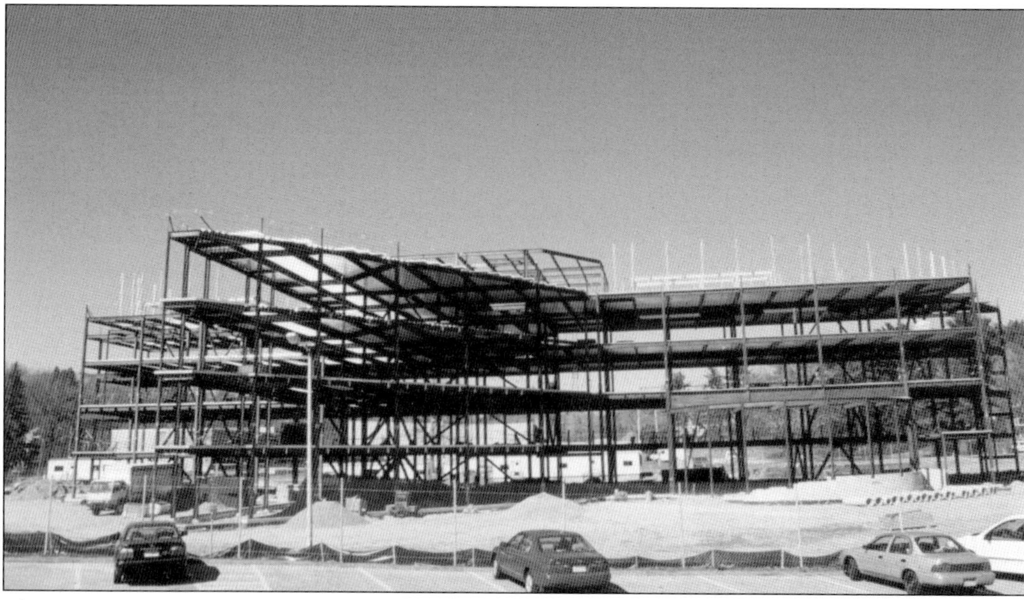

The science building that would ultimately be the Ghosh Science & Technology Center was erected in the northeastern corner of Worcester State's main campus. Previously, this space had been a large field used for recreational purposes and varsity sports practice.

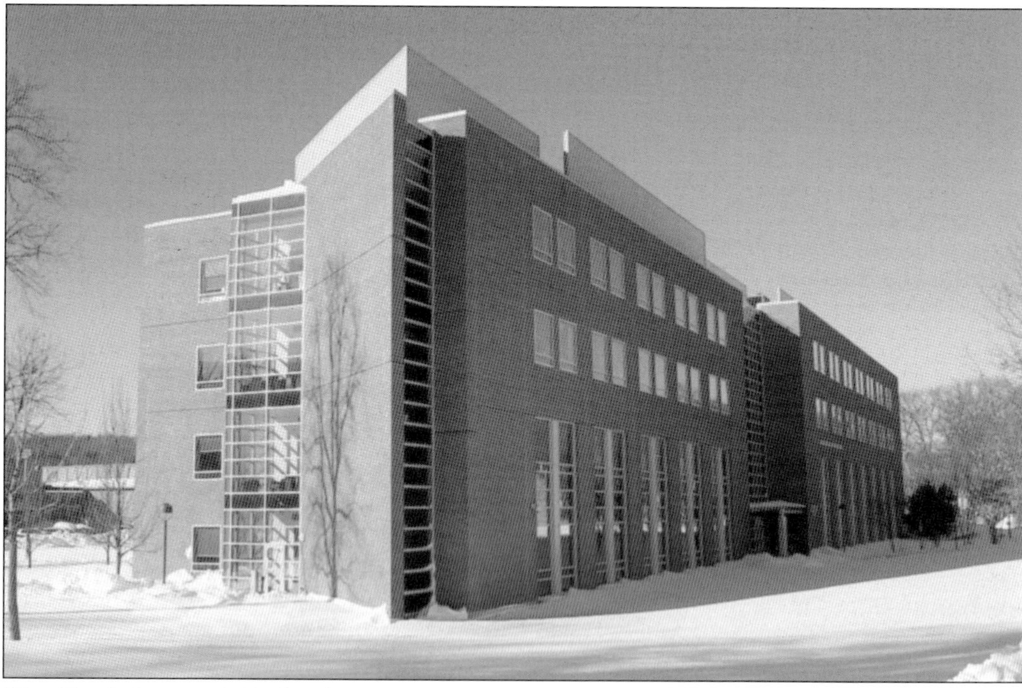

The Ghosh Science & Technology Center, named for the university's ninth president, Kalyan K. Ghosh, is a five-story, 97,300-square-foot structure opened in 2000. It contains academic offices, computer labs, clinics, science and spatial labs, and a 196-seat multimedia auditorium. The completion of this building with its modern lab and technology facilities precipitated a major shift of academic spaces that had rippling effects as the science departments moved from the "old" to the "new" science building. (WSU Office of Marketing.)

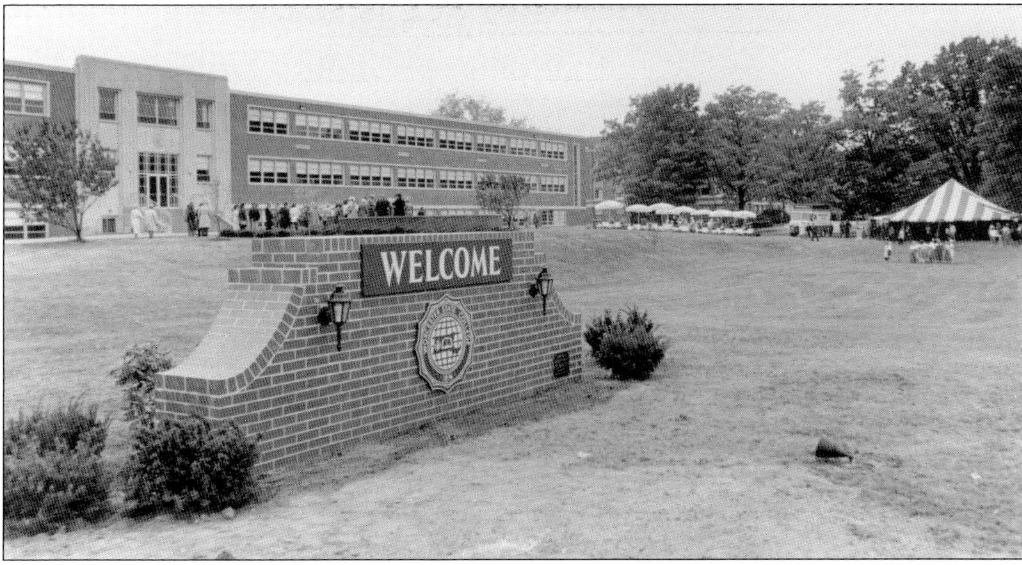

As science departments moved from the Sullivan Building to the new Ghosh Science & Technology Center, a mix of other departments began to backfill the evacuated spaces. These departments were relocated primarily from the LRC and main building, which cleared the way for expansion of new programs and for the main building's transformation into the administration building. In turn, the Sullivan Academic Center went through a $14.6 million renovation of its own. By 2005, new systems were installed, classrooms were upgraded with technology, and departments saw cosmetic upgrades. (WSU Athletic Department.)

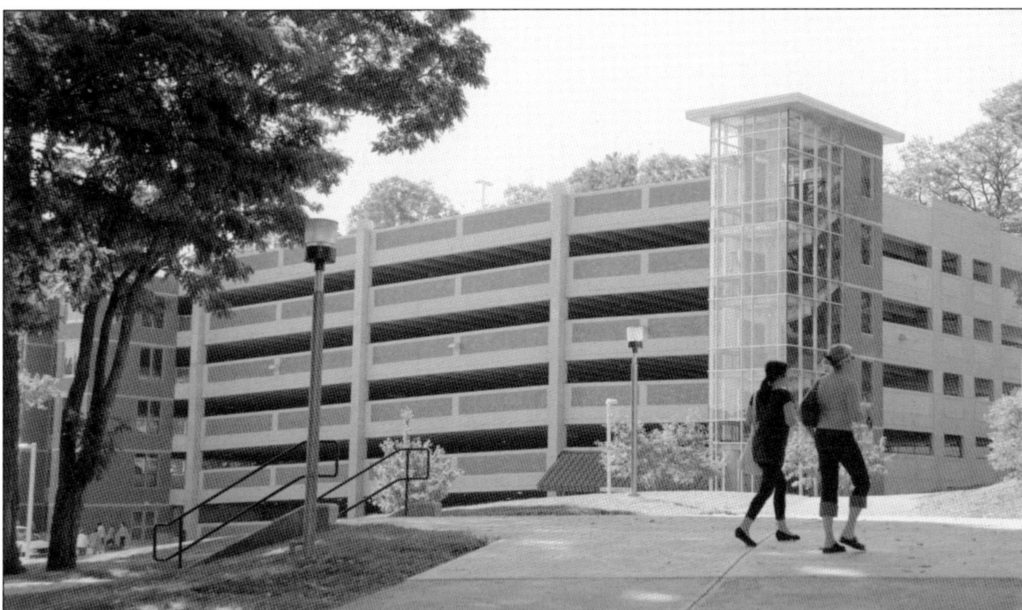

The Campus Garage opened for use in August 2007. While today's students talk about the problems of campus parking, in fact, WSU yearbooks show it has been a perennial issue on campus for decades. With six stories and 554 spaces, the $10.8 million garage project actually improved the situation—although at 10:00 a.m. while classes are in session that is often easy to forget. (WSU Office of Marketing.)

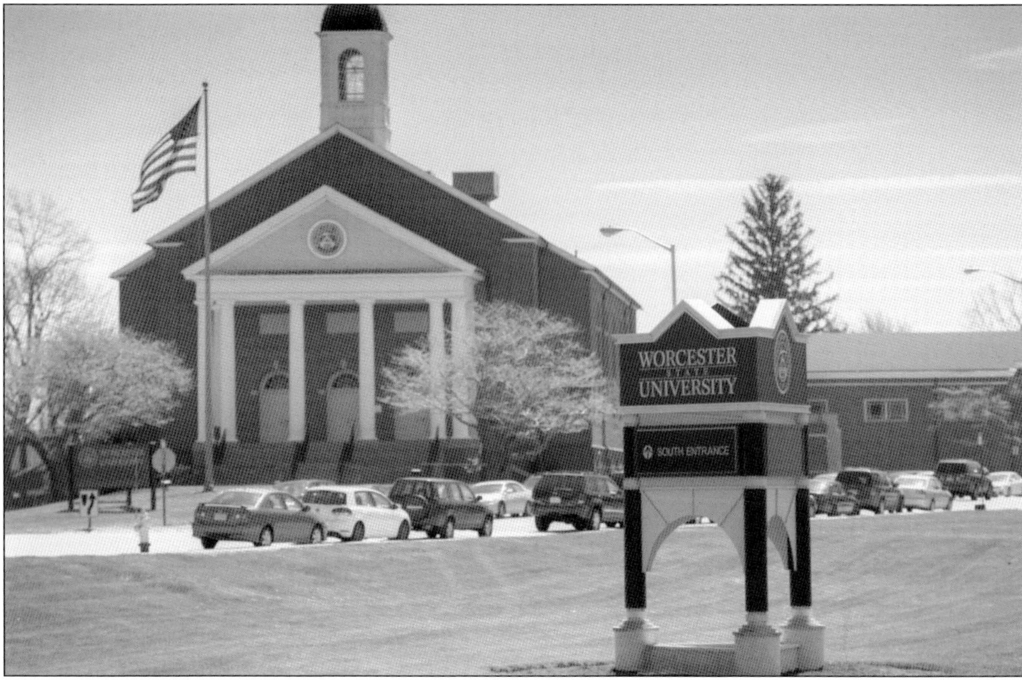

In 2015, the university completed the purchase of Temple Emanuel across the street from campus. The congregation, which had roots in the 1920s, built this structure in the late 1940s and moved to it in 1949. With Jewish congregations consolidating on Worcester's west side, the temple community sold it to the Worcester State University Foundation. It contains classrooms, a large auditorium, and a sanctuary; the university is currently exploring reuse options. (WSU Office of Marketing.)

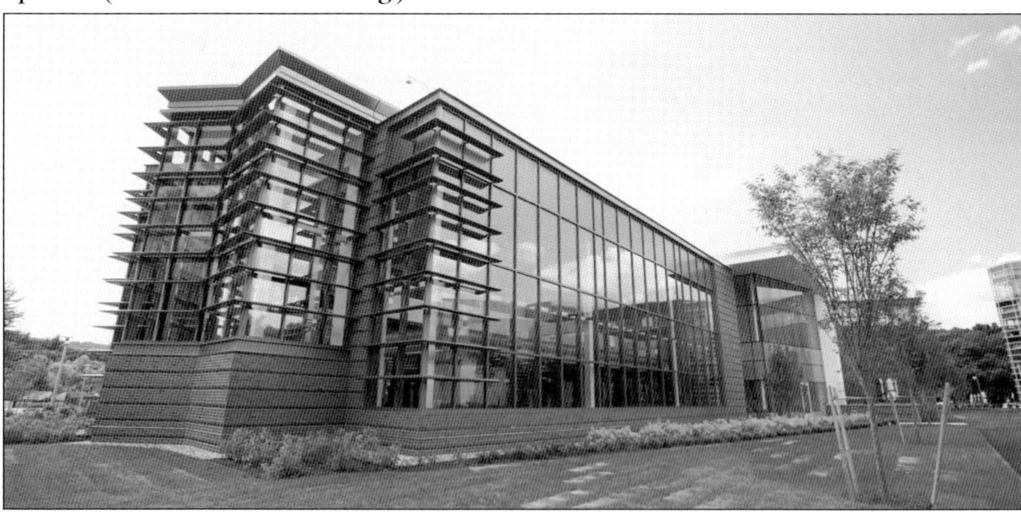

The Wellness Center is WSU's replacement for the 1950s gym. The two-story, 99,000-square-foot complex was completed in 2016. It contains the athletic department offices and classrooms as well as a trainer's suite, team locker rooms, exercise rooms, a golf simulator, batting cages, a 1,500-seat competition gymnasium, a multipurpose gym, and a raised walking track. Located on the northern edge of the campus buildings, its two-level fitness center faces in to the campus. (WSU Office of Marketing.)

Two

Leading the Institution

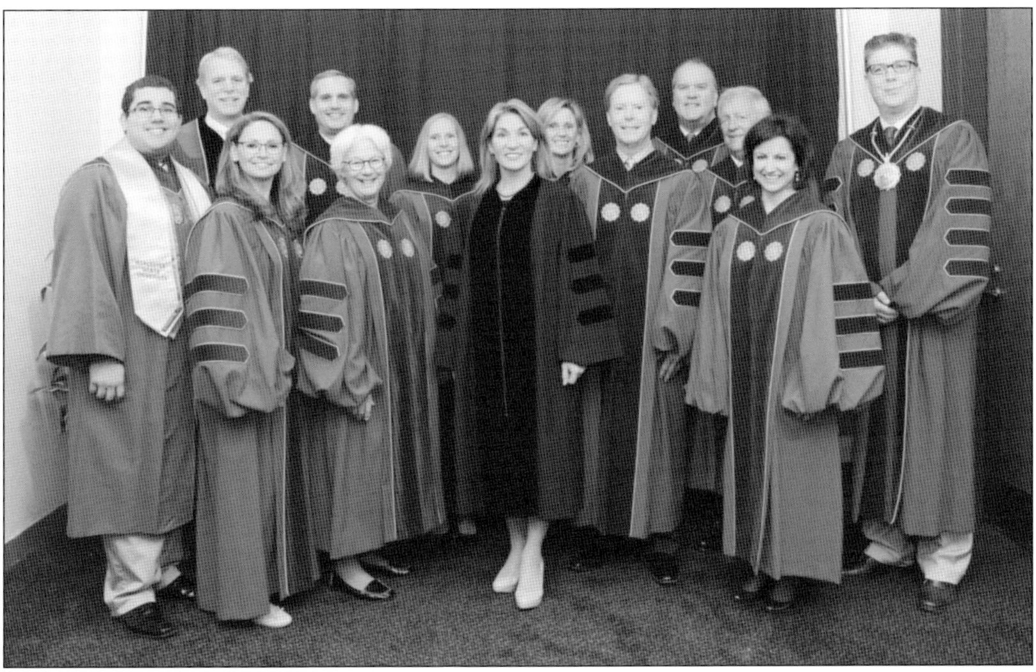

The Worcester State University Board of Trustees has governing authority over the university on behalf of the Commonwealth of Massachusetts. Among other things, it appoints the president, confirms presidential hires, tenures and promotes faculty, approves academic programs, ensures financial stability, and provides guidance on major university initiatives. Pictured here are the trustees and President Maloney with Lt. Gov. Karen Polito at the 2016 commencement. (WSU Office of Marketing.)

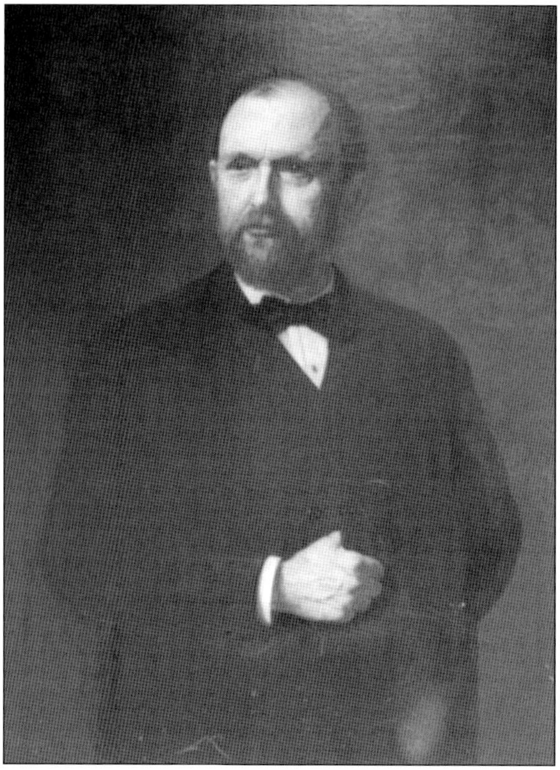

The first normal school principal was Elias Harlow Russell. Born in New Hampshire, Russell was a teacher and principal at New York and New England schools before taking the reins in Worcester. He established the school's early educational blueprint, particularly for student teaching, and made the normal school a laboratory for work in the child-study movement pioneered by colleague G. Stanley Hall of Clark University. Russell retired in 1909. (WSU Office of the President.)

By the early 1890s, the school acquired a house for the principal and his family. Connected to Stoddard Terrace, it was both a residence and an active place in the school's social life. State and city officials, faculty members, and leaders of other schools, often with their families, were received here. No longer in university hands, it is the only structure that remains from the original campus.

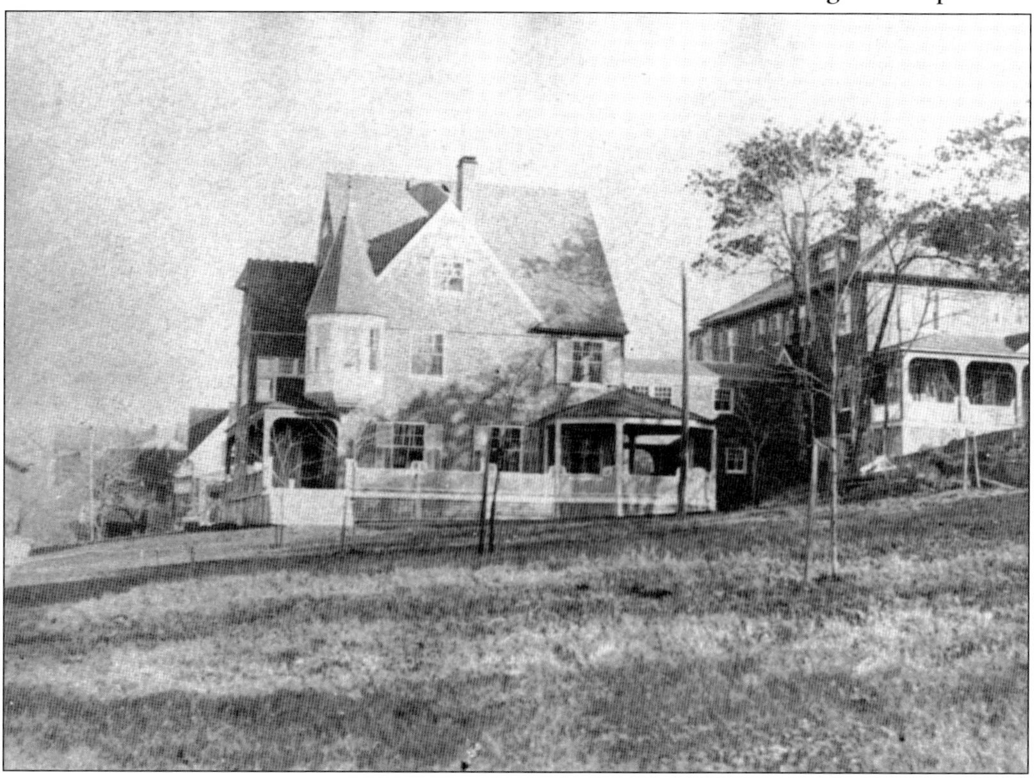

There was a change to centralize and credential state higher education when the new principal, Francis Random Lane (1909–1912), a medical doctor, came to the normal school. Even before arriving, he suggested removing the school to a new site because of its age and location. Unsuccessful in this, he refurbished classroom spaces, added a kitchen at Stoddard Terrace, and introduced a kindergarten for local children in the normal school building. (WSU Office of the President.)

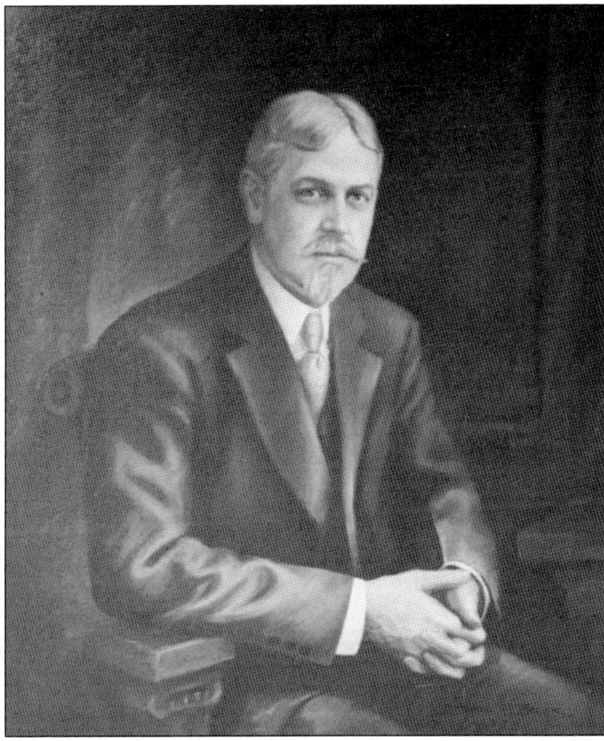

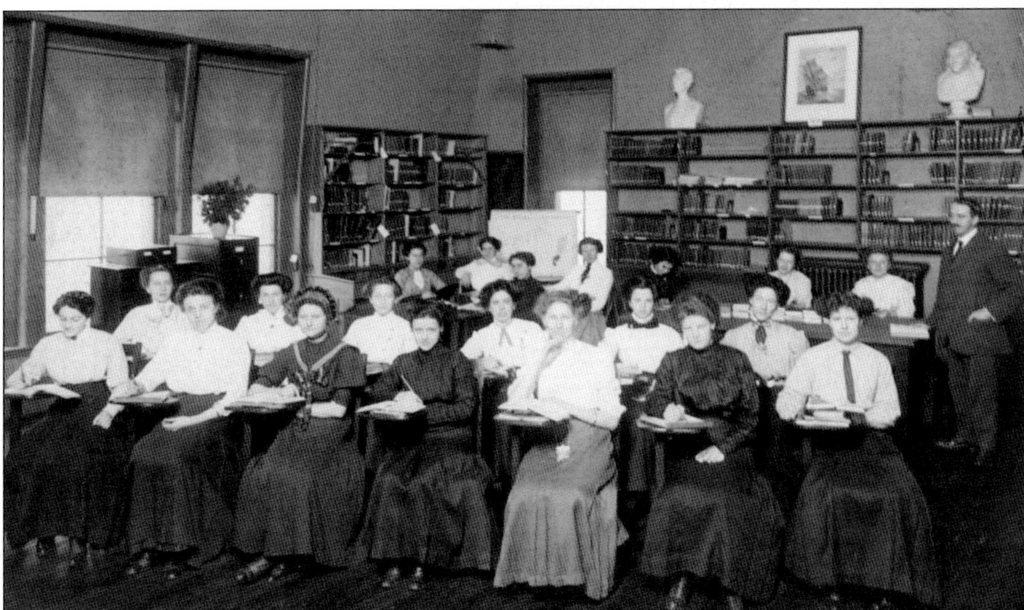

Lane kept one of the Russell administration's greatest innovations: supervised student teaching done both on campus and in public schools. Rebecca Jones, supervisor of apprentice teaching, had managed this aspect of the curriculum for 34 years. While Lane believed in the primacy of the textbook to standardize learning, perhaps because of his medical training, he saw the utility of practical application associated with what would now be called experiential learning.

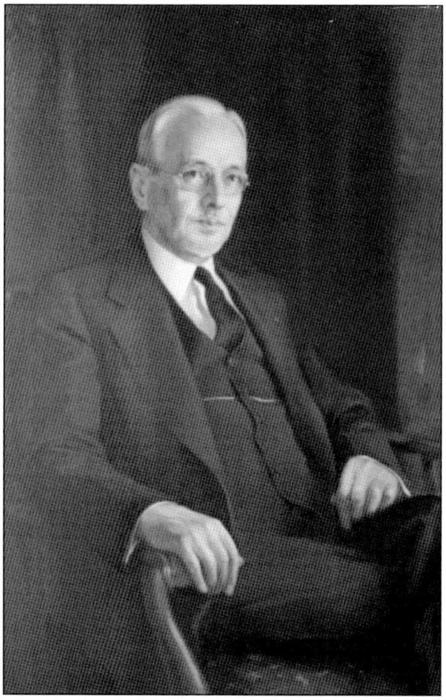

Dr. William B. Aspinwall (1912–1940) was the last principal of the normal school and first president of Worcester State Teachers College. His administration saw the shift from one to the other, the move to Chandler Street, and the evolution from a two-year degree program to a four-year bachelor degree–granting school. Aspinwall also steered the college through an attempt to liquidate it prompted by financial dislocations of the Great Depression. (WSU Office of the President.)

Though not without some controversy, Aspinwall was well liked and well respected. He and his wife, Aurelia (Hyde) Aspinwall, entertained a variety of guests regularly at their house. He encouraged faculty scholarship and publishing, and created academic conferences. Students referred to him as "eminent scholar and leader." Indeed, the class of 1940 dedicated its yearbook to Aspinwall, noting "his sympathetic guidance, his inspiring example, and his personal interest in developing our minds and personalities." (WSU Office of University Advancement.)

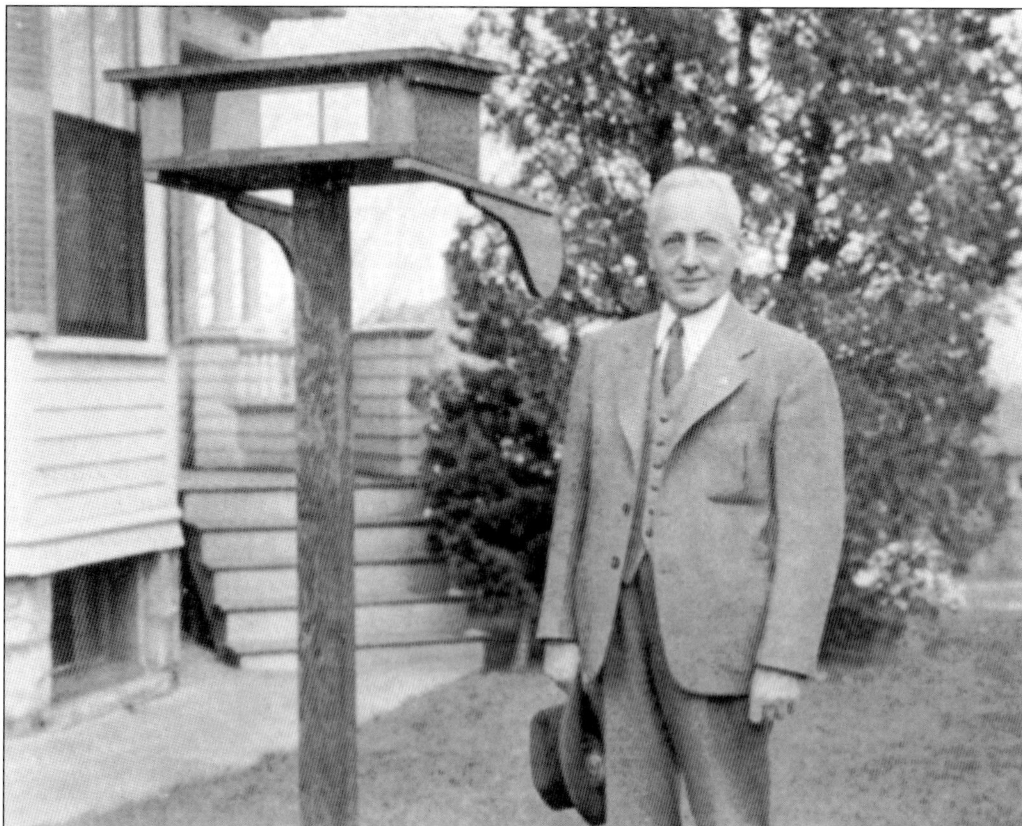

Clinton E. Carpenter became president in 1940 and led the institution during the World War II years. Under his administration, men were readmitted, and Carpenter accordingly emphasized more of a coed social life on campus with the student tea, college dances, junior prom, and the introduction of men's sports. Dying unexpectedly in June 1946, Carpenter was replaced by Dr. Albert Farnsworth (acting president), who pushed many of his predecessor's initiatives to completion. (WSU Office of the President.)

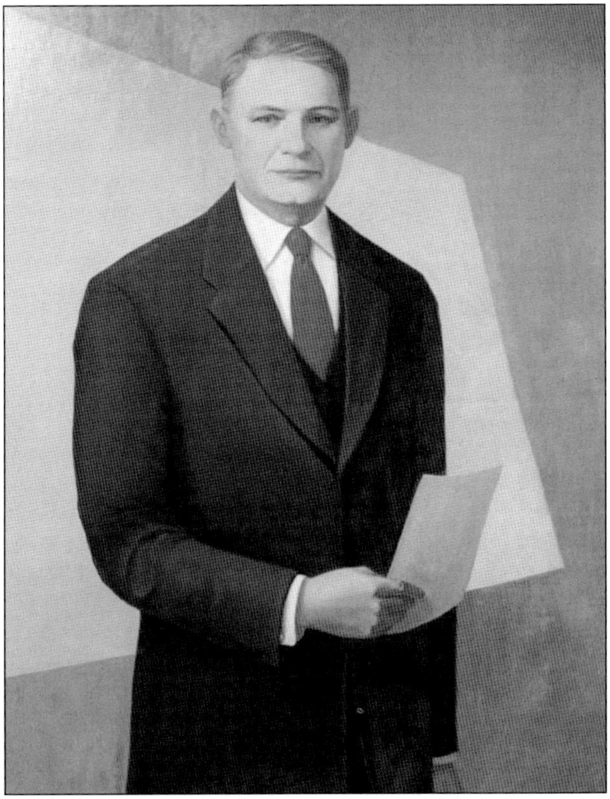

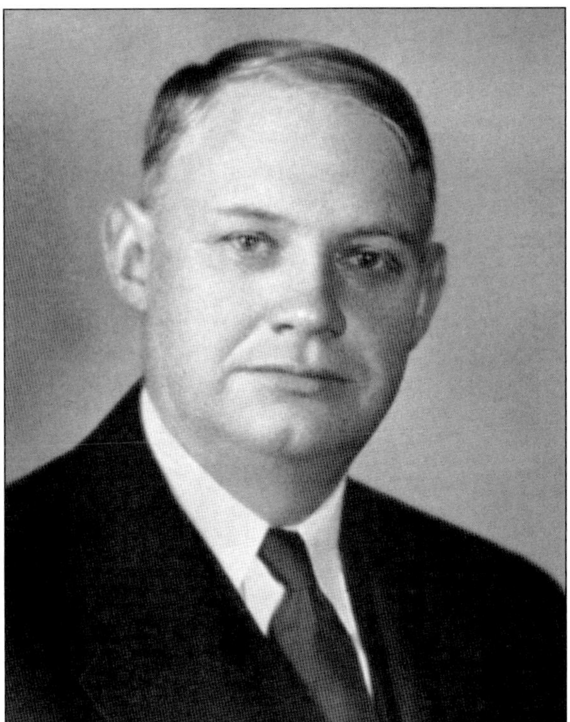

World War II seemed to profoundly influence Carpenter's thinking about the role of WSTC graduates. An unprecedented item in the 1943 yearbook reproduces a short quote under this picture that reads, "[You are] graduating in the midst of the chaos of war. You are becoming teachers at a time when our land desperately needs you in its schools . . . when the chaos of war gives way to the chaos of peace." (WSU Office of University Advancement.)

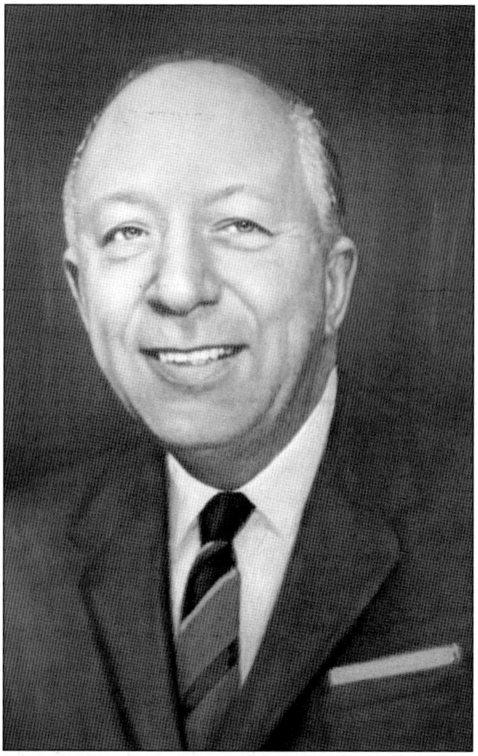

Eugene A. Sullivan's presidency (from 1947 to 1970) saw a tremendous expansion of the physical site, a curricular evolution beyond teacher education, and the first moves toward a modern collegiate athletic system. Under his administration, three major buildings were erected—a multipurpose athletic complex, science building, and learning center with a library—all of which suggested something more than teacher training, though that remained a vital function of the institution. (WSU Office of the President.)

Significant curricular changes occurred during the Sullivan years, too. Through President Carpenter, sciences played a limited part in the humanities-heavy teaching-oriented curriculum. In 1932, only Dr. Lawrence Averill had a small research-oriented lab for experimental psychology. The new science building (today's Sullivan Academic Center) invited more robust scientific research and training. By 1963, the evolution to a more comprehensive program was acknowledged when the school became Worcester State College.

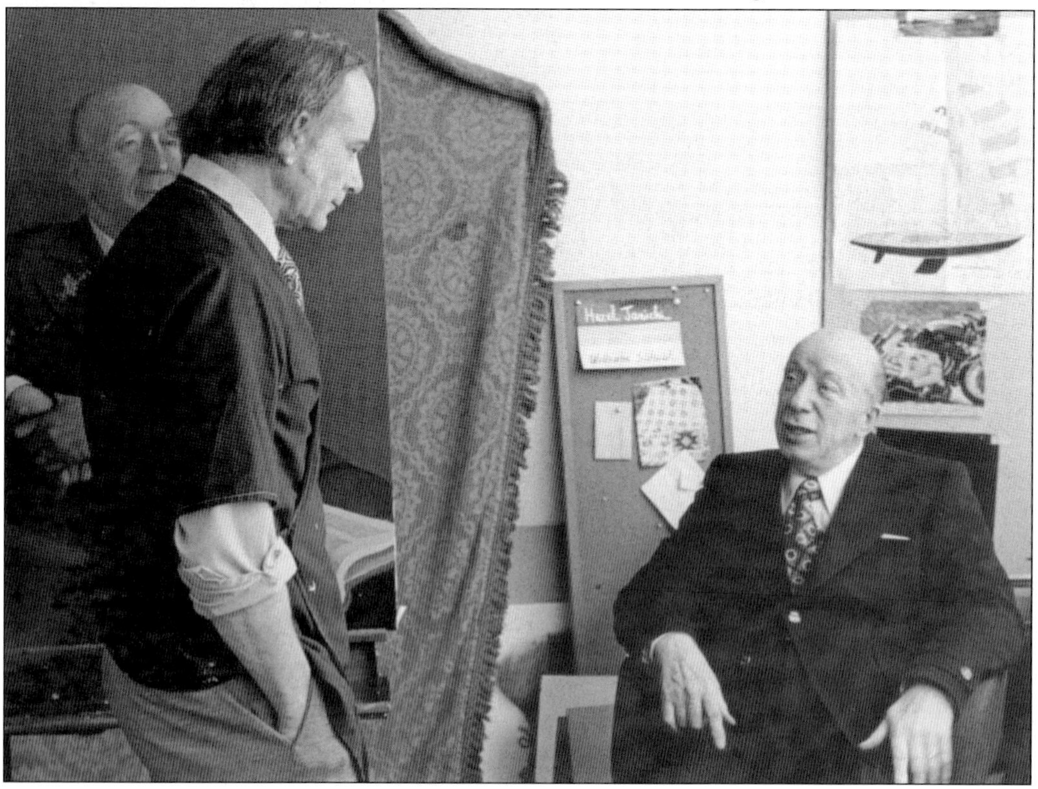

Robert E. Leestamper's presidency lasted from 1970 to 1975. Beyond marking the school's centennial in 1974, his tenure saw two major changes with far-reaching consequences not fully realized at the time. The first was the creation of Chandler Village, 26 townhouse-style apartments for 440 students, the first dorms on the current campus. The second was the creation of graduate programs, which would later help the state colleges become state universities. (WSU Office of the President.)

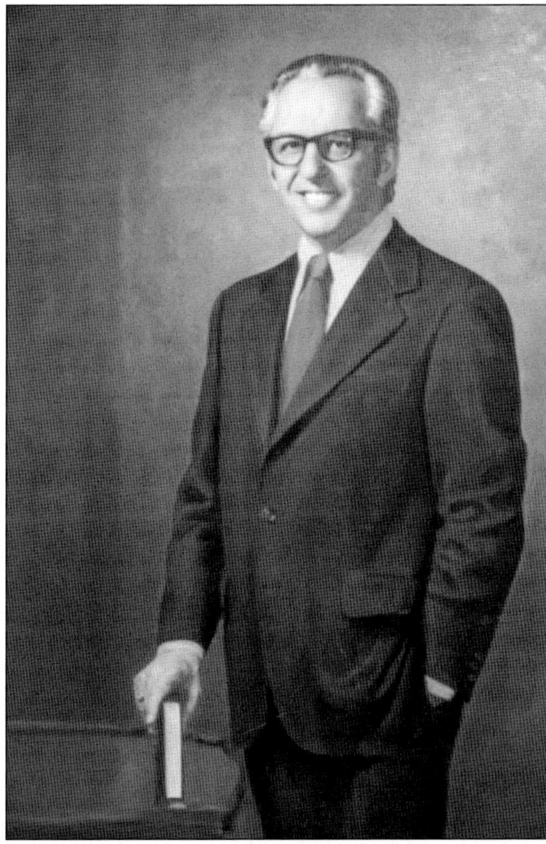

Leestamper's presidency saw a few pioneering curricular changes. The backdrop was a world in which baby boomers were entering the professional workforce and American cities experienced profound difficulties. Accordingly, the college established professional programs in business and nursing to provide job avenues, and it created an interdisciplinary urban studies academic program to look at cities and their people. All three led to bachelor degrees.

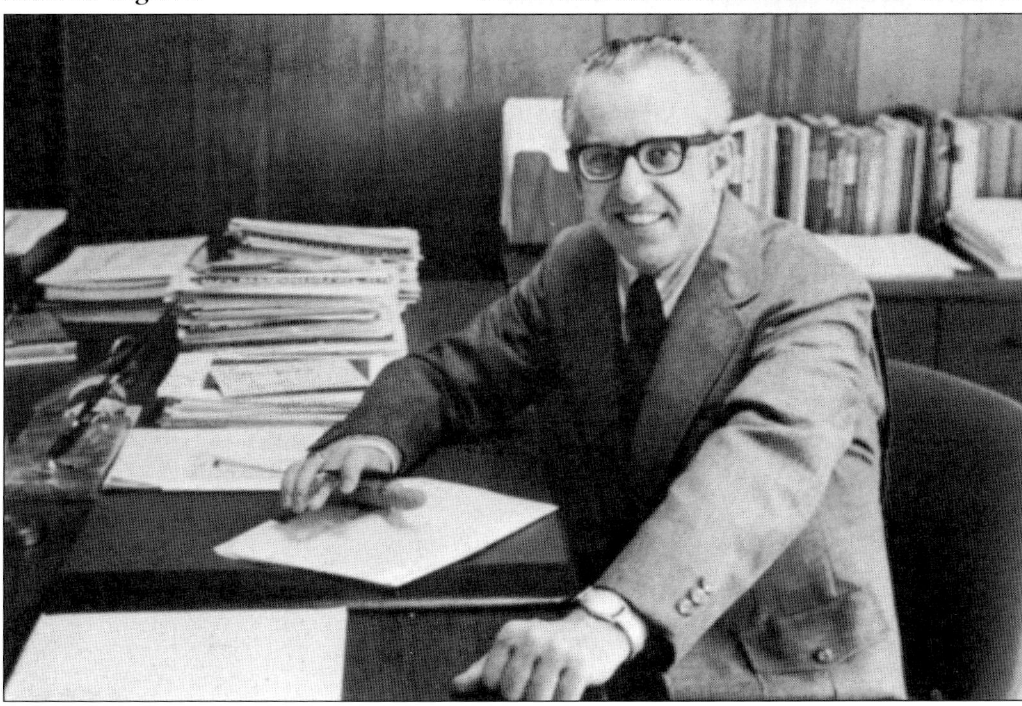

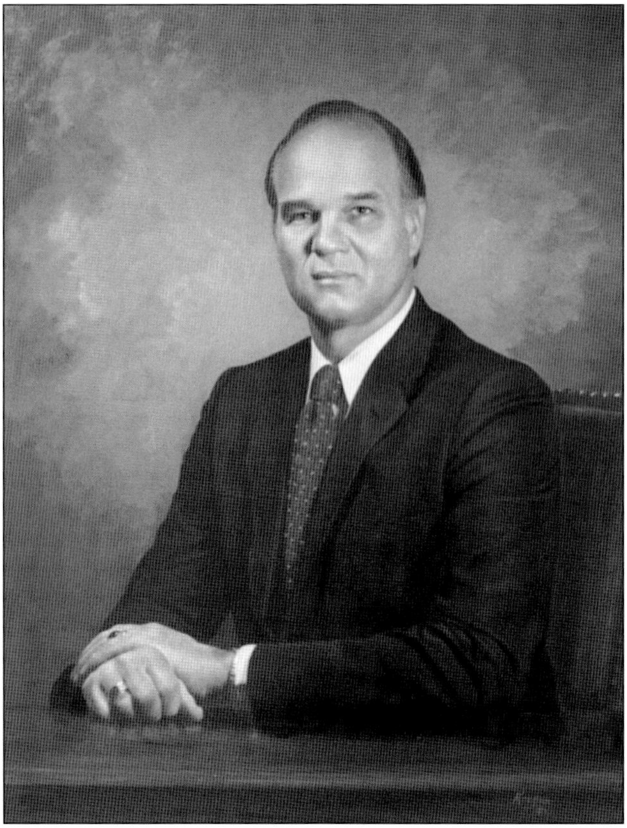

Joseph J. Orze, the seventh president of Worcester State, served from 1975 to 1982. During his tenure in office, the Student Center opened. Built in the center of campus and set amid Chandler Village, the academic buildings, the library, and gym, it quickly became a hub on campus with several dining areas (including the main cafeteria), student activity offices, the bookstore, meeting rooms, and event space. (WSU Office of the President.)

Pictures in the college yearbook and personal accounts indicate that President Orze frequently appeared at school events, often smoking a pipe and interacting warmly with students. He was a strong supporter of varsity sports. In 1982, Orze left Worcester State to become the 15th president of Northwestern State University of Louisiana.

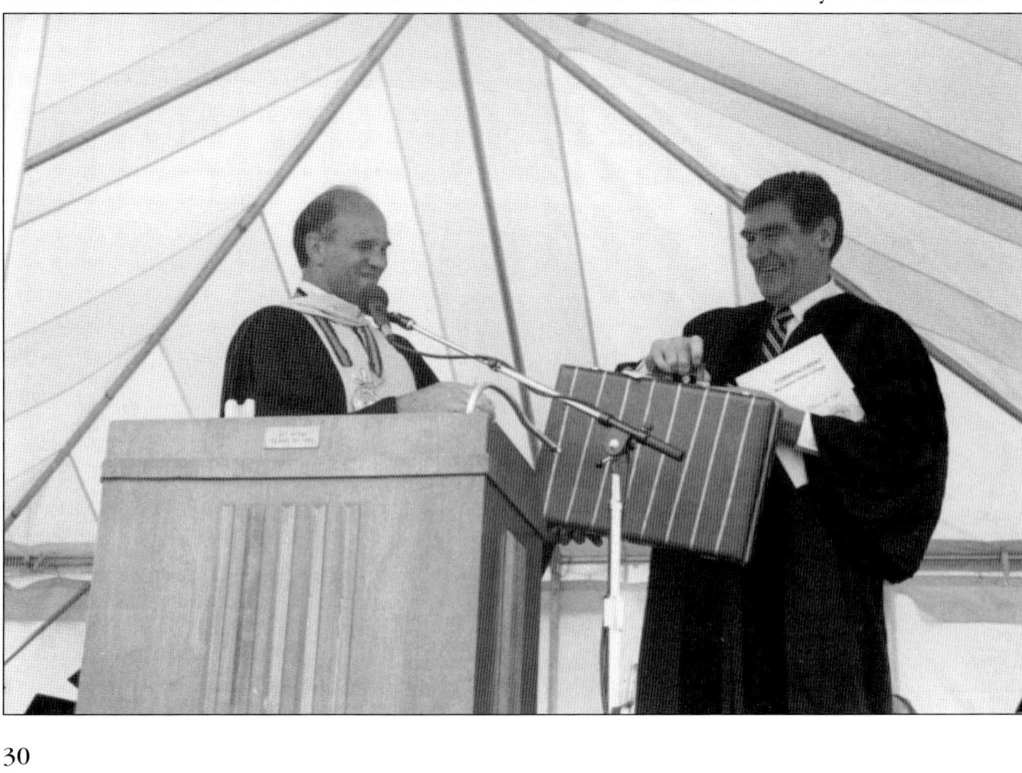

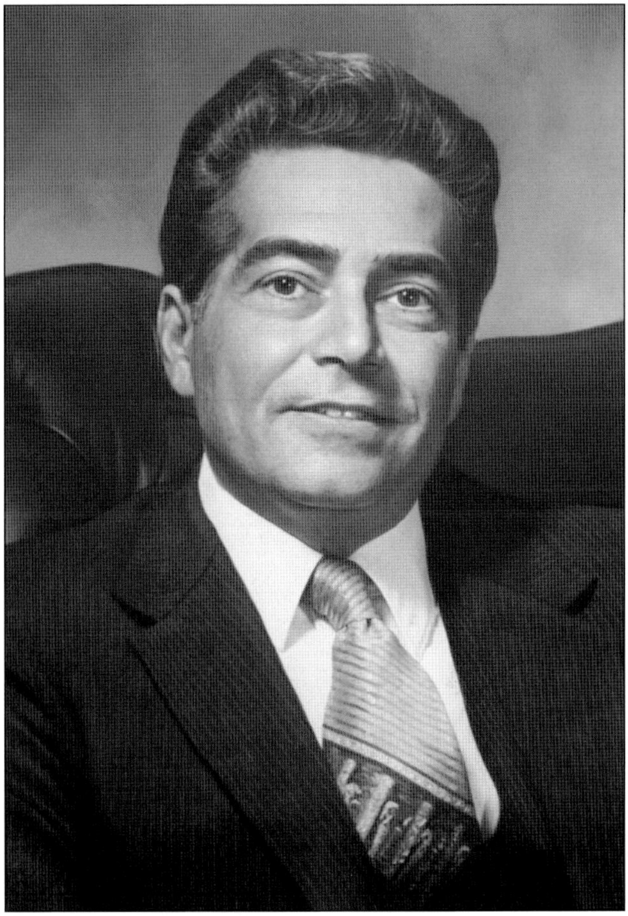

Philip D. Vairo was the eighth Worcester State president in a tenure that spanned the decade from 1982 to 1992. His administration saw the building of the college's second dormitory, Dowden Hall, named for Vera M. Dowden, Worcester State's first dean of students. Accommodating 240 students, this traditional dorm was erected next to Chandler Village. Vairo also championed student participation in city events, especially the Columbus Day Parade. (WSU Office of the President.)

President Vairo, shown here with some faculty members and the portraits of previous presidents, also oversaw the further expansion of academic programs including an MS in speech-language pathology and the first BS degree in occupational therapy in the state system. (WSU Student Involvement and Leadership Development Collection.)

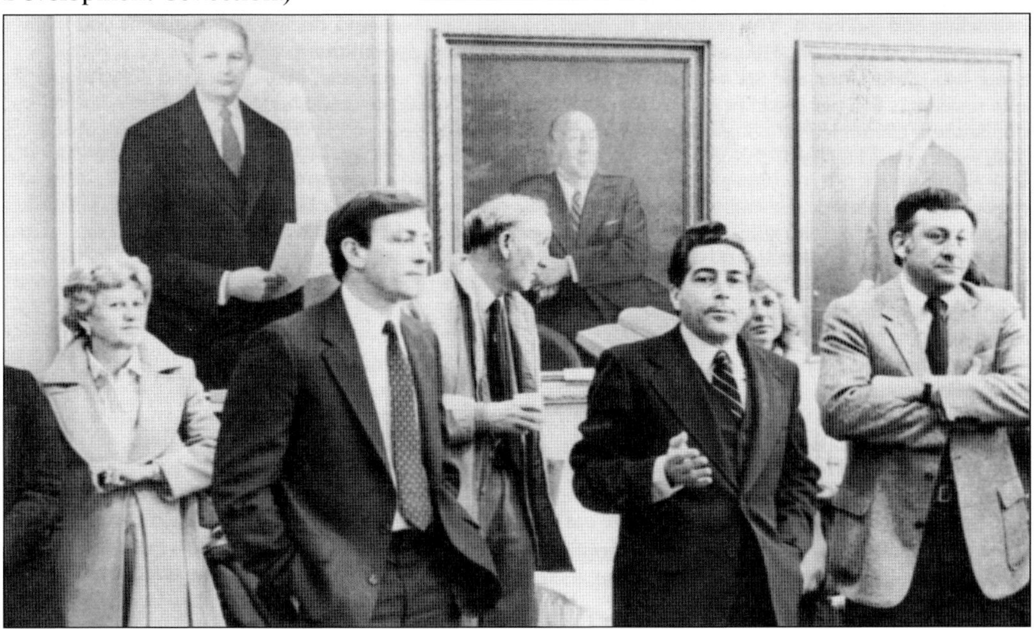

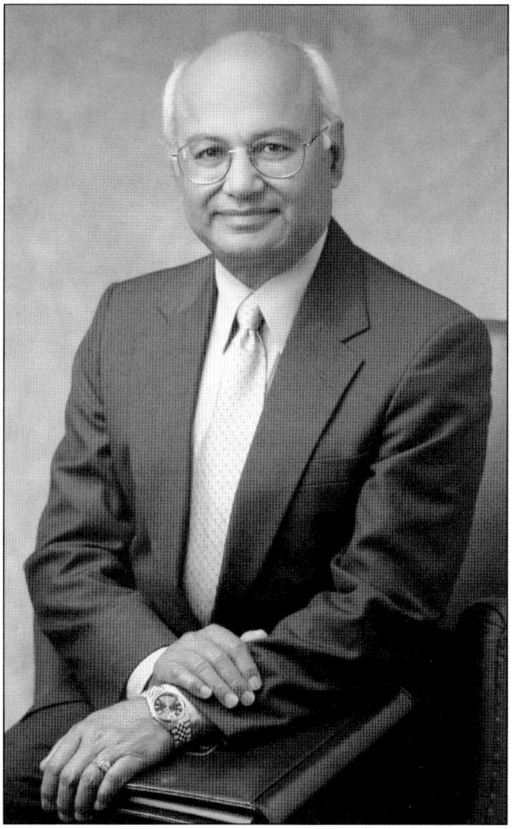

Ninth president Kalyan K. Ghosh served from 1992 to 2002 and helped meet the state's growing technology sector needs in the early 2000s. Ghosh's presidency saw the building of the science and technology center that bears his name, and he is known on campus for advancing the sciences. At the same time, he also helped create the Worcester State Foundation, a 501(c)3 nonprofit involved in soliciting funds from alumni, corporations, and foundations to provide scholarships, program support, and capital improvement initiatives. (WSU Office of the President.)

While the Ghosh presidency is often associated with campus advances in the study of science, his tenure also coincided with new initiatives in experiential learning and community engagement/research. Under his watch, the Intergenerational Urban Institute (now the Urban Action Institute), the WSU CityLab, and the Latino Education Institute were developed. Ghosh also looked to the past, as when he dedicated Founders Park in 1999 (shown here).

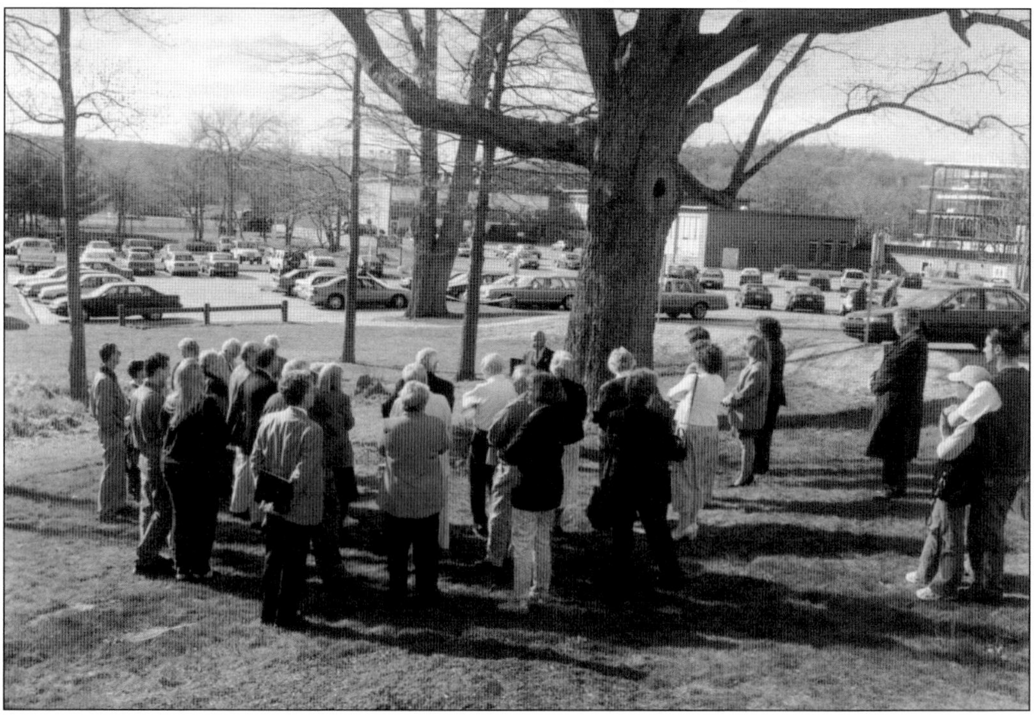

The 10th president, Janelle C. Ashley, oversaw the college from 2002 to 2011. During her tenure, the college built a six-story residence hall for 348 students (Wasylean Hall) and a 554-space parking garage. She also presided over the transition from Worcester State College to Worcester State University in 2010, when the state legislature made all Massachusetts state colleges into universities. (WSU Office of the President.)

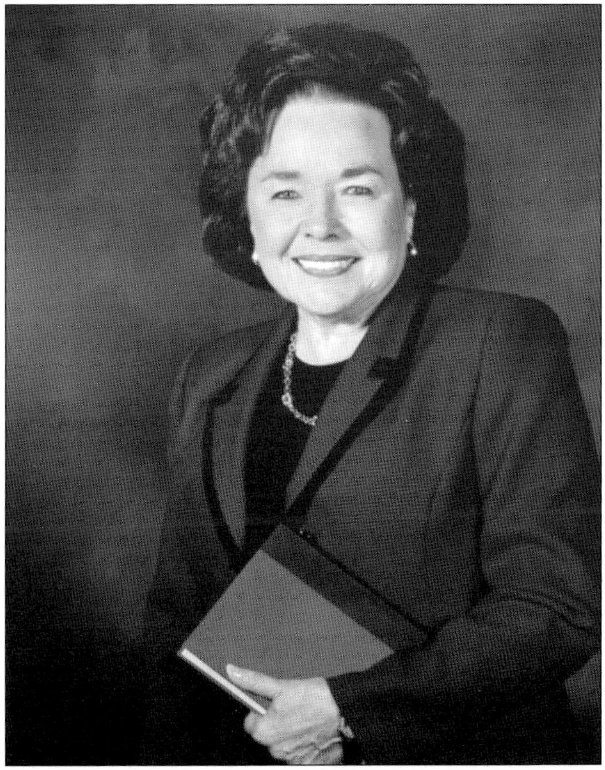

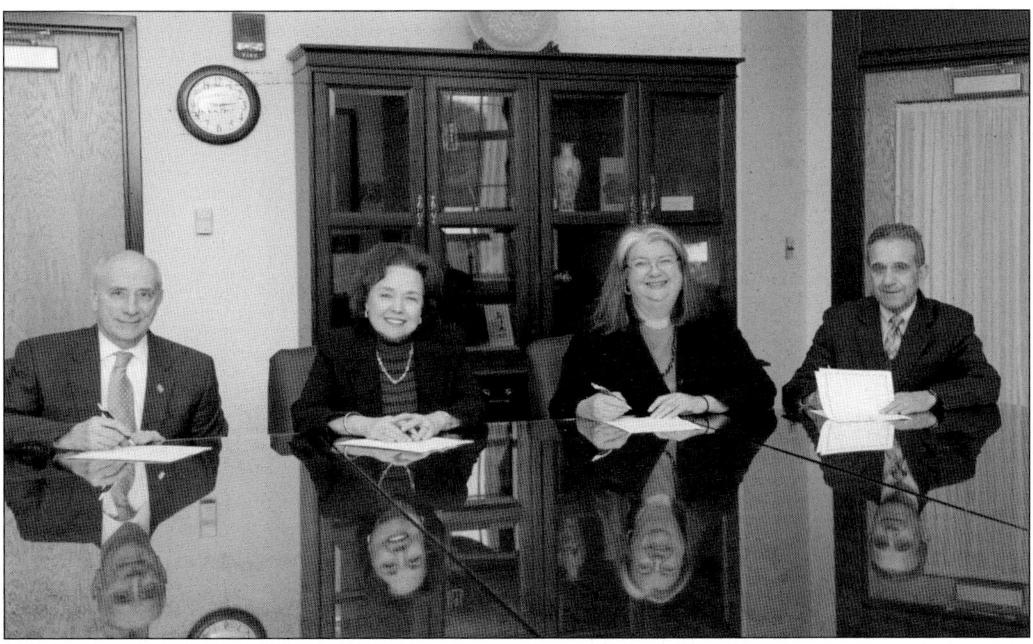

The presidents of Fitchburg State College, Worcester State College, Quinsigamond Community College, and Mount Wachusett Community College are pictured from left to right in the Worcester State President's Conference Room. President Ashley cultivated academic and administrative ties among area public higher education institutions. (WSU Office of Marketing.)

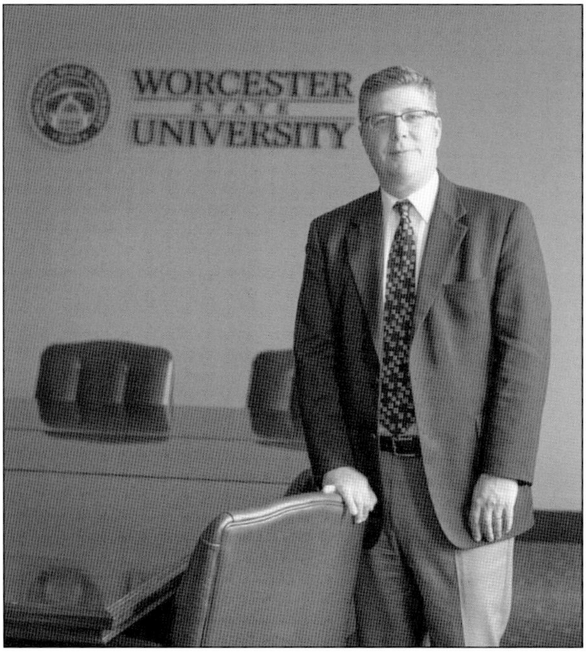

Barry M. Maloney became the 11th president of Worcester State University in 2011. One of the most student-centered presidents in the university's history, he has improved student spaces, built Sheehan Hall, a 400-plus bed dorm with a new university cafeteria, and erected a new Wellness Center to replace the old gym. The acquisition of the Temple Emanuel Buildings, called the May Street Complex, represent an opportunity for the university to expand humanities, arts, and social science spaces as well as community-engaged initiatives. (WSU Office of the President.)

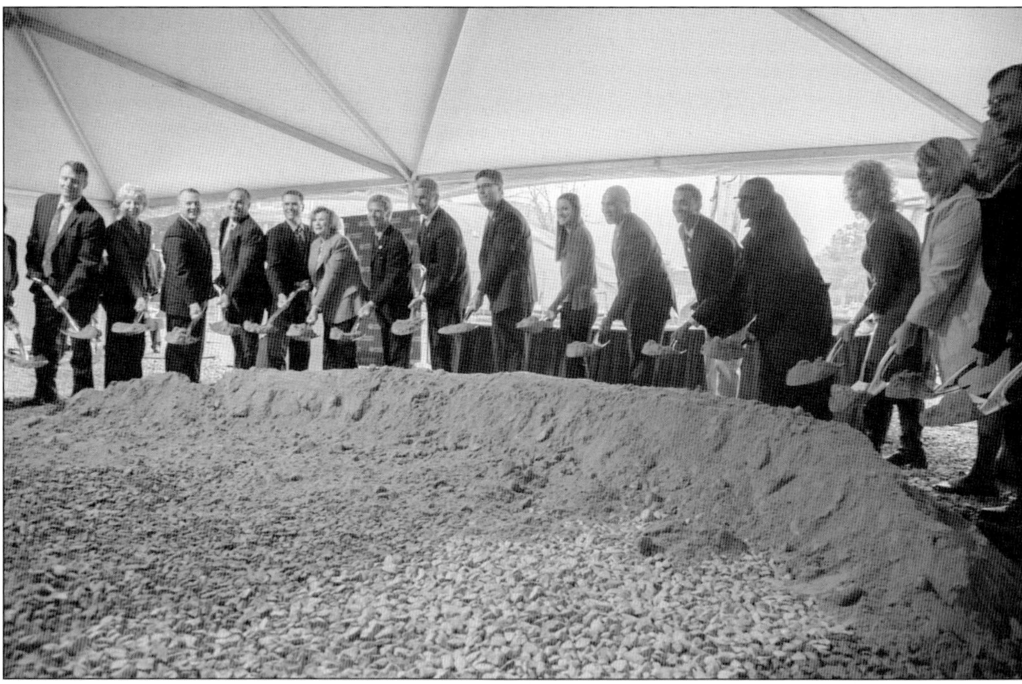

In addition to large-scale building projects—this image shows the Wellness Center ground breaking—President Maloney's tenure has seen important smaller initiatives across campus. During his presidency, new learning spaces such as the Aisiko STEM Center and the WSU Teaching Garden have come online, and full-time faculty hires and student enrollments have increased, graduation rates have improved, fundraising targets have been surpassed, community-based learning and research have expanded, and student-exchange/study-away opportunities have multiplied. (WSU Office of Marketing.)

Three

Methods of Learning

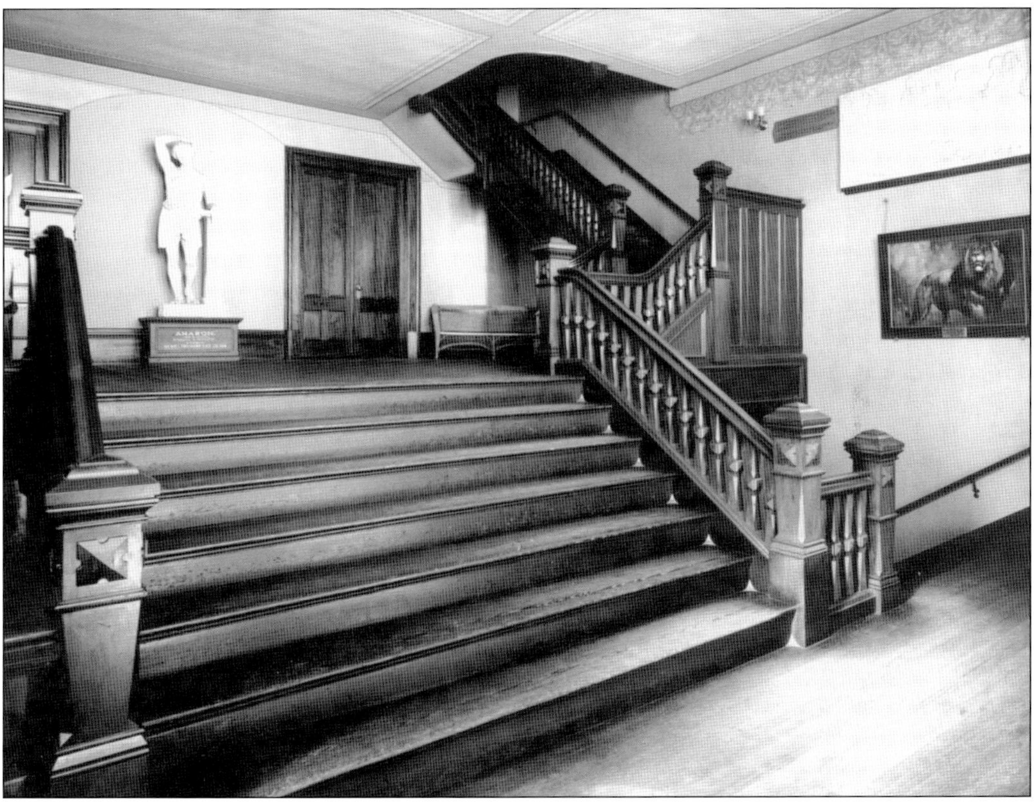

On September 15, 1874, the first WSU students, 69 out of 90 applicants, ascended these stairs and assembled in the normal school's Great Hall. There, they embarked on a course of study that prepared them for professions in public school classrooms. If they took up that work, their educations were free. This chapter looks at the curriculum, methods of learning, faculty, and academic lives over Worcester State University's history.

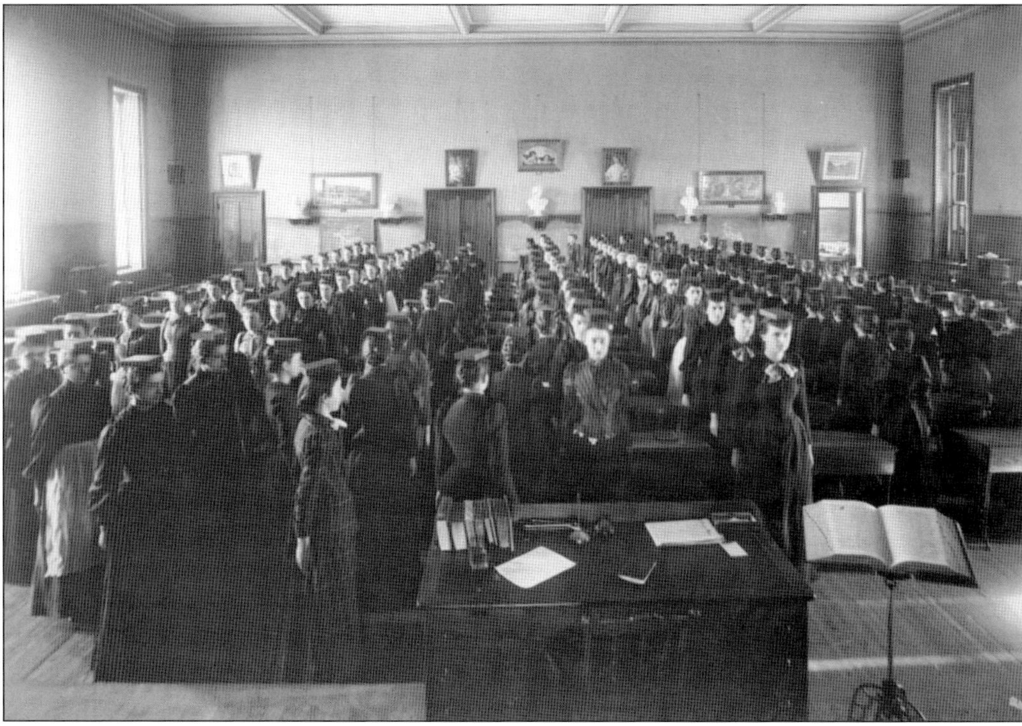

The curriculum for aspiring teachers at the normal school stressed subject matter proficiency in multiple disciplines, the acquisition of skills that befit young women of the day, and practice on proper classroom conduct, teaching, and deportment. Assemblies in the Great Hall, something of a large homeroom, were often school announcements and presentations. But they also included posture exercises, such as balancing writing blocks on one's head (above), and group stretching (below) or calisthenic activities to start the day.

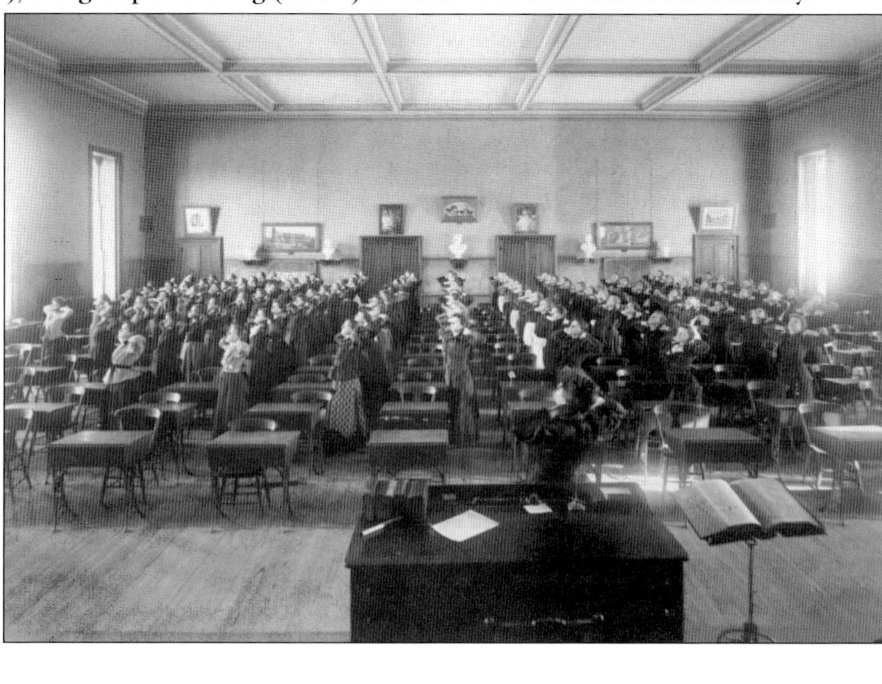

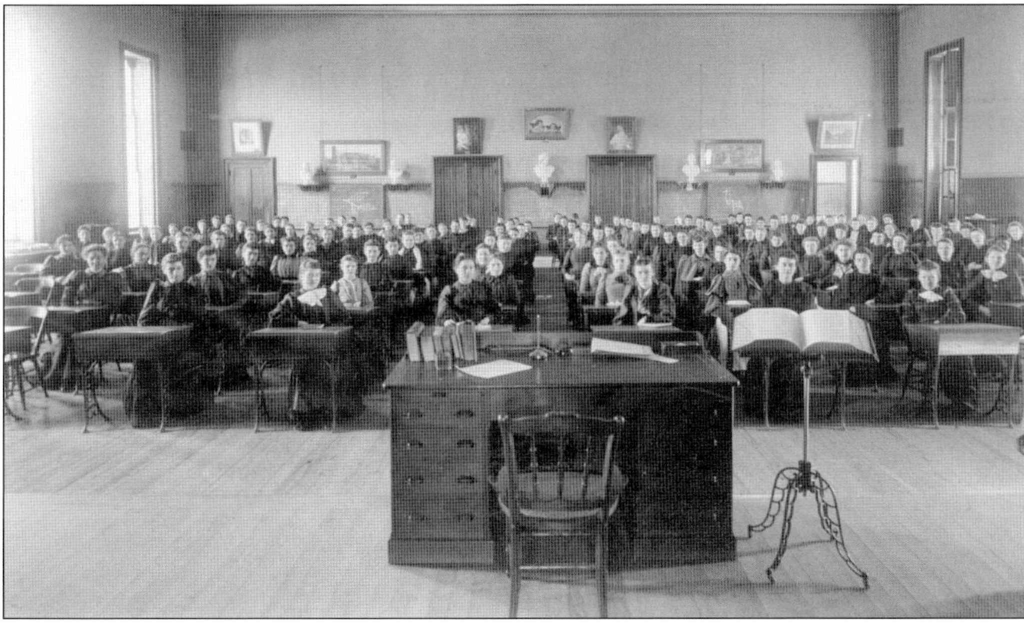

The Great Hall assemblies were also used for academic programs called "platform exercises." As described in the school catalog, these consisted of "speaking, reading, drawing, etc., on the platform in the presence of the school." Students or groups presented a lesson of not more than four minutes, but questioning from the faculty and other students expanded that time to forty minutes a day. As the catalog claims, "The exercise has the somewhat comprehensive aim of helping pupils to command their faculties and use their mother-wit amid the interruptions and distractions of the school-room."

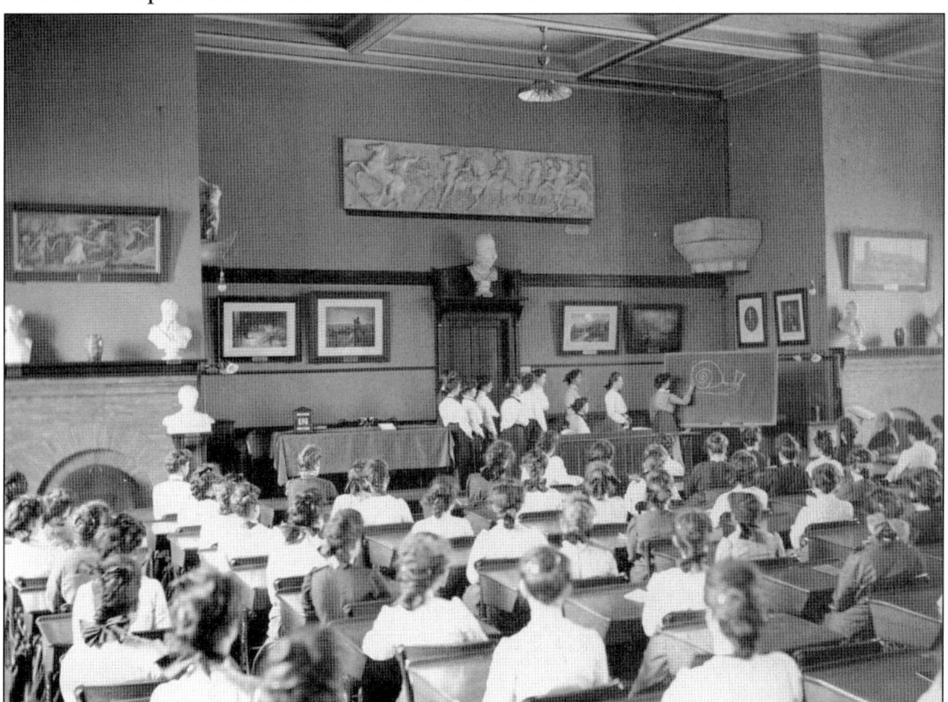

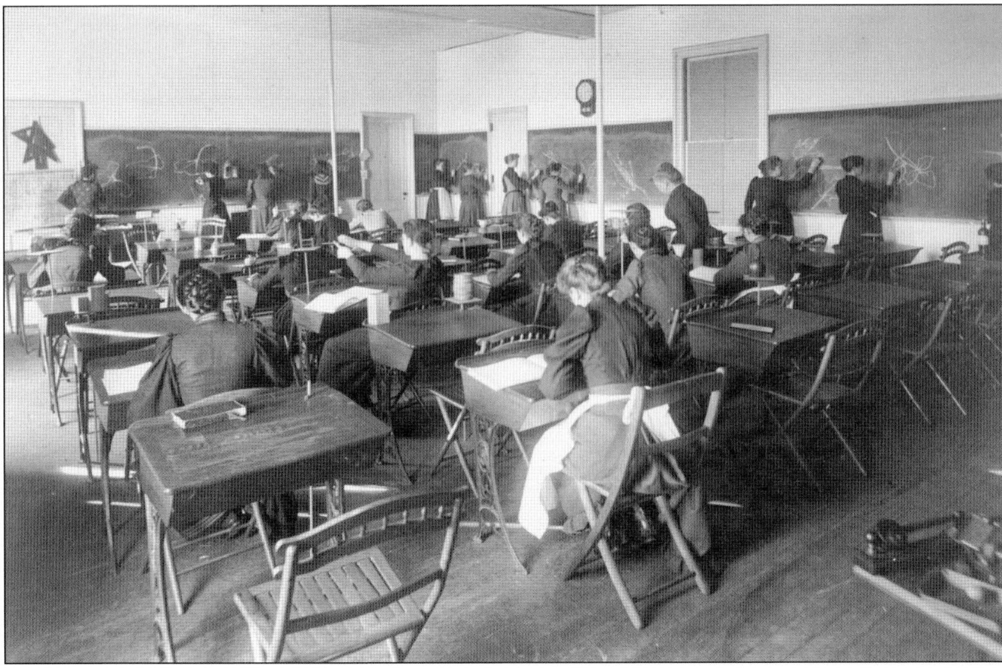

When teaching candidates were not in Great Hall assemblies, they might be found in classrooms spread throughout the building, mainly on the third and fourth floors. Here, they learned a variety of subjects they would have to teach in elementary and secondary programs. Art class was a particularly hands-on subject class.

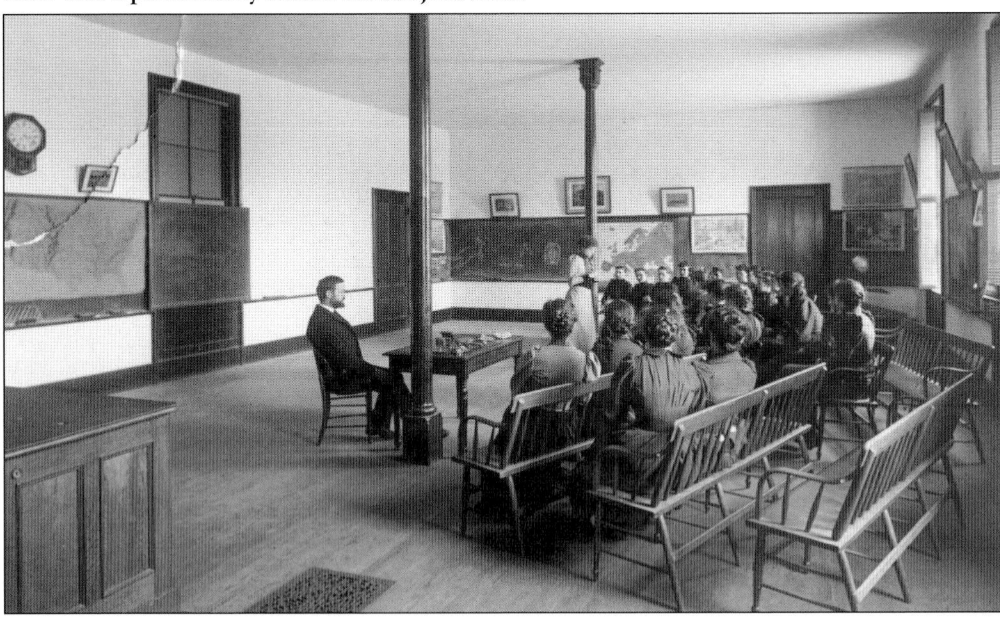

Classes might also be lecture- and discussion-based such as this geology class. In 1874, the faculty consisted of Principal Russell, who also taught, and four other faculty members who covered English, history, geography, music, sciences, and teaching theory/practice. By the turn of the century, three more faculty members were added—in mathematics and physiology, drawing and art, and literature and grammar.

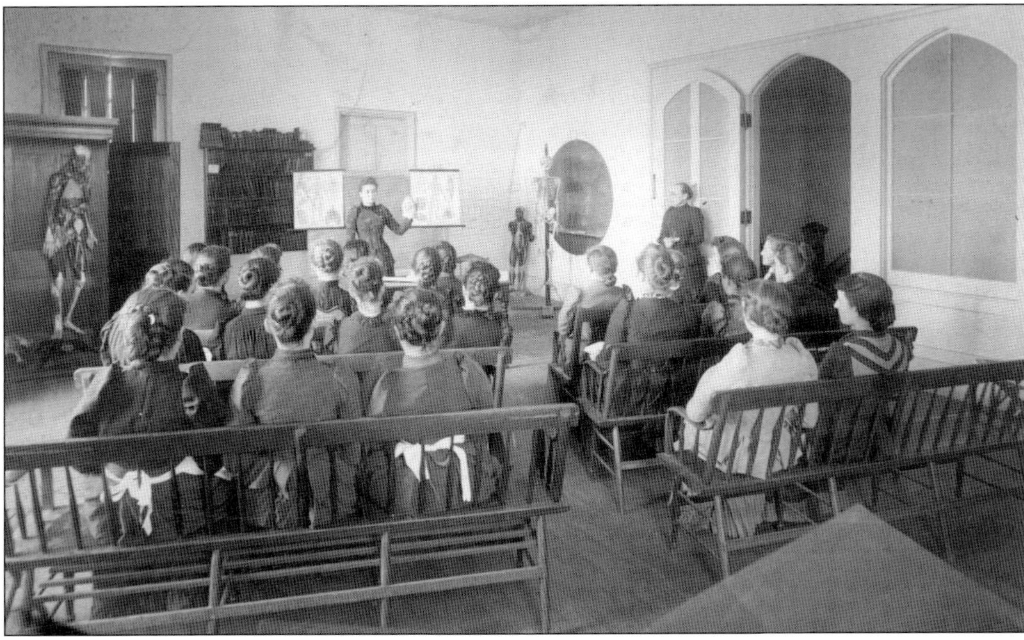

Physiology was one of the sciences on which students were tested for graduation. Also a lecture-based class, it relied on a variety of visual aids such as organ and musculature models as well as skeletons. One history records that a physiology skeleton was the last item moved out of the old building during the December 1931 removal to the new site.

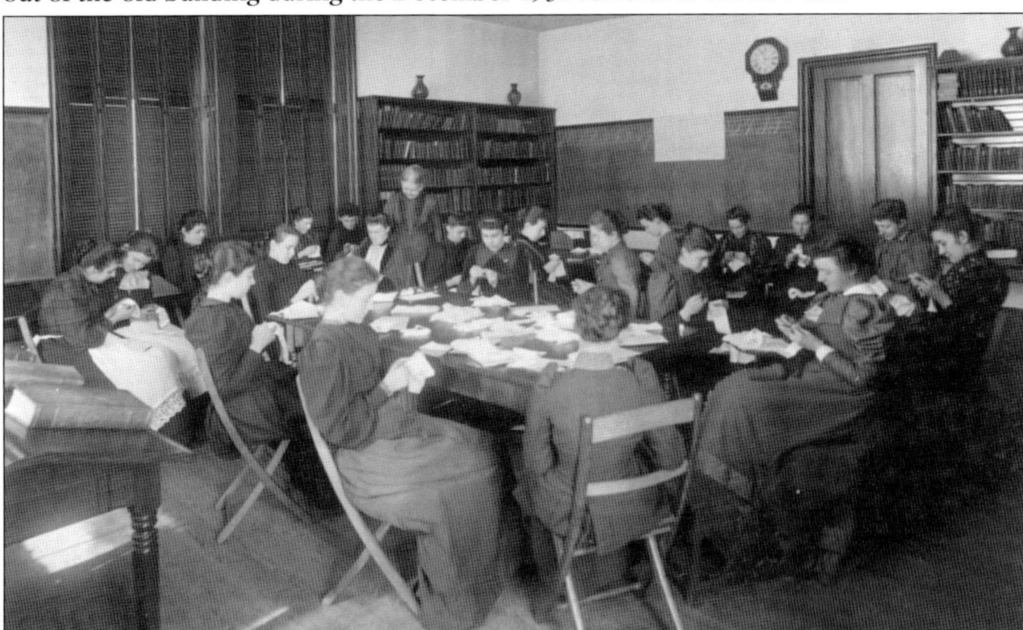

Sewing class was taught for students to gain this skill, but it was not part of the graduating examinations. For those, students had to prove proficiency in five areas: languages (English and either Latin, French, or German); mathematics; history and geography; sciences (including hygiene); and drawing and music. Candidates might also be required to sit for an oral examination.

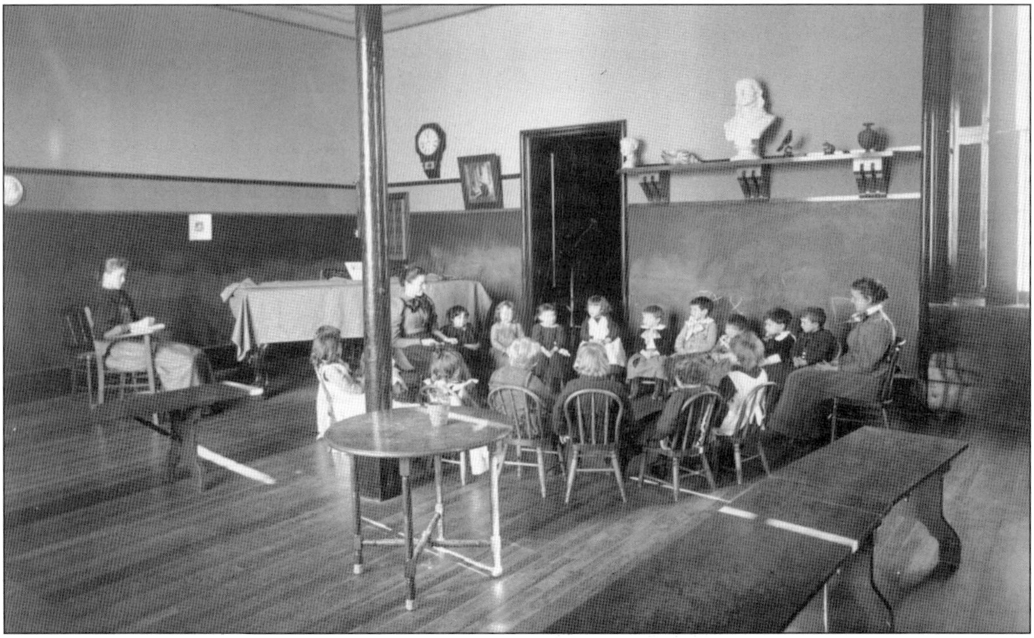

While it is a fundamental part of teacher training today, apprentice teaching in schools was relatively innovative at the time. Initially, it was more common to see apprentice teachers in front of a classroom of students on the normal school campus, than it was to see them enter urban schoolhouses and work there for a term. Both methods were practiced in Worcester as apprentices went into the city's classrooms to teach a range of students in kindergarten (above) to upper grades (below). These methods of teaching in an active urban classroom were so innovative that the federal Bureau of Education included a chapter on the school's approach in an 1891 survey of professional teaching education.

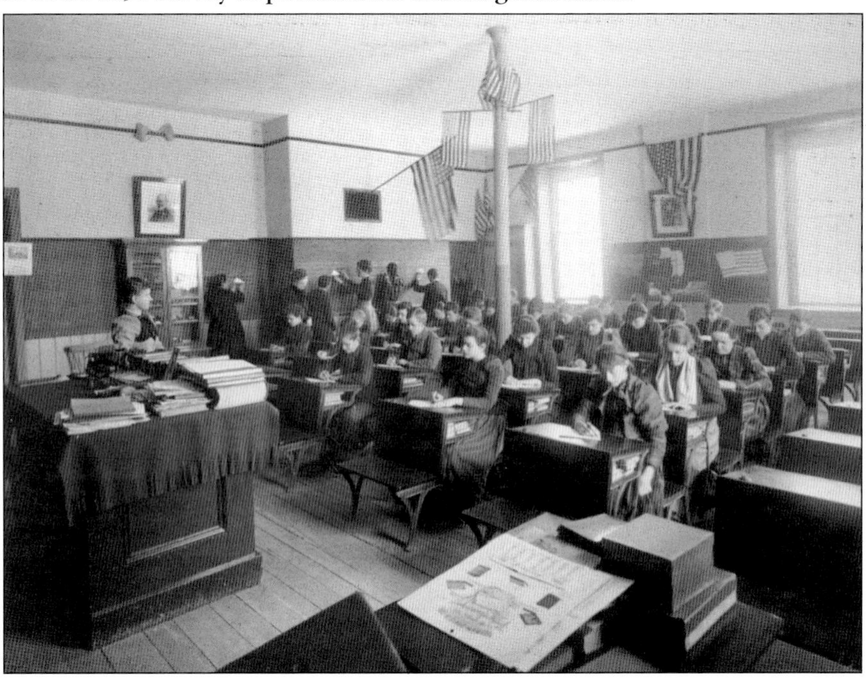

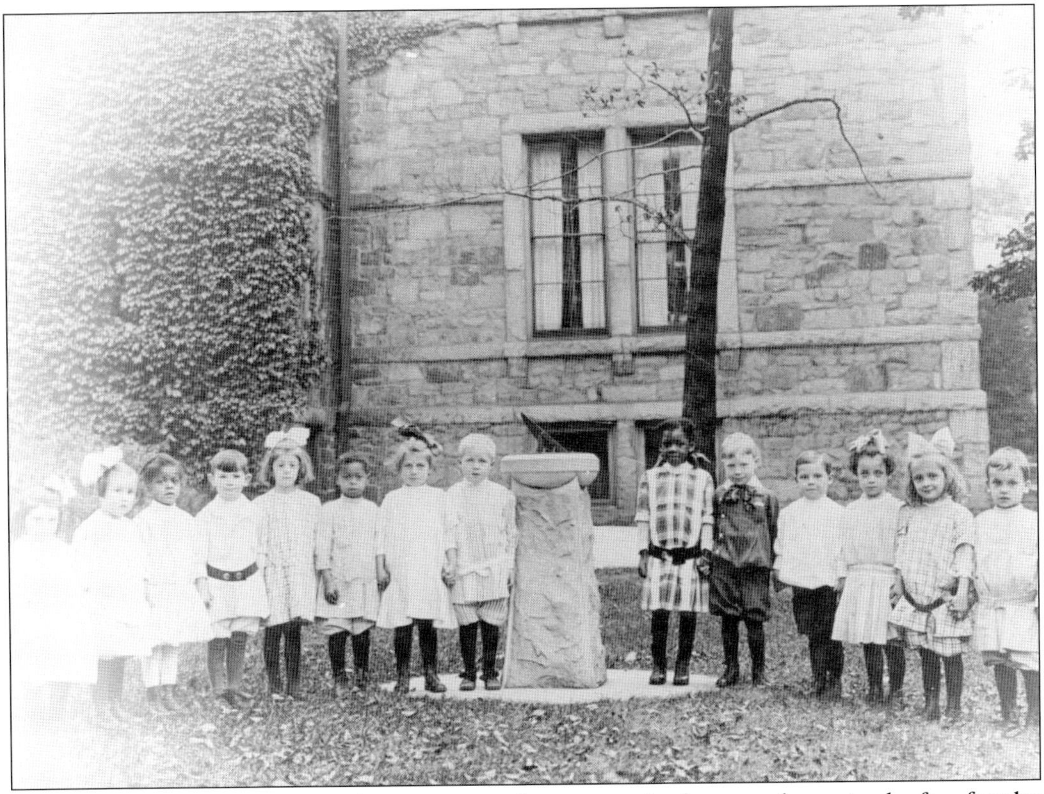

Over time, the apprentice teaching program became quite large and required a few faculty members and staff to manage it. The normal school even built a regular kindergarten on-site in addition to apprentice programs happening on campus. Consequently, young students were a regular part of campus scenes such as this one (above) in which they gathered around the sundial commemorating Principal Russell's first 25 years. Student teachers were thereby ably trained to enter the city's classrooms. (Below, Maryanne Hammond.)

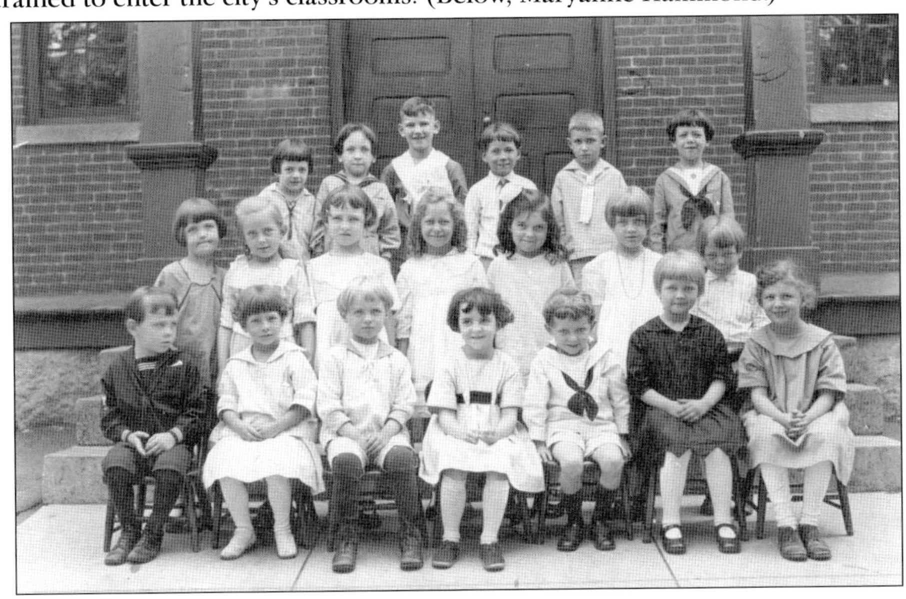

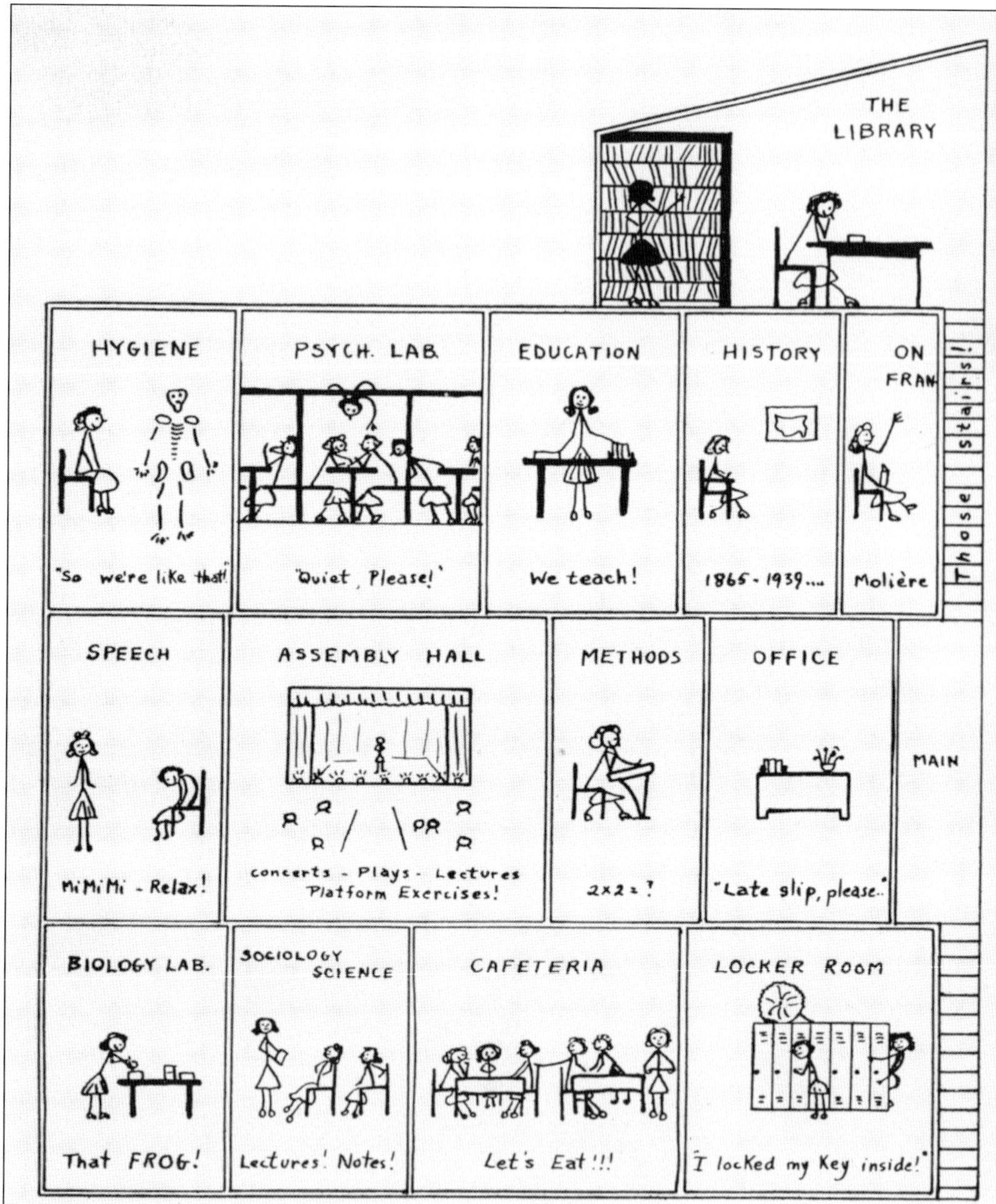

The move to the new campus afforded a larger space for the entire student body, president, and faculty to work together under one roof. (WSU Office of University Advancement.)

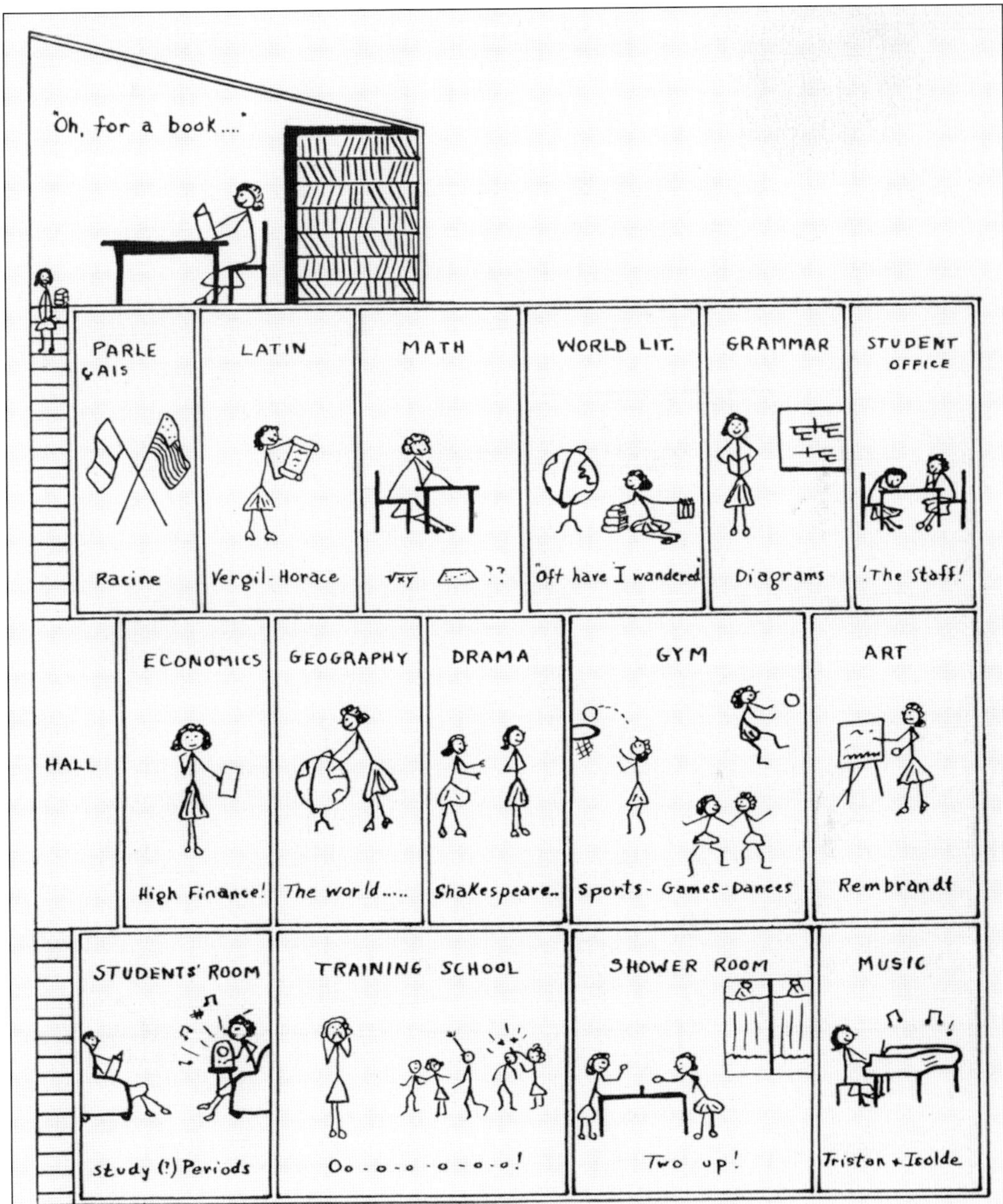

What is difficult to see in this image, though, is the depth of the building. Two three-story wings protruded back (west) from the south and north ends of the structure. As suggested on the previous page, an assembly hall and theater occupied the southern wing; a two-story gymnasium and shower facilities, which can be seen in the image on this page, occupied the northern wing. (WSU Office of University Advancement.)

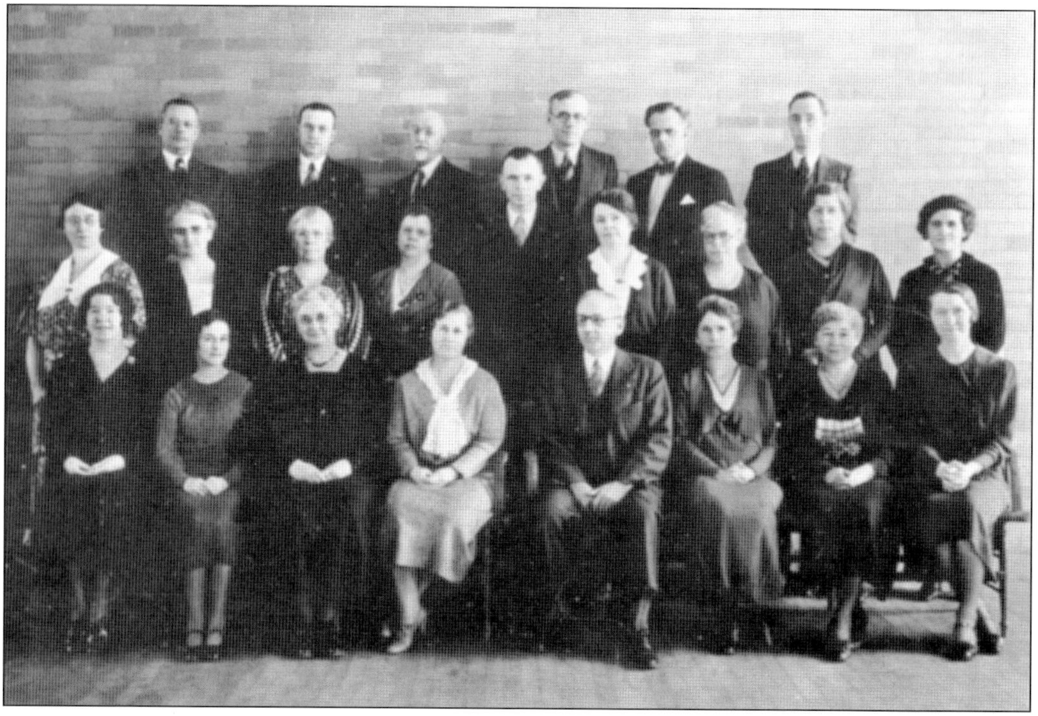

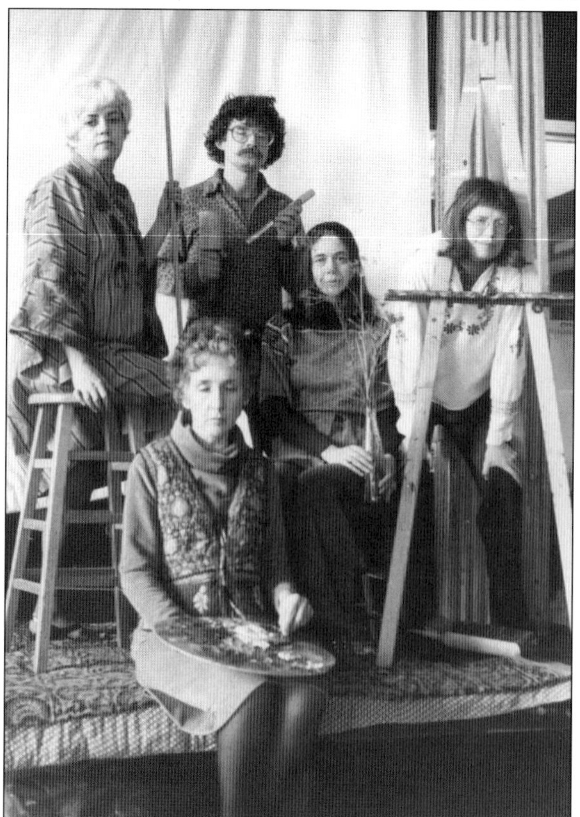

This image shows President Aspinwall and the Worcester State Teachers College faculty in 1935. Annual photographs of the faculty regularly featured the president because there was a clear relationship between them at such a small school and they collectively managed the institution. Faculty stepped into leadership positions when required, becoming deans or administrators when necessary. Some returned to the faculty and some did not, but they all started out in the same place. (WSU Office of University Advancement.)

By the 1960s and 1970s, the college had grown to such a degree that posed pictures of presidents and all professors together were no longer possible. Far more common were candids of presidents with smaller groups of faculty members or departmental photographs, such as this 1979 image featuring the art department.

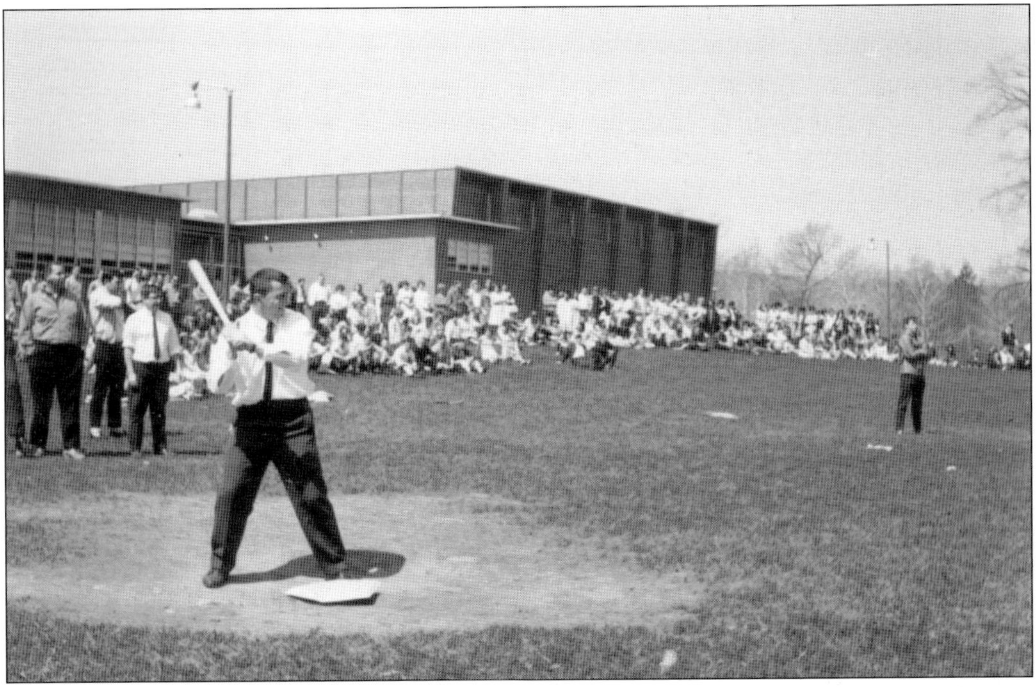

Even as the college grew and different relationships between administration and faculty formed, faculty members retained their bonds with the student body. Indeed, even outside the classroom, the faculty had professional relationships with students that resulted in moments such as this: a faculty-student baseball game. Above at bat is Prof. Vito Campo from the mathematics department, and below, students follow the progress of a game.

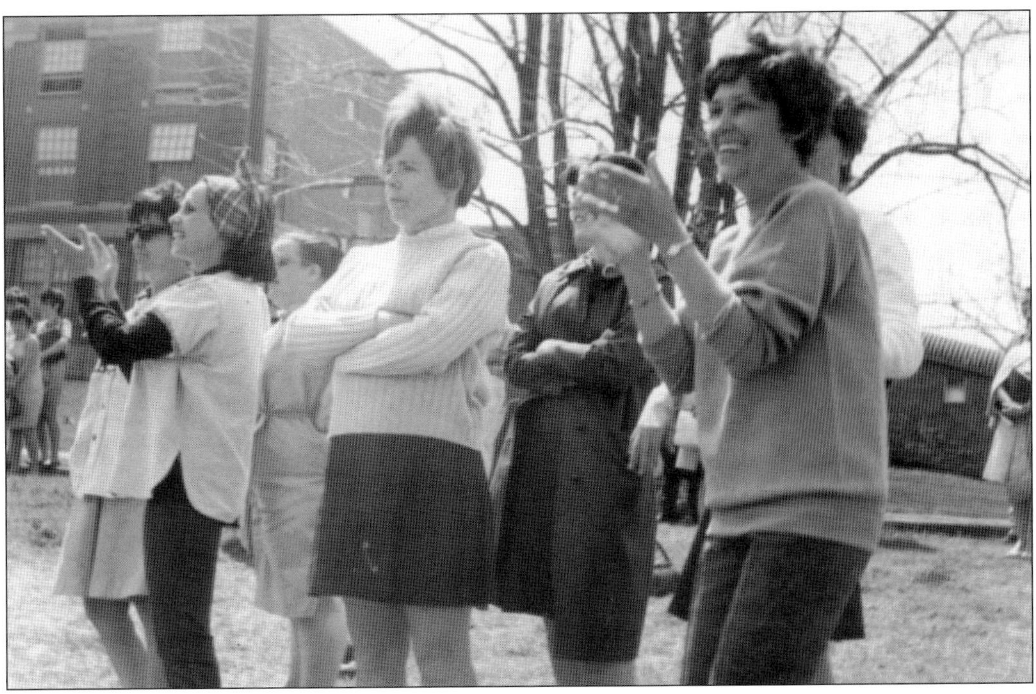

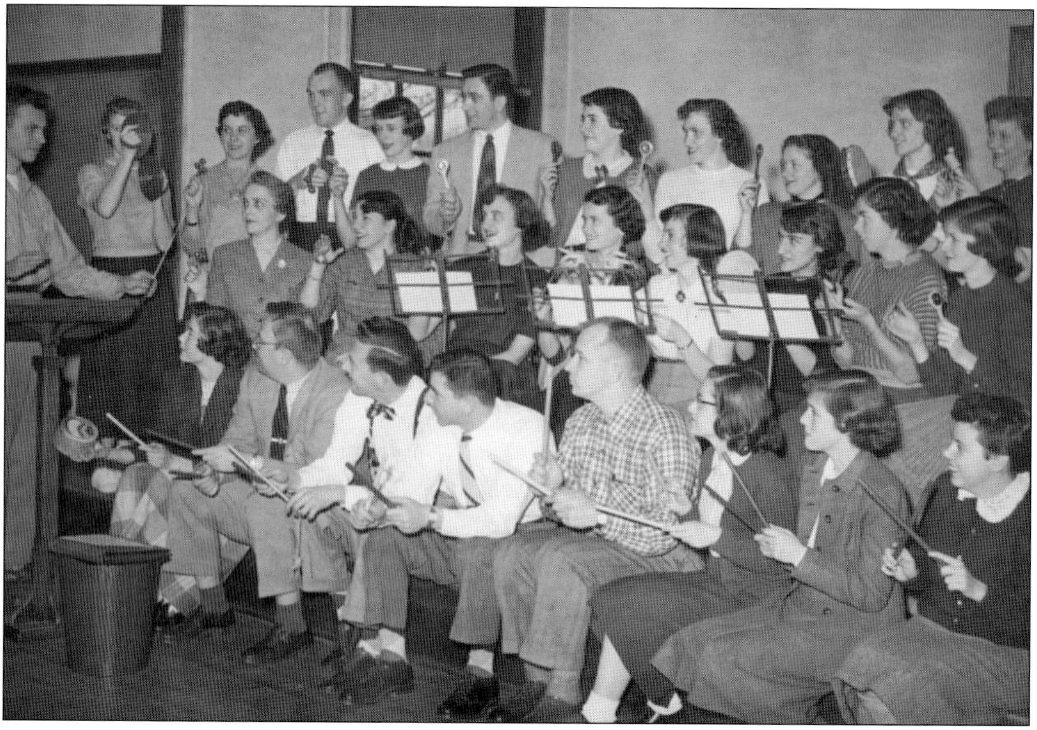

The pictures on these two pages show classrooms at different points in the 1950s, 1960s, and 1970s. Images such as these afford viewers moments to contrast them with images from earlier points in the school's history to glimpse what has changed over time and what has not—fashion, gender balance, facilities, pedagogical approaches? The pictures on these pages show music instruction for teaching students (above, this page), discussion in a social studies course (below, this page), a physics lab (above, next page), and a sculpting class (below, next page).

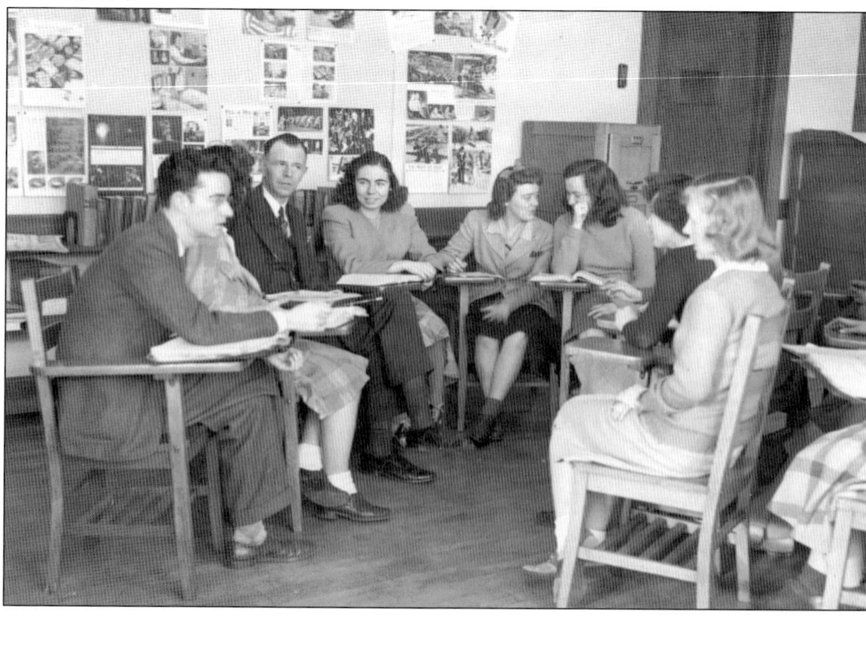

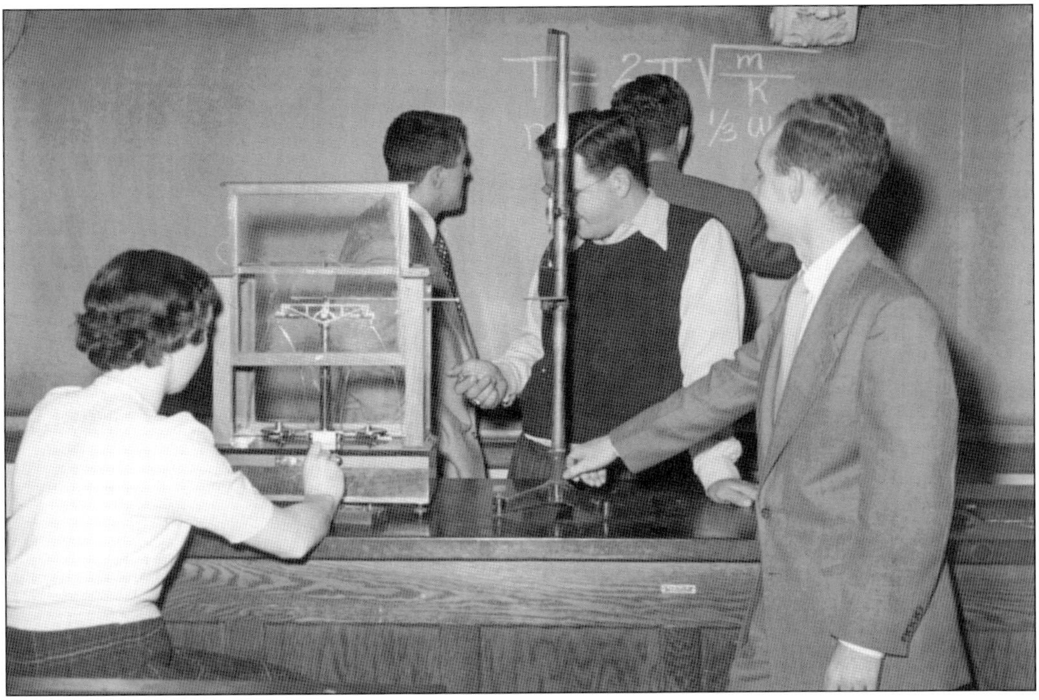

Some things are not readily observable from images. For example, over time, the faculty has become considerably more credentialed. While few teachers held doctoral degrees in the early decades of the normal school, it is overwhelmingly the situation today that faculty members have doctoral or other terminal degrees in their areas. (Below, WSU CityLab, Vincent "Jake" Powers Archives.)

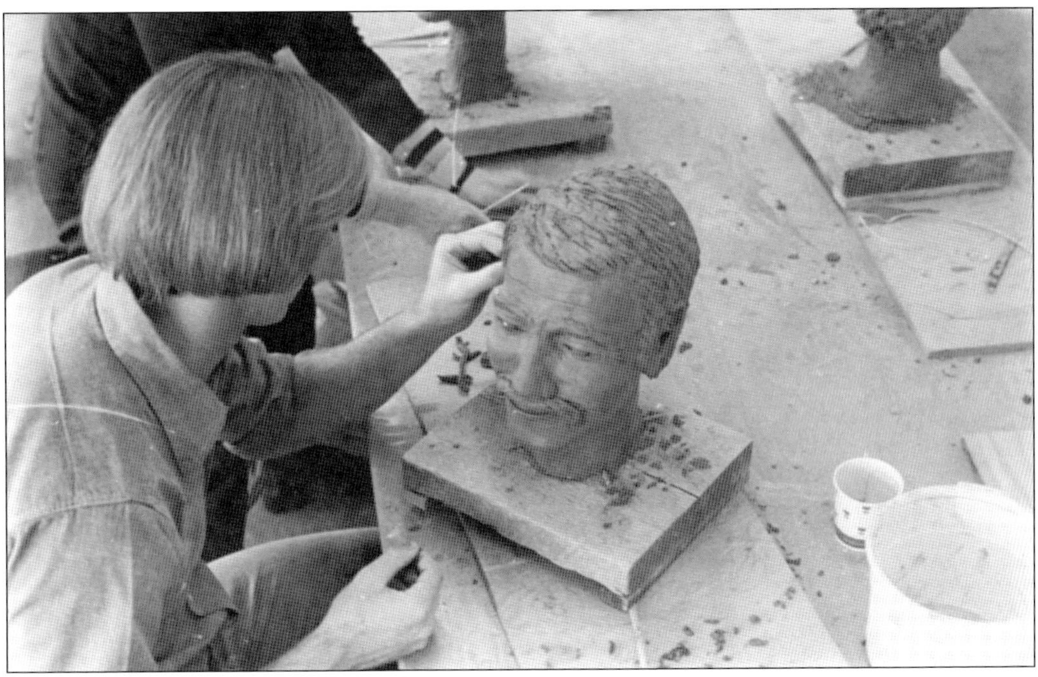

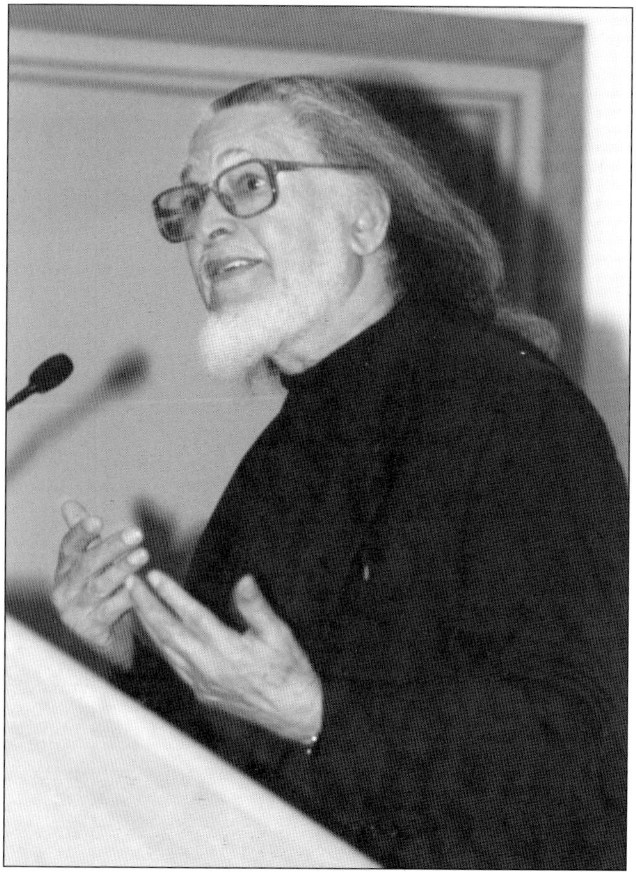

As with any school, Worcester State has a history of bringing experts and notable persons of local, regional, and national prominence to augment classroom education. These visits take on a variety of configurations from formal lectures to informal panels, and conference presentations to guest lecturing in specific classes. Pictured at left is South African activist, poet, and educator Dennis Brutus speaking on campus; his papers are preserved in the WSU Archives and Special Collections. Below, Massachusetts governor Michael Dukakis kicks off a conference on aging held in the Sullivan Building.

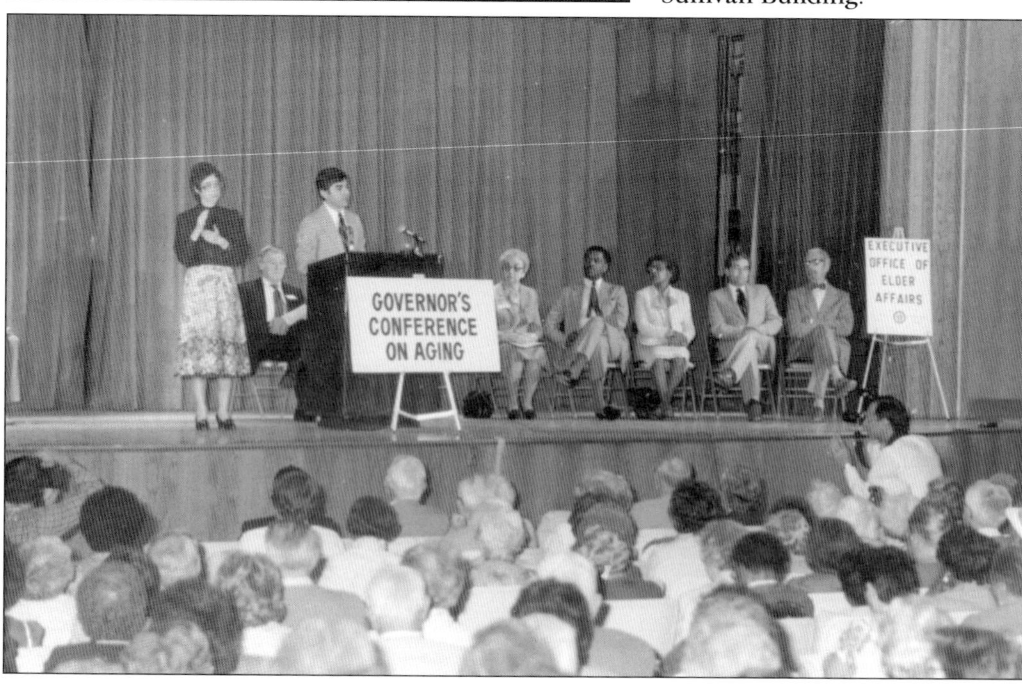

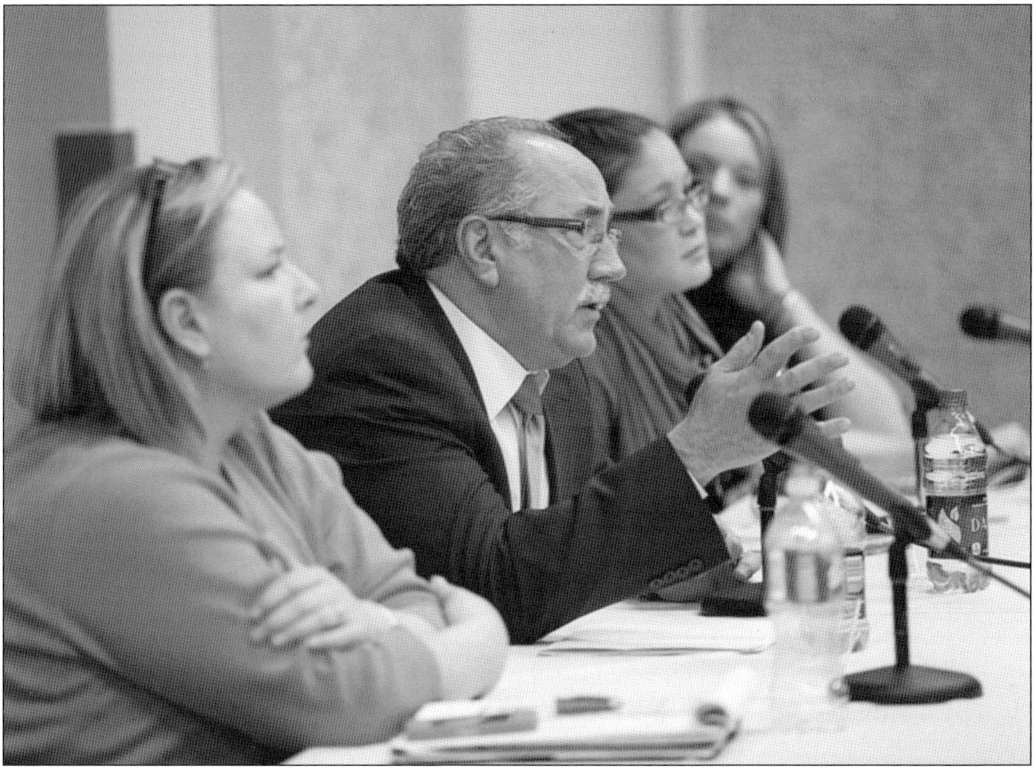

Above, state legislator James O'Day, Kate Kerr, and Amanda Herron (all WSU alumni) participate in a panel discussion on homelessness with current students. In a more formal setting, US secretary of education Richard W. "Dick" Riley addresses the campus community about the importance of and challenges facing public education in the late 1990s. (Above, WSU Office of Marketing.)

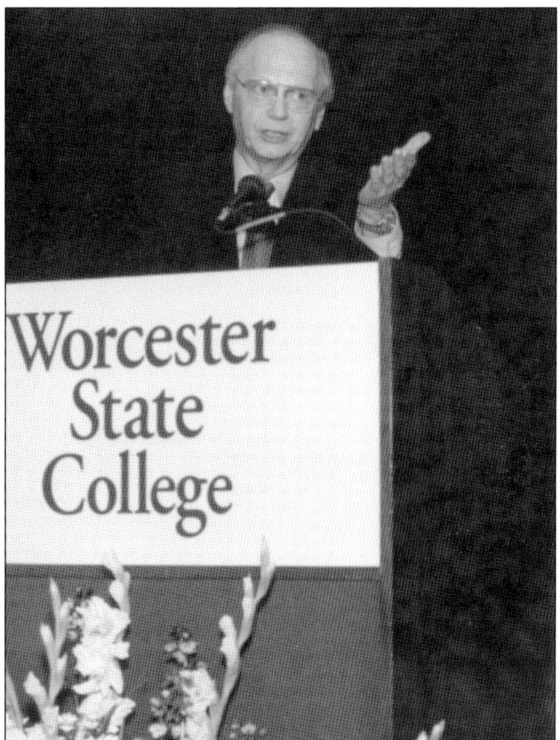

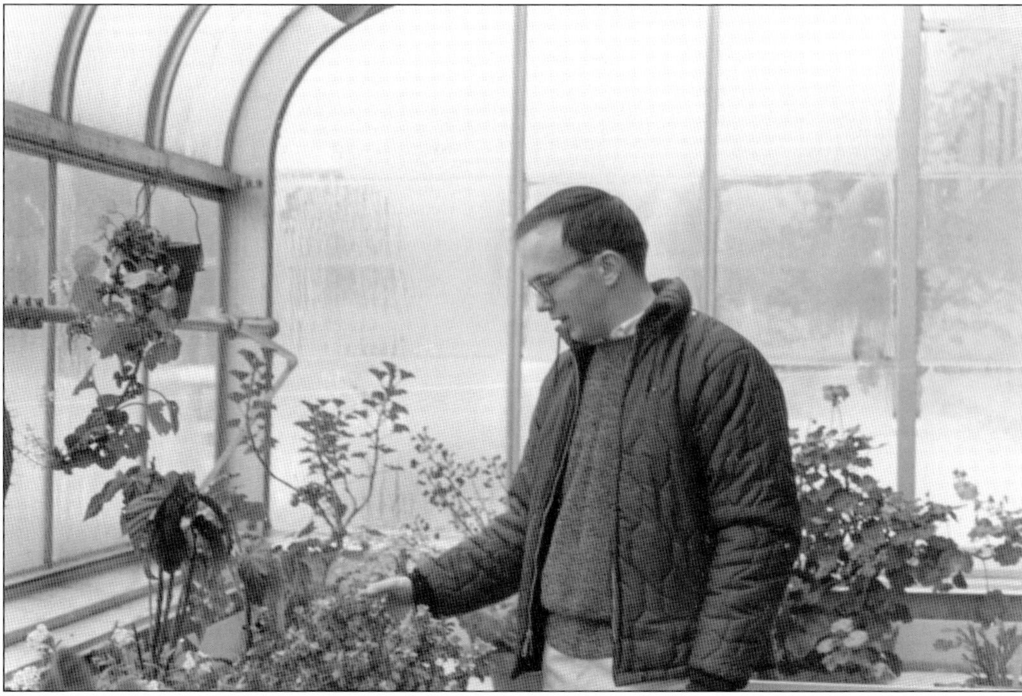

Plant biology had been a subject of study at the normal school from its early days. Even the grounds of the original site had "pocket gardens," areas with beds of specific flowers, and a variety of trees planted around the grounds. Plant biology continued to be studied at the Chandler Street campus, and when the new science building (now the Sullivan Building) was erected, a greenhouse was attached on the first floor (above). While the greenhouse moved to the completed Ghosh Building, a newer form of outdoor classroom has been created in the WSU Teaching Garden, located across the street from campus and overseen by the Urban Action Institute (below). (Below, WSU Office of Marketing.)

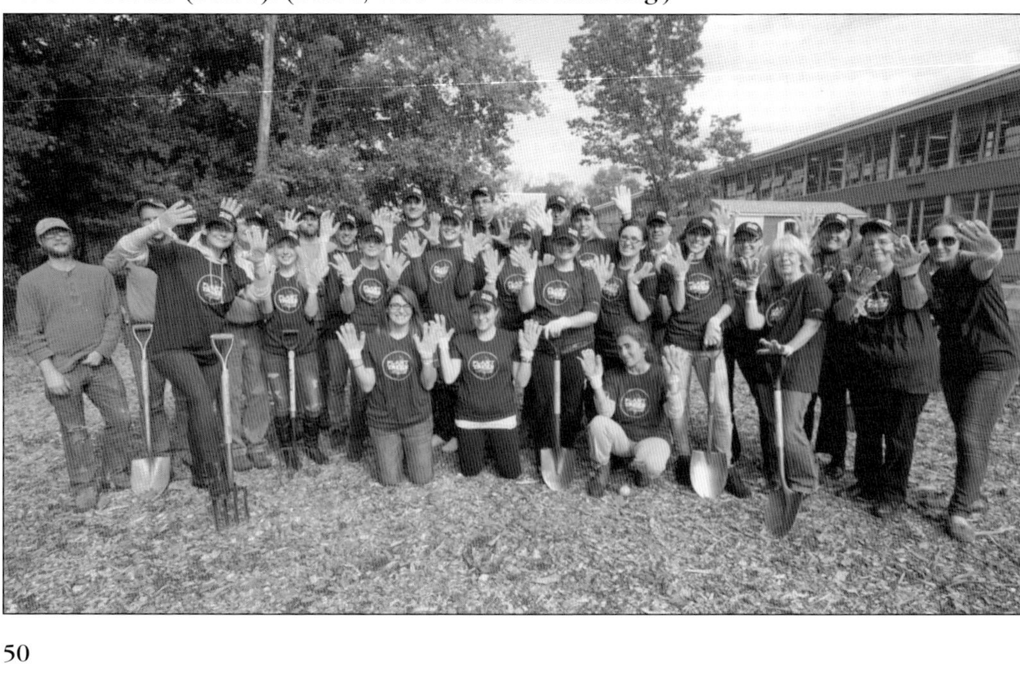

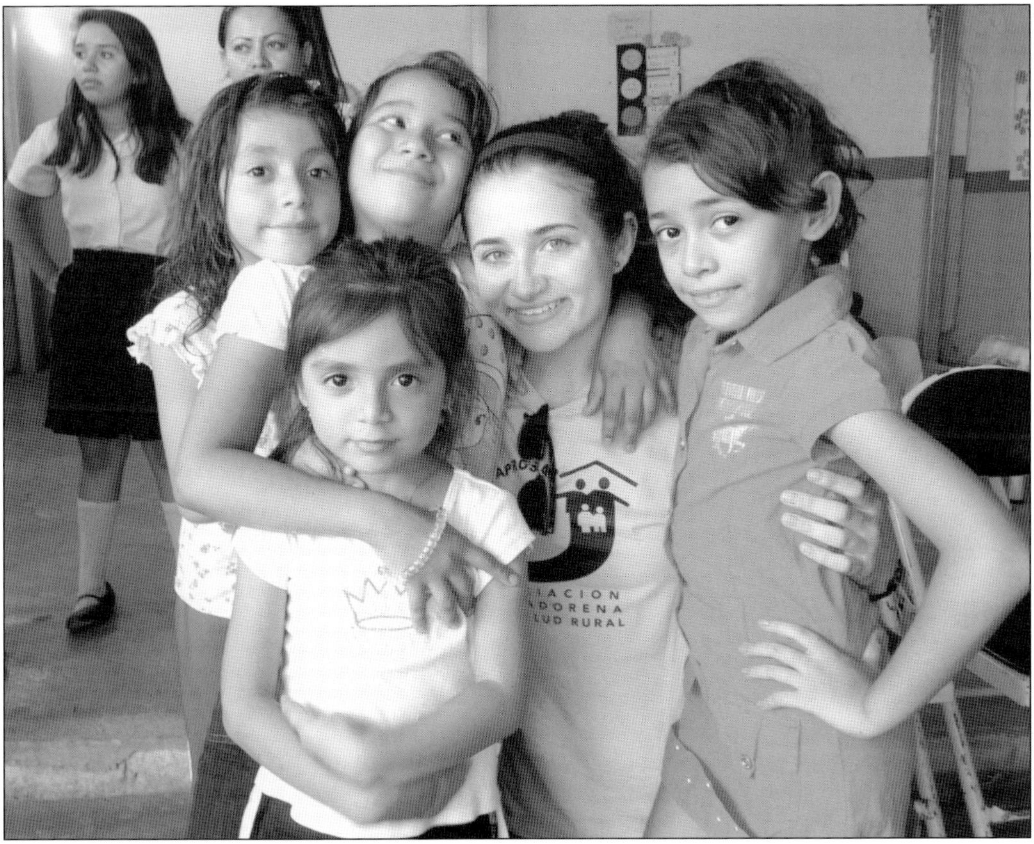

More recently, Worcester State University, like many American universities, is emphasizing the importance of cultural exchange and intellectual exploration through study abroad and study away programs. These take students to different parts of the world to experience life and learning in different contexts. Two examples of study abroad trips are pictured here: one to El Salvador (above) and the other to the Dominican Republic (below). Other university students and faculty have gone abroad to Europe, Africa, Asia, and South America, and to other cities in North America, including Chicago, New York, New Orleans, Detroit, and Los Angeles. (Both, WSU Office of Marketing.)

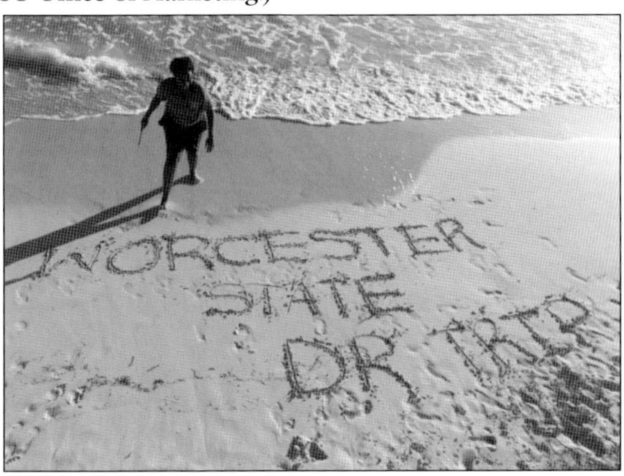

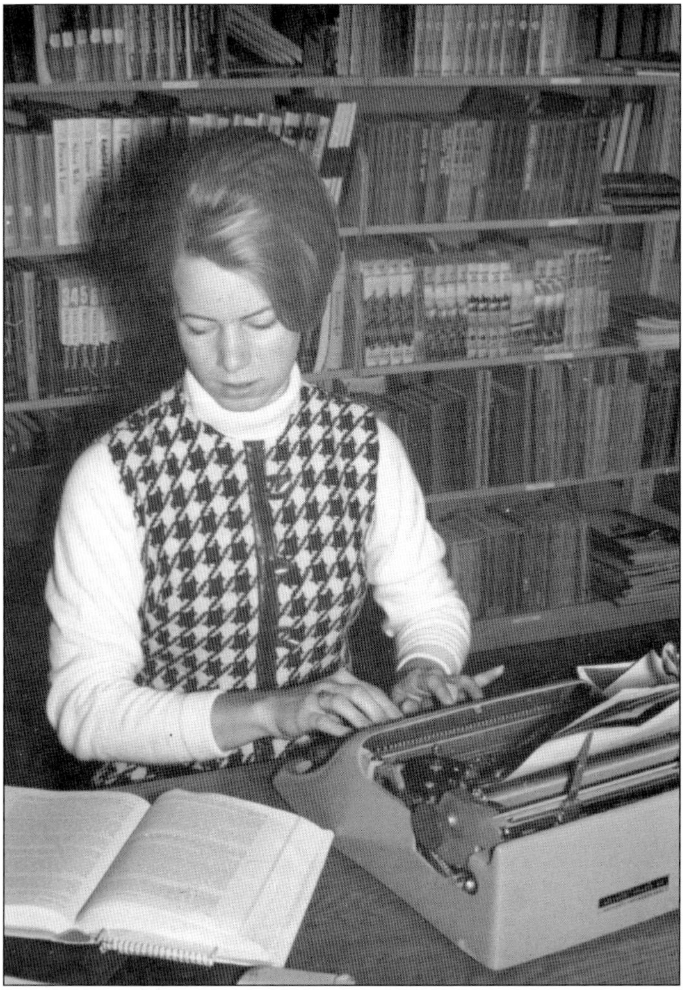

Two elements of the college experience offer interesting (and entertaining) contrasts over time. The first is the methods by which students prepare written work for professors. Before Internet-based collaborative software packages that allowed students to work in "the cloud," students used word processors that required saving work on disks; typewriters, as this student is using in 1967 (left); and handwriting. Especially in the 1970s and 80s, pie-eating contests accompanied larger festivals and events. Yearbooks from these decades and candid pictures in the university archives include many images of pie-eating contests indoors (most frequently in the Student Center) and outdoors, at homecoming, winter carnival, and interclass events (below).

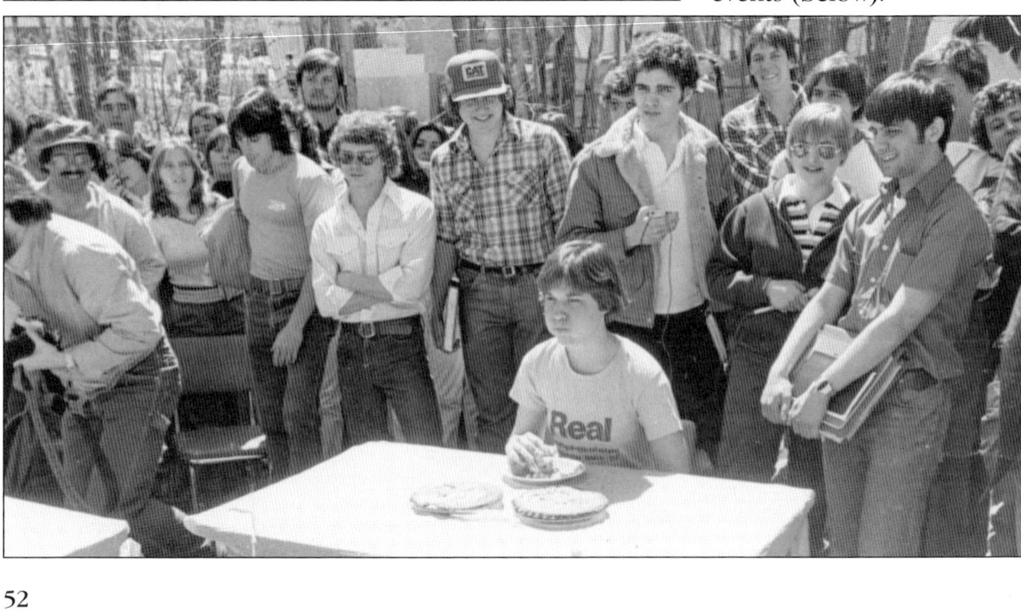

Four

DORMITORIES

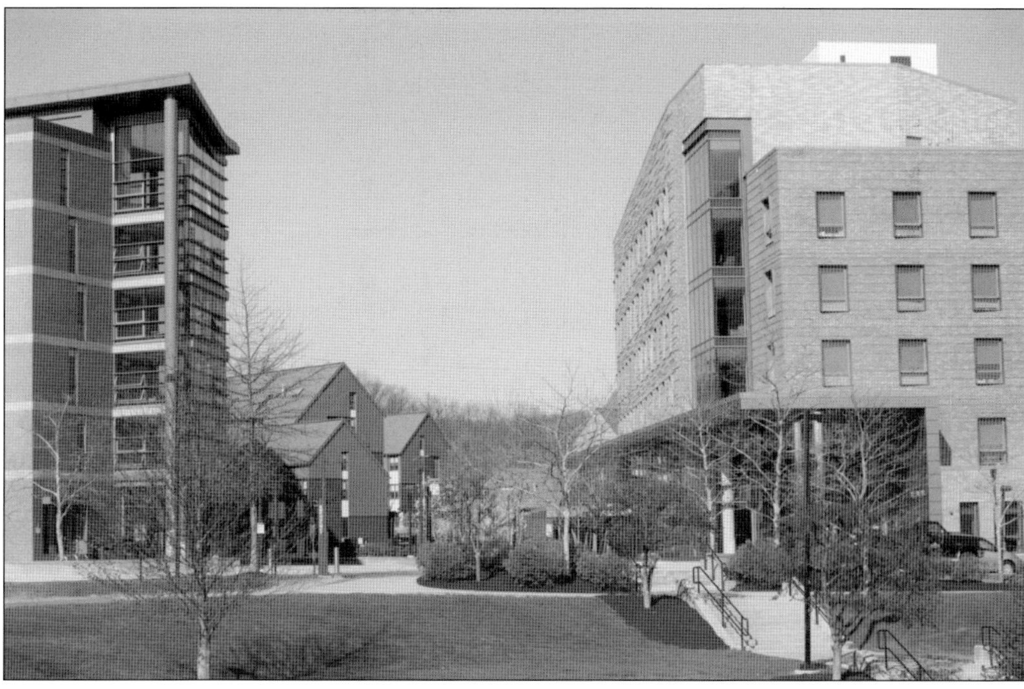

A familiar scene for today's students, staff, and faculty is the residence area of upper campus. This large campus district is only a relatively recent addition to Worcester State, one that was not initially connected to the academic buildings as closely as it is now. This chapter looks at Worcester State University's residential areas over time.

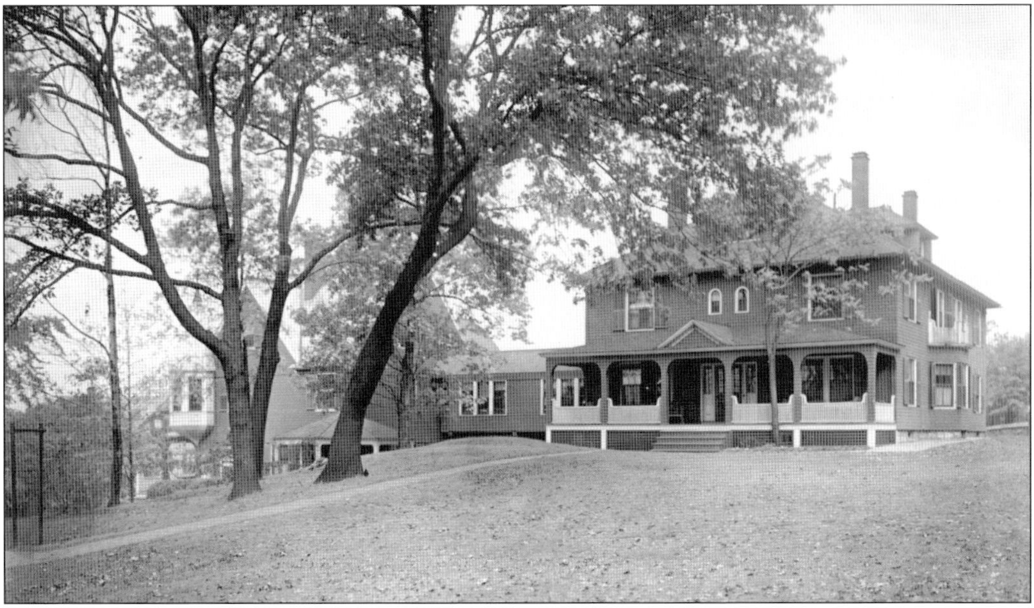

Attached to the west side of the principal's house, Stoddard Terrace was built in 1891 to accommodate about 20 young women and a few teachers. Prior to this, normal school students who lived far from campus sought room and board with nearby families, often introduced through faculty members. Because Stoddard Terrace initially had neither a dining hall nor a kitchen, those students who lodged here still had to make arrangements for board with neighboring families. Cost of board in this fashion was approximately $4 per week. Room rent at this dormitory was $38 for the school year, and two girls shared a furnished room. By the end of the dorm's use in 1931, annual costs had risen to $325 per year, but this amount included meals.

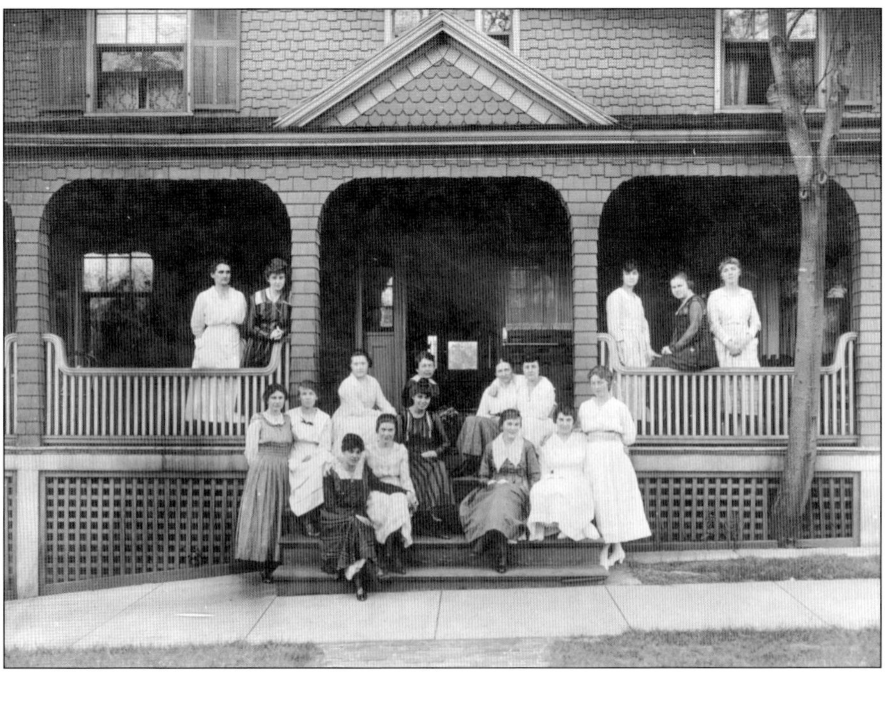

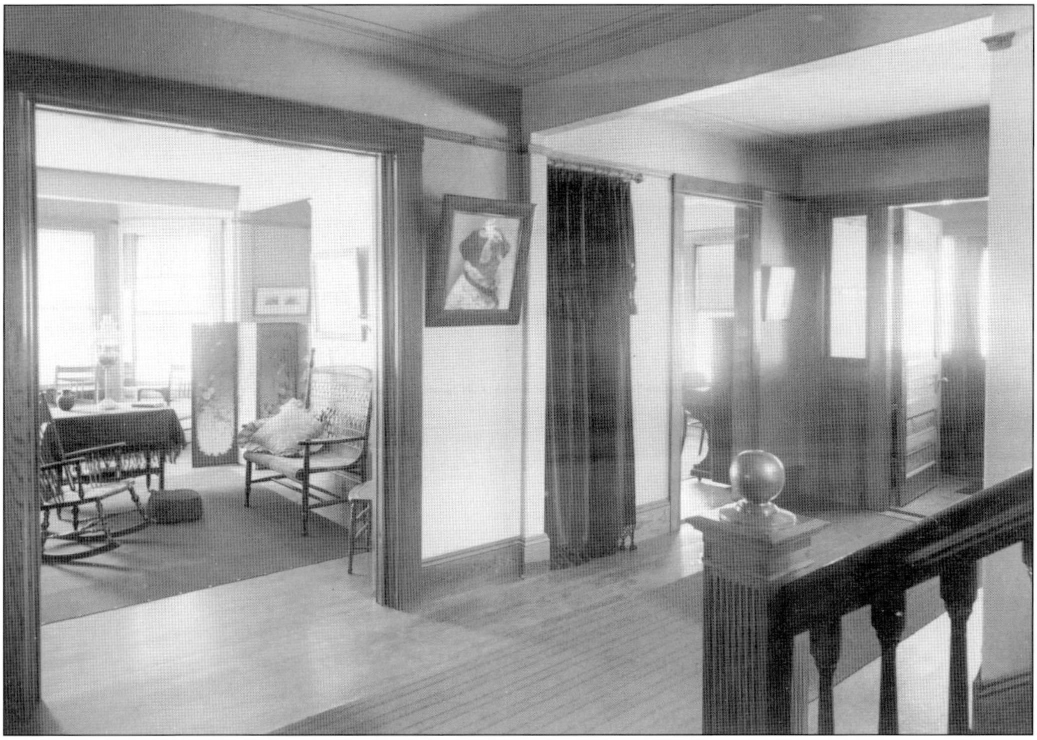

There were many common spaces in Stoddard Hall. The main foyer and hallway (above) connected sitting and receiving rooms although the presence of faculty and the proximity of the principal ensured gatherings were restrained and well-chaperoned. Still, there was clearly a social life at the dorm both inside (below) and around the outside.

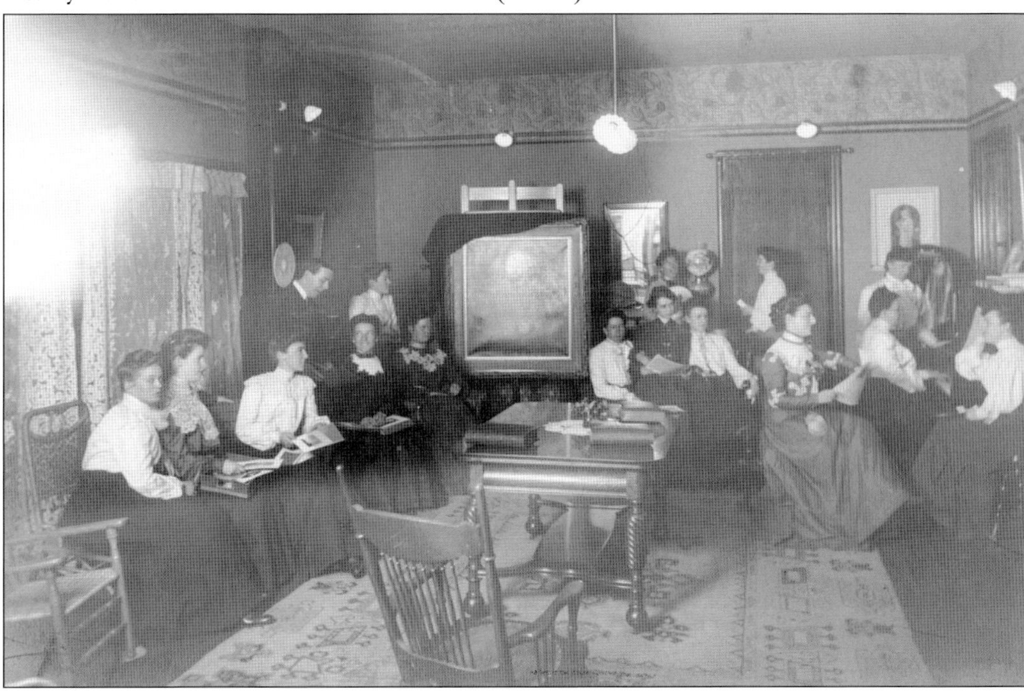

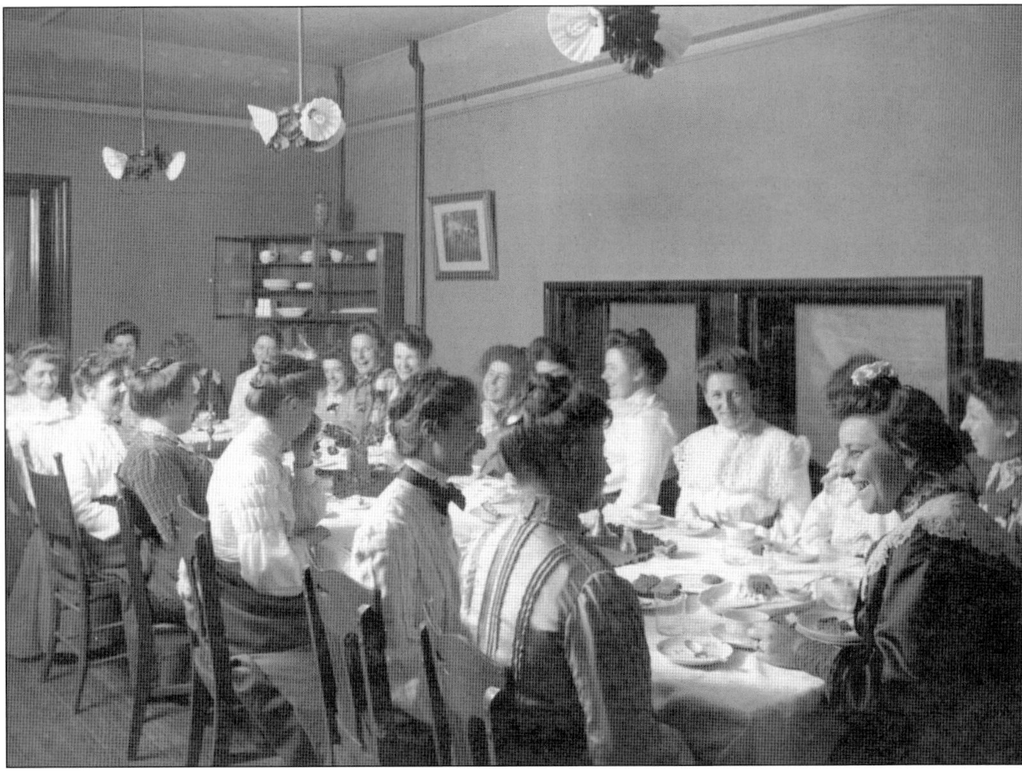

By the time Francis Random Lane became principal in 1909, the need for some sort of food preparation and eating facilities at Stoddard Terrace had become a much-discussed issue. He quickly moved to create both, which deepened the social connections among the residents. Living quarters in the furnished rooms were perhaps more spacious than those of modern-day students, but there were also fewer items and accoutrements to locate in the rooms.

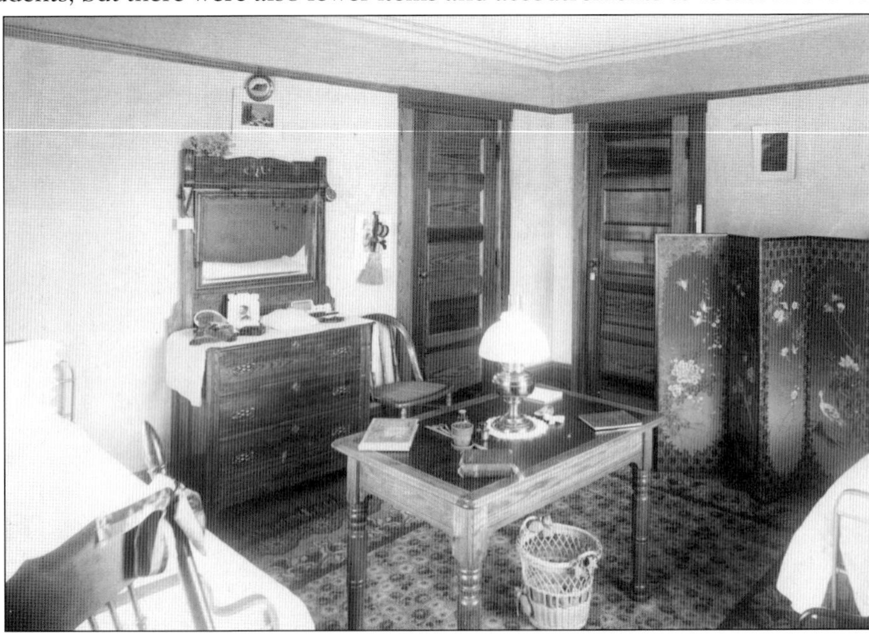

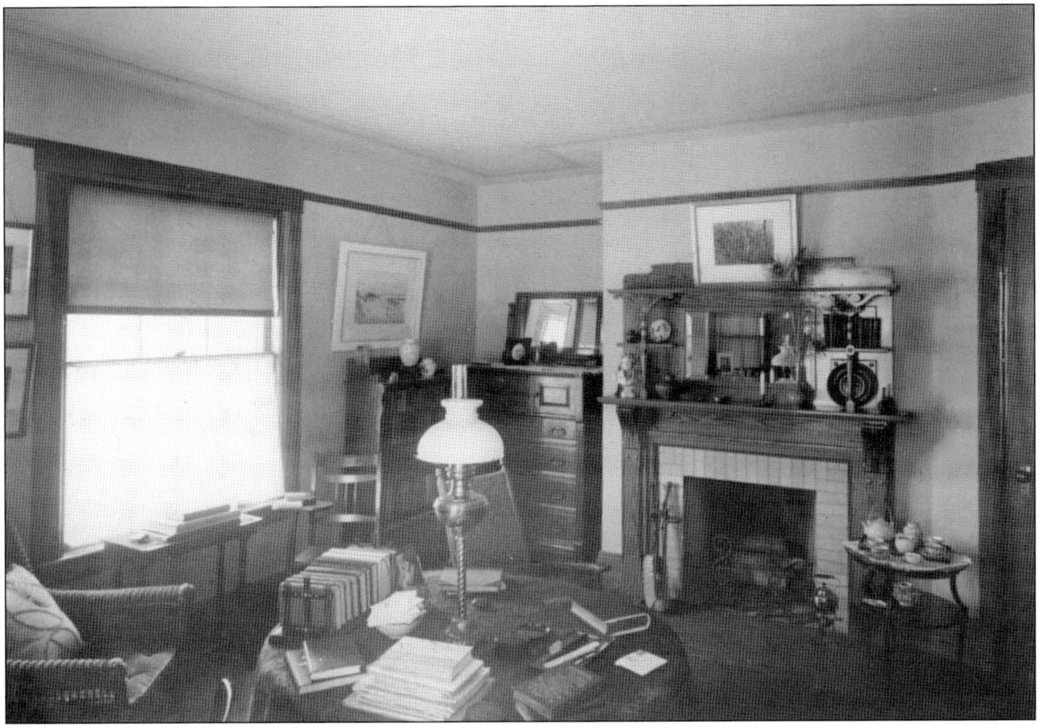

Teacher's rooms at Stoddard Terrace appear to be single-occupancy rooms with enough space for work areas that included books, desks, and furniture for more personal touches.

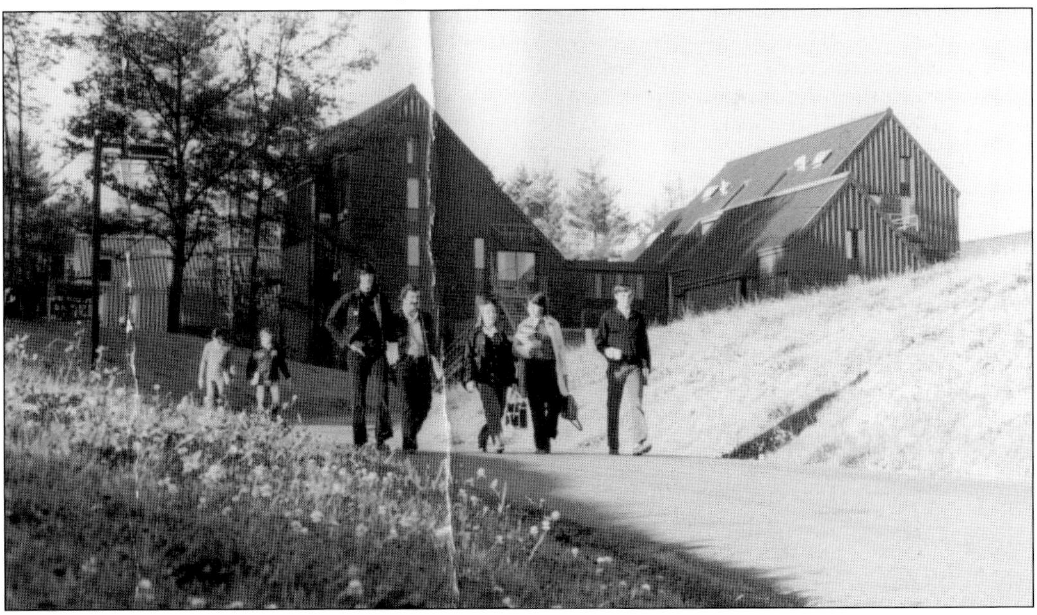

Chandler Village consists of 63 apartments in a series of 26 townhouse-style units. Opened in 1973, they house 440 students with common living spaces and kitchens. In some ways, Chandler Village is a clear, though larger, descendant of Stoddard Terrace. When Chandler Village was built, it was located on the western edge of the campus, a short distance from the academic buildings but isolated enough from them nevertheless.

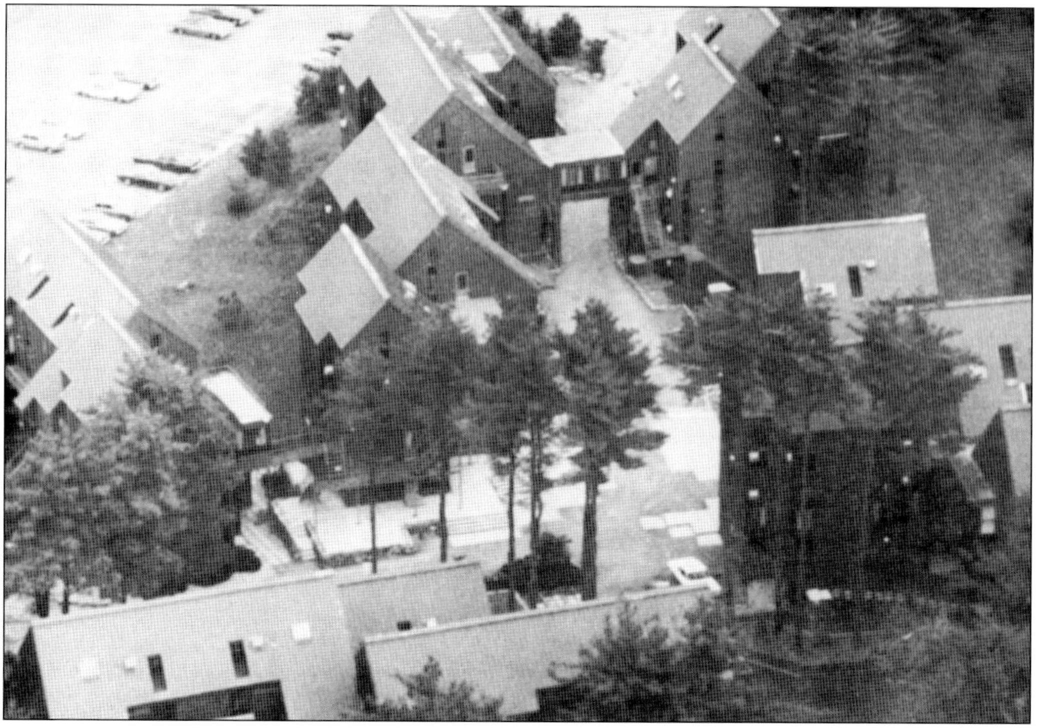

Because Chandler Village was set apart from the academic core and its residents did not have the president and faculty members living next to or among them, those students enjoyed a level of independence and freedom that Stoddard Terrace residents could not have imagined a half century earlier. (Both, WSU Student Involvement and Leadership Development Collection.)

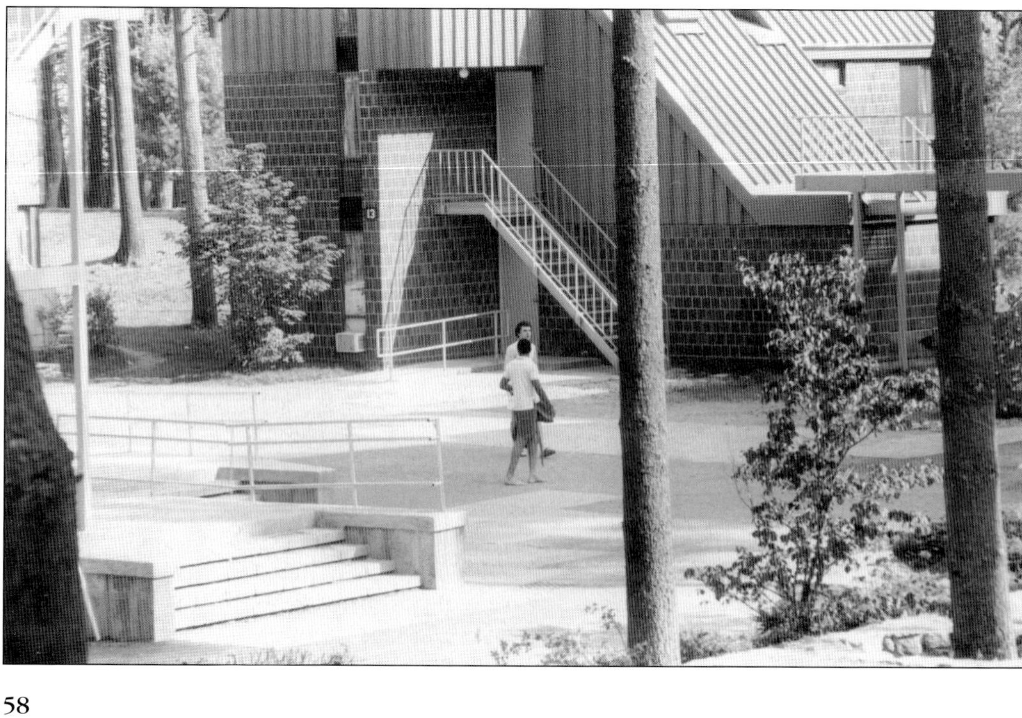

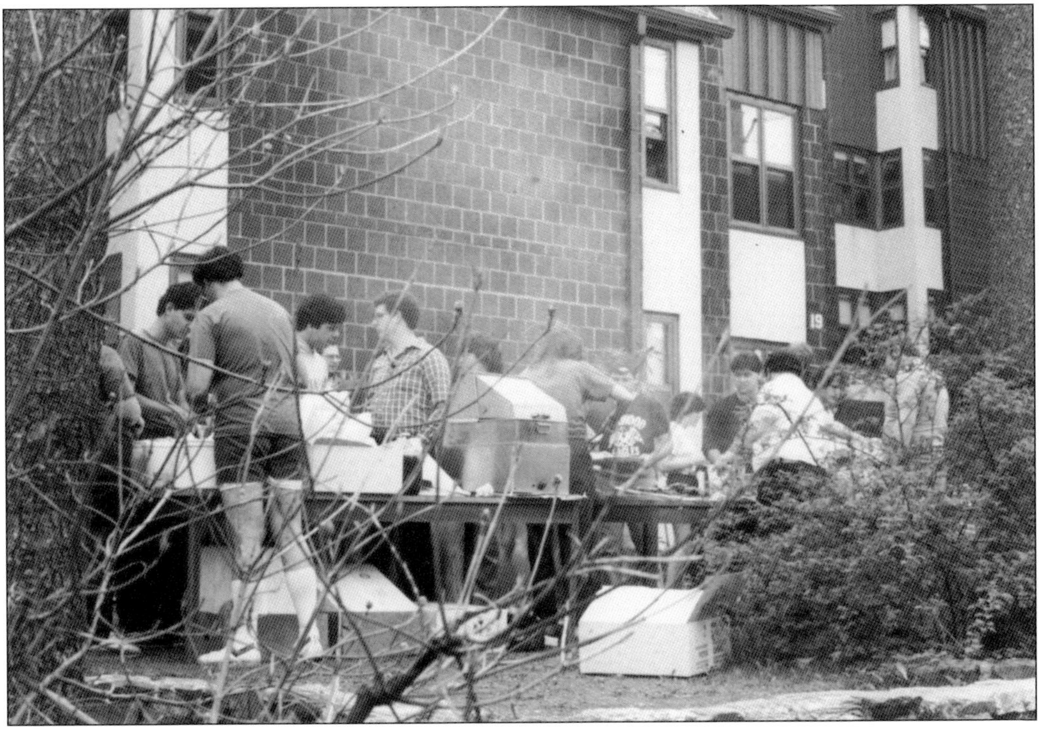

Combined with its physical layout—not a traditional dorm but rather something of a neighborhood—Chandler Village saw a lot of community-style events such as games, cookouts, and concerts. (Both, WSU Student Involvement and Leadership Development Collection.)

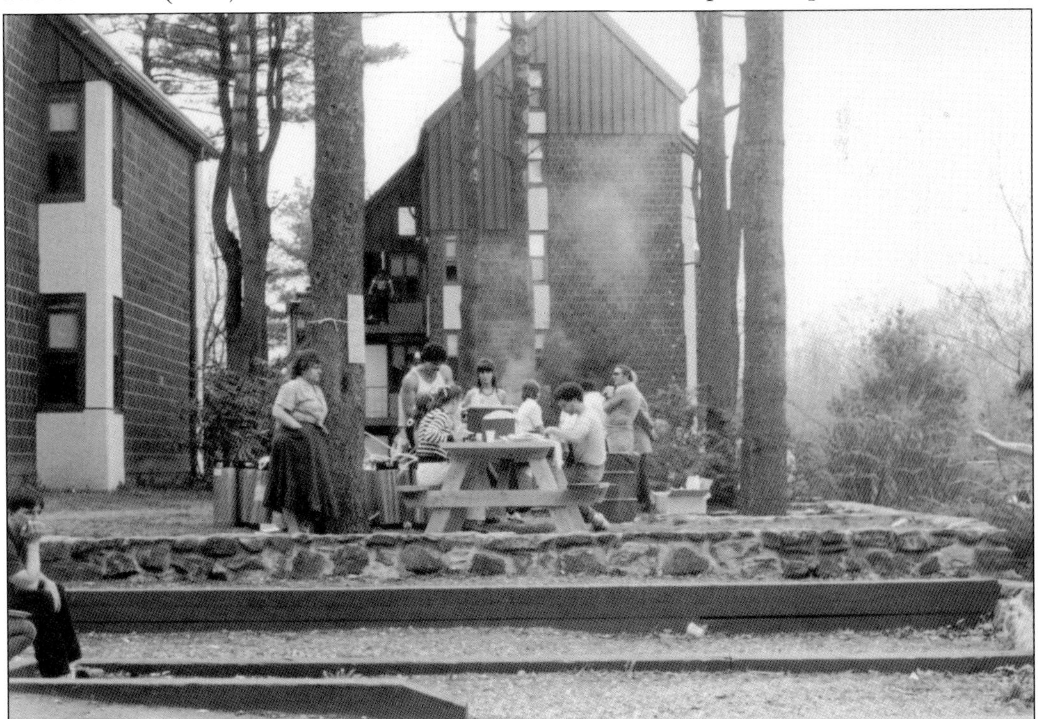

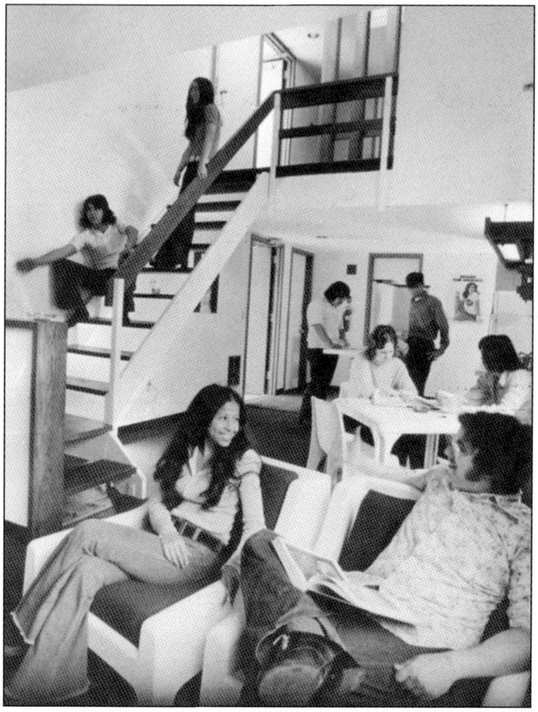

Even the interior suite-style arrangement of Chandler Village dorms fostered community and an independent home-away-from-home feeling for many students. Occupancies of each unit are four, eight, nine, ten, or eleven students, and roommate choices are allowed, of course.

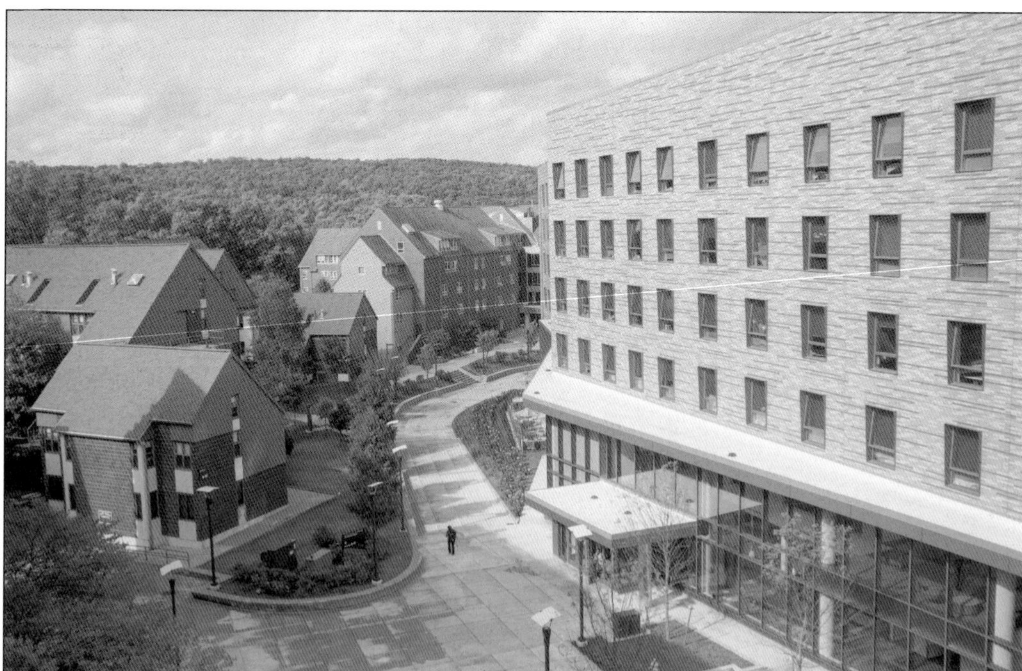

This image shows the spatial and physical relationships between Chandler Village, on the left, and Dowden Hall on the right. Dowden is a five-story, more traditional dormitory opened in 1990, and from this angle dwarfs the Chandler Village units. Initially built to house 240 students, the residence hall is named for Vera Dowden, the first dean of students at Worcester State. (WSU Office of Marketing.)

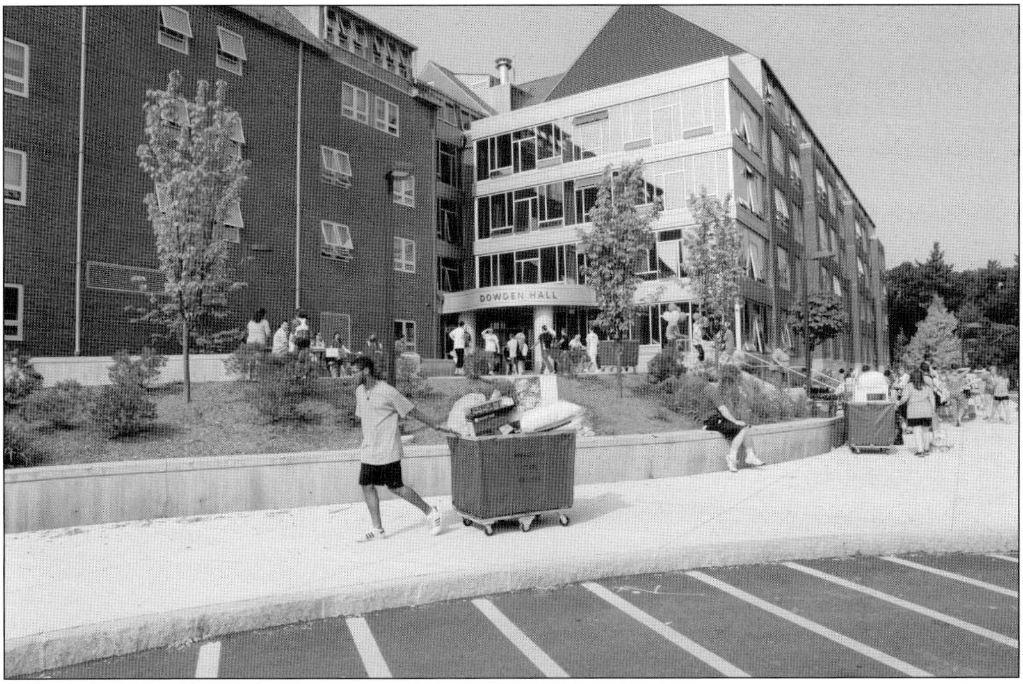

Dowden Hall was substantially expanded in 2010 with an addition that provided 177 new beds. It also created new student life components including a convenience store, student common rooms, private study areas, and a fitness center. Neither Dowden Hall nor its addition much shortened the space between residences and main academic buildings, but the LRC and Student Center had begun to close the gap by the 1980s. (WSU Office of Marketing.)

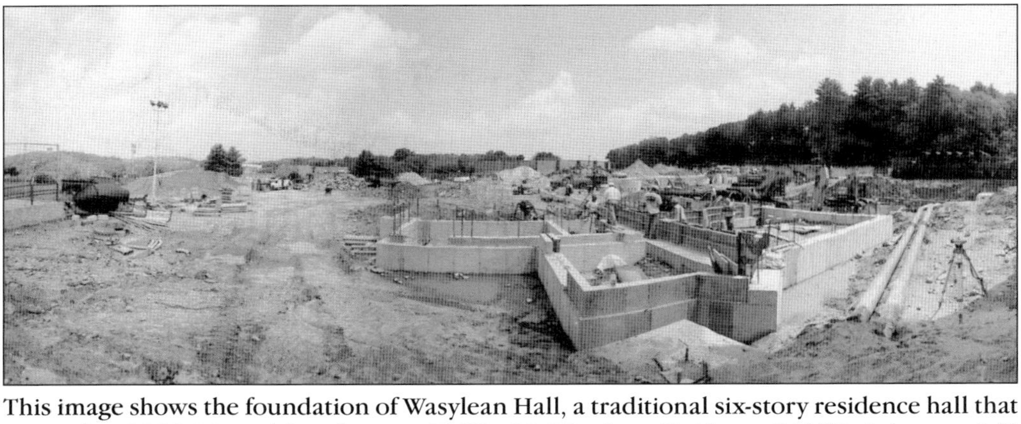

This image shows the foundation of Wasylean Hall, a traditional six-story residence hall that opened in 2004. Named for alumnus Phillip M. Wasylean II (class of 1963), it houses 348 students, a cafe, student lounges, a function room, and the university police.

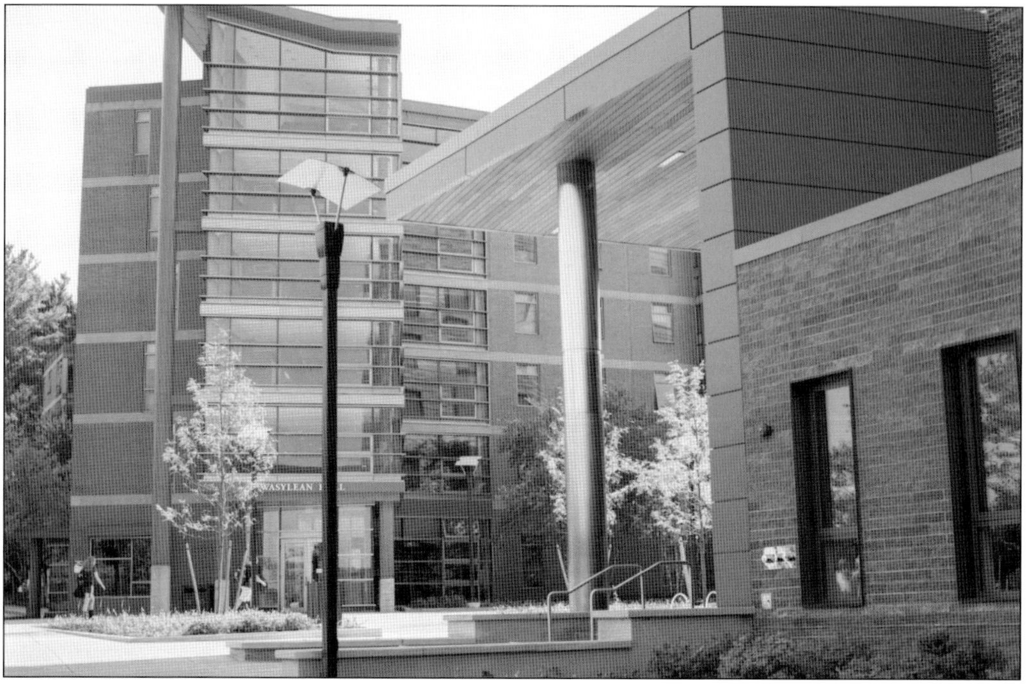

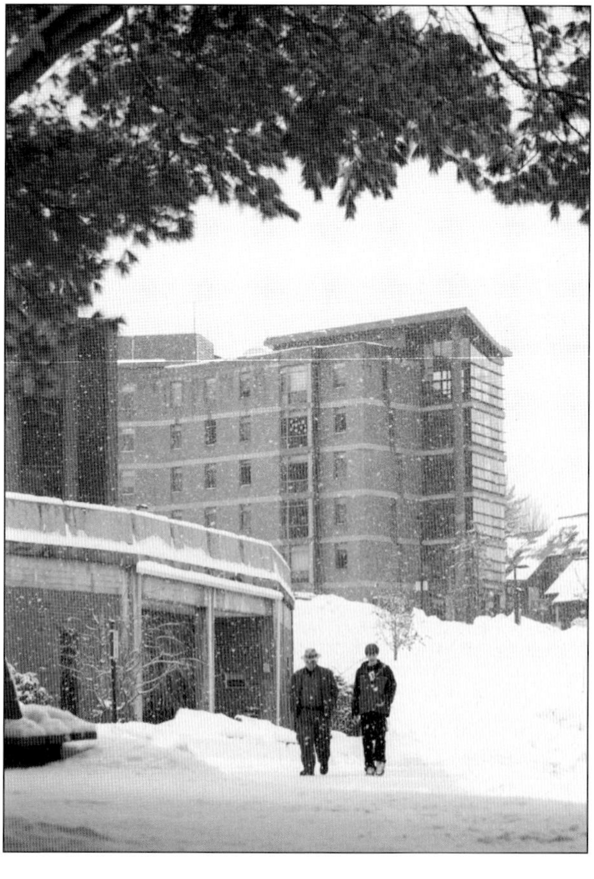

Importantly, Wasylean Hall (to the left in the above photograph) and eventually Sheehan Hall (on the right) closed the geographic gap between residential area and the academic area, or what might be called the residential upper campus and academic lower campus. These two buildings sit directly behind the LRC and Student Center and in front of Chandler Village and Dowden Hall. (WSU Office of Marketing.)

Sheehan Hall, shown here from the front of the LRC (foreground), was named for Lt. Col. James Sheehan, USMC (Ret.), a member of the class of 1955. Opened in 2014, it is a six-story traditional dormitory that houses 400 students. It also contains residence life offices, health services, multipurpose spaces, a game room, a student fitness area, and the university's 575-seat cafeteria. (WSU Office of Marketing.)

Five

STUDENT LIFE

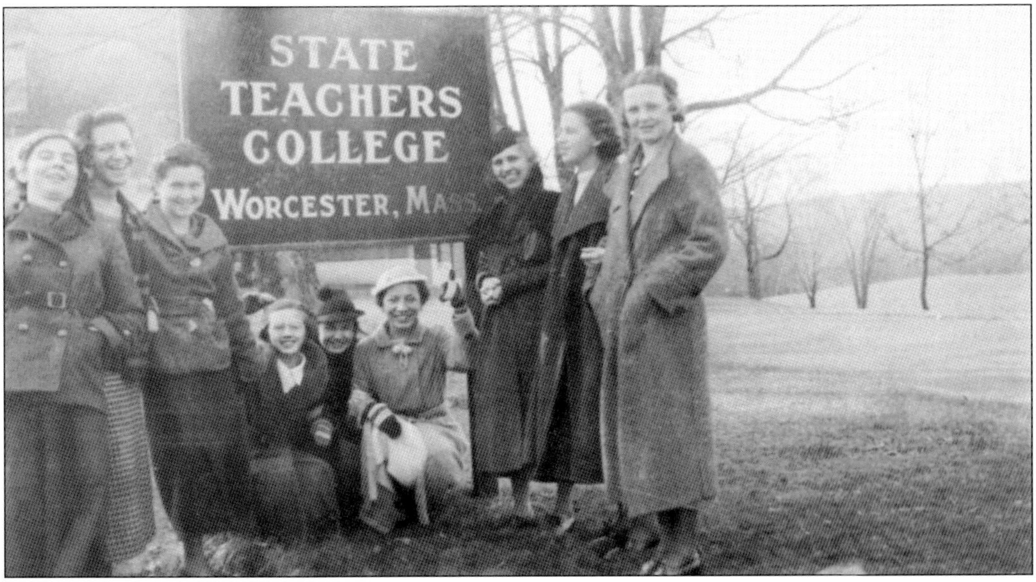

In this image, members of the class of 1936 pose in front of the State Teachers College sign, a favorite site for student photographs. This picture also shows a glimpse of campus behind what is now the Shaughnessy Administration Building long before dorms and student spaces were constructed. This chapter looks at the variety of events, clubs, and experiences that punctuated the lives of Worcester State students.

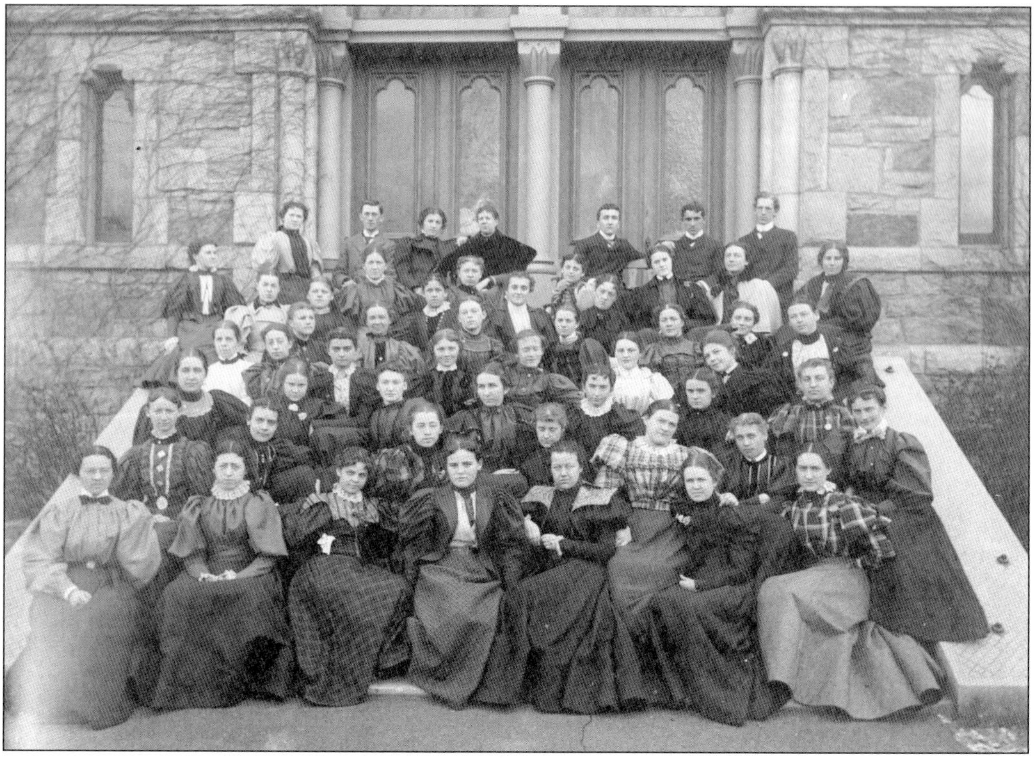

As classes got larger over time, it became more difficult to take class pictures. Accordingly, smaller cohorts—friends, classmates, majors, and more—became integral to student identities and photographs on campus. The above formal picture was taken at the normal school site and includes most of a large 19th-century graduating class. Below, classmates from the class of 1937 pose for a candid picture at the new site, but there were many more students in the class than those seen here. (Below, Maryanne Hammond.)

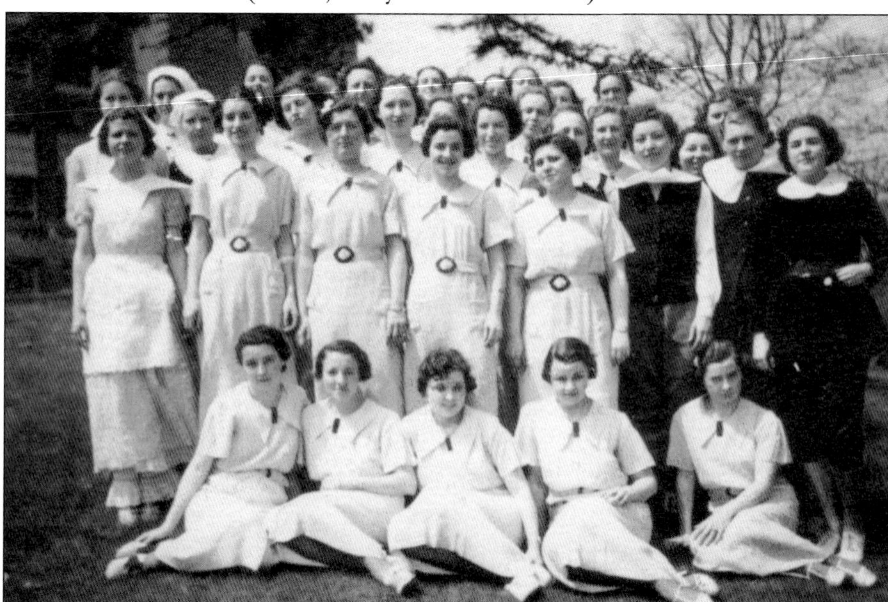

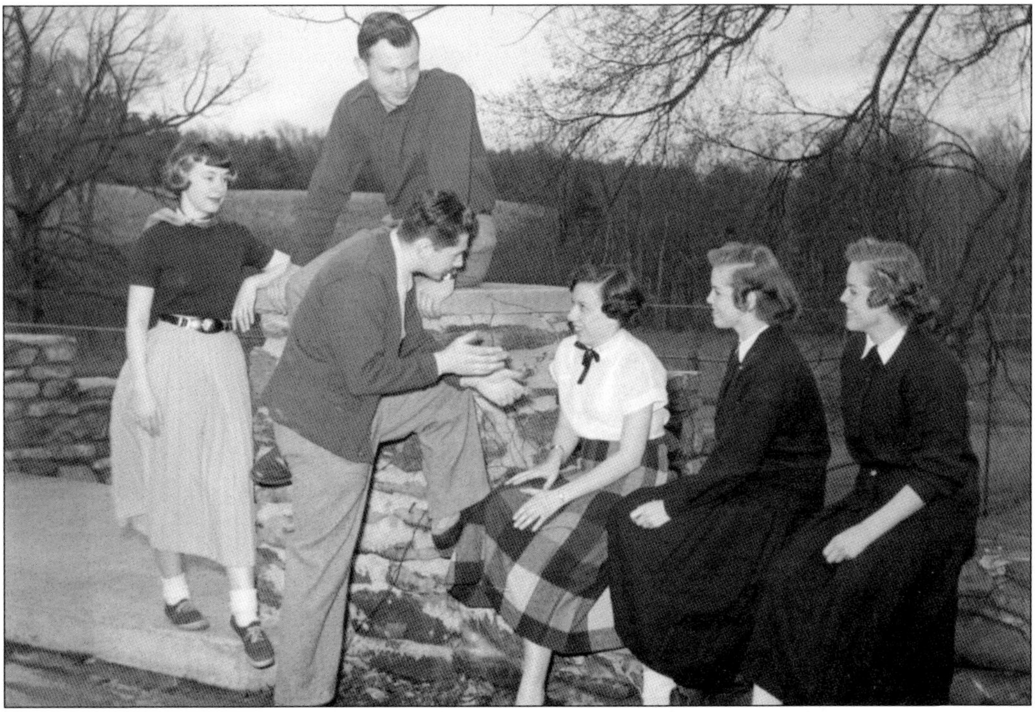

Although it is assumed the earliest years of Worcester State were female-only, there were male students—63 of them to be exact—who attended between 1874 and 1915. From that latter year, attendance was limited to women only until 1940. This later image also shows the largely undeveloped area behind the Shaughnessy Administration Building. (WSU Office of University Advancement.)

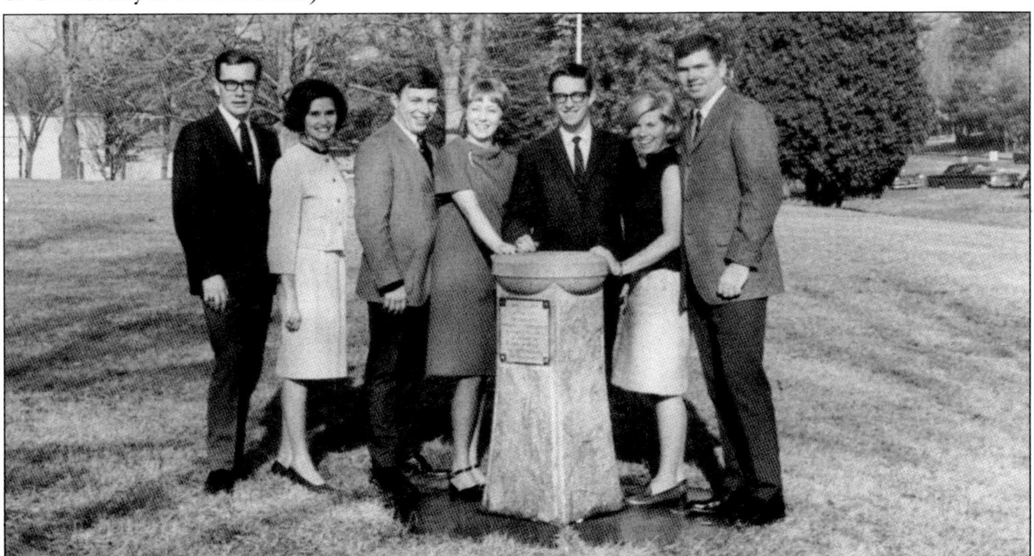

Another favorite location for school photographs was "the sundial." An 1899 gift from the normal school alumni, it commemorated E. Harlow Russell's first 25 years at the school. The memorial was located on the grounds of the old site; when the school moved to the new campus, the sundial came with it, and it continues to be a focal point of the grounds.

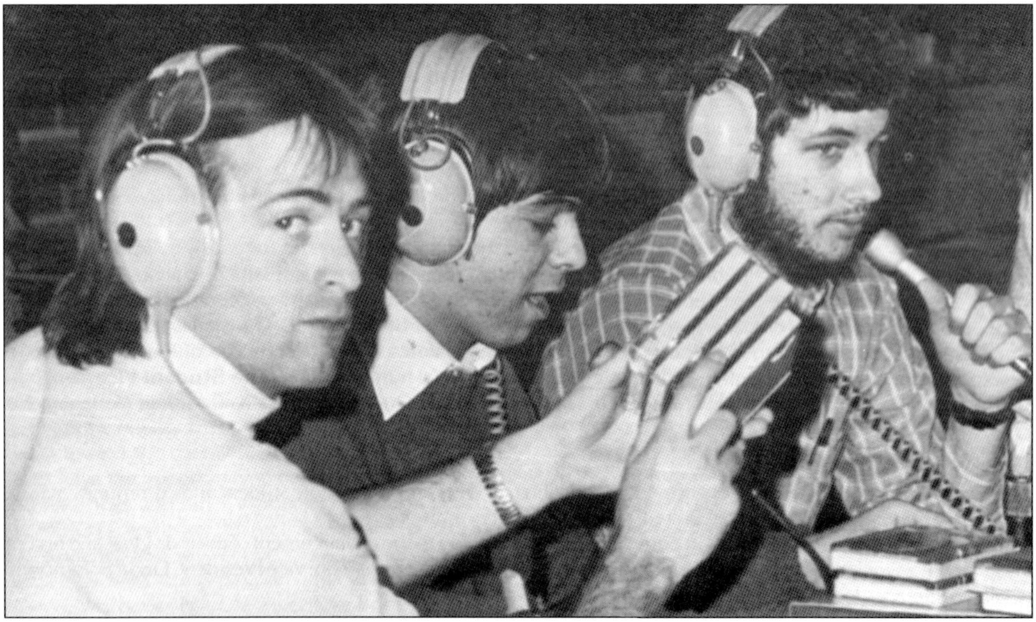

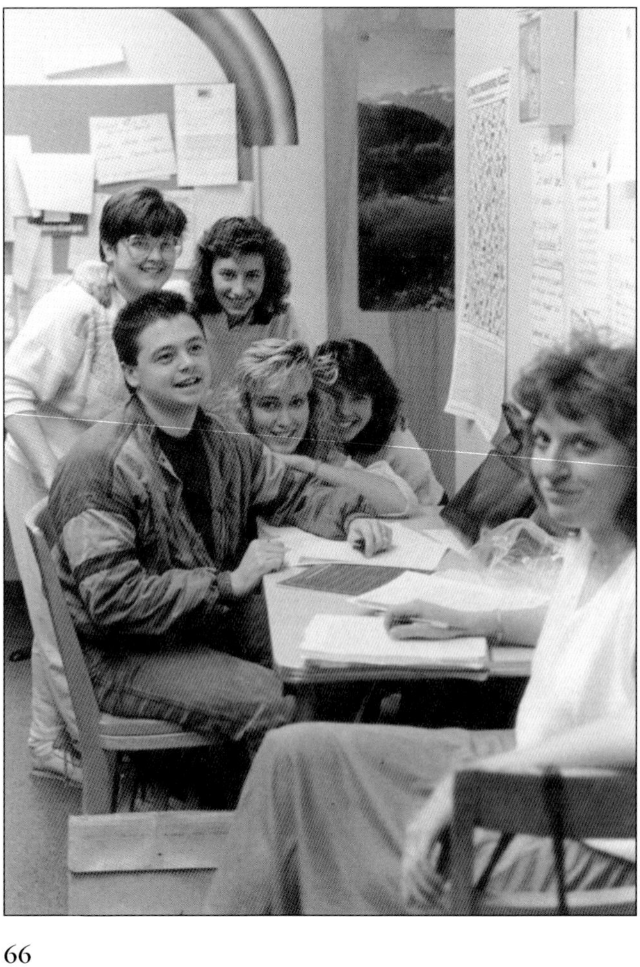

Like any institution of higher learning, Worcester State University and all its previous incarnations have had a variety of clubs, groups, and initiatives for students to get involved. These are a few of them, all before the 1990s. The radio club and station staff (shown above in 1979) operated an on-campus station known today as WSUR. (Both, WSU Student Involvement and Leadership Development Collection.)

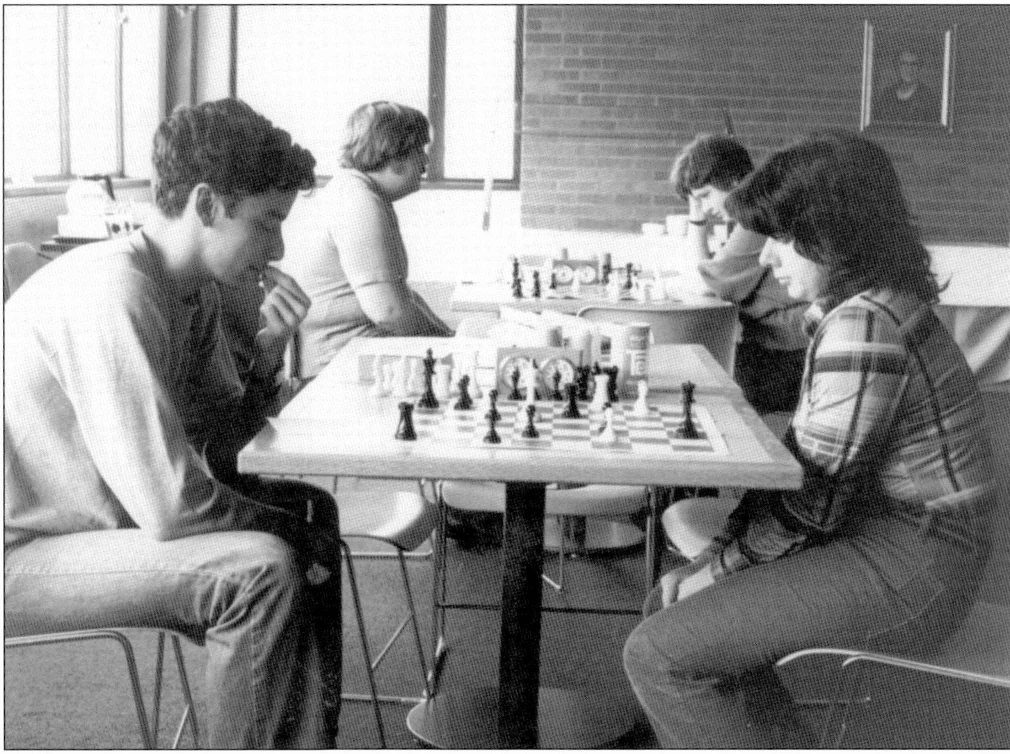

The chess club (above) plays in the Blue Lounge of the Student Center. Meanwhile, two student staffers from the *Student Voice*, the student newspaper, are pictured here (below) with one thoroughly enjoying the *Voice* and the other bored to sleep by the *New York Times*.

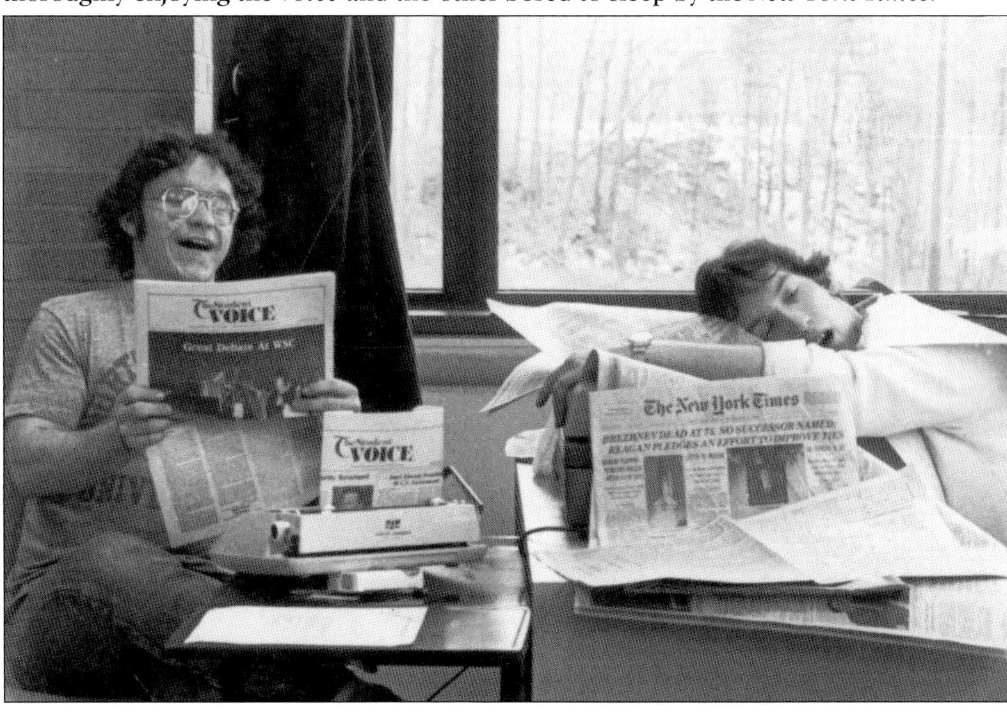

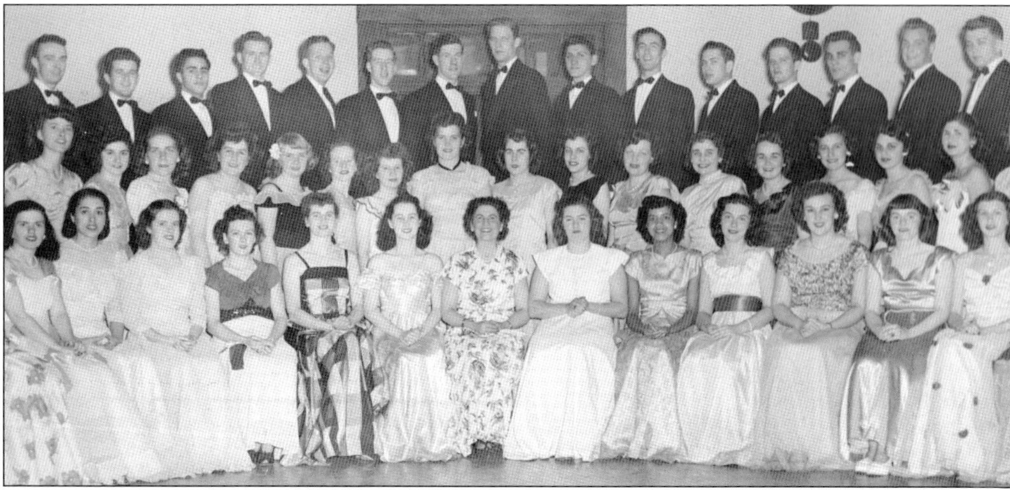

Particularly before the 1980s, dances were especially popular events that punctuated the academic year and provided social outlets for students. Proms, such as the one shown above at midcentury, were exceptionally formal affairs. Decorating took on special importance considering the dances were frequently held in the gym. Below, one can even see how columns are formed by dangling streamers from basketball hoops. (Below, WSU Student Involvement and Leadership Development Collection.)

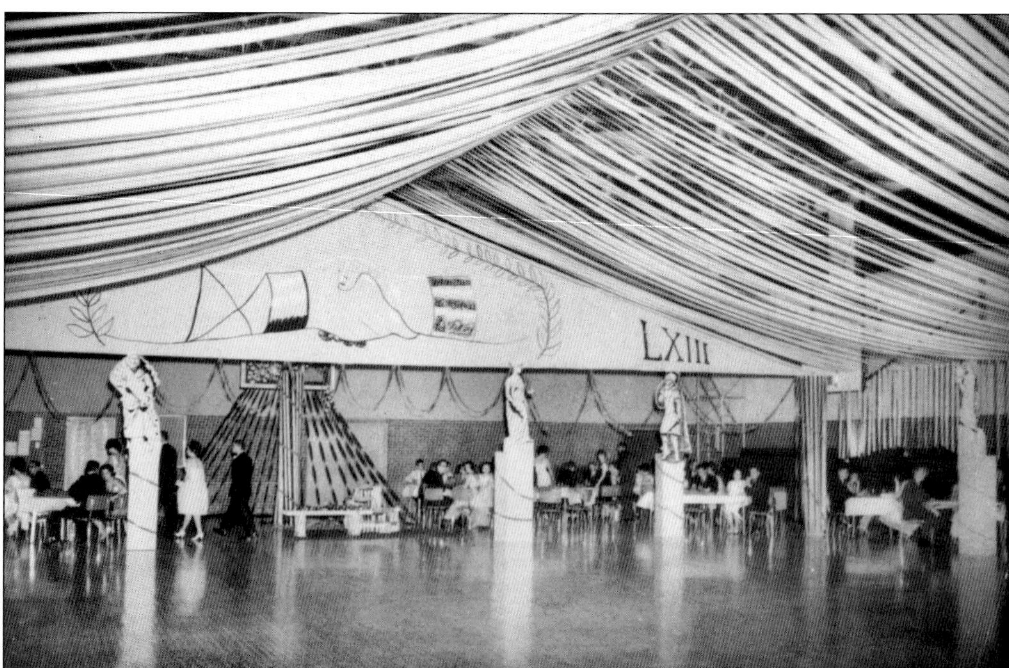

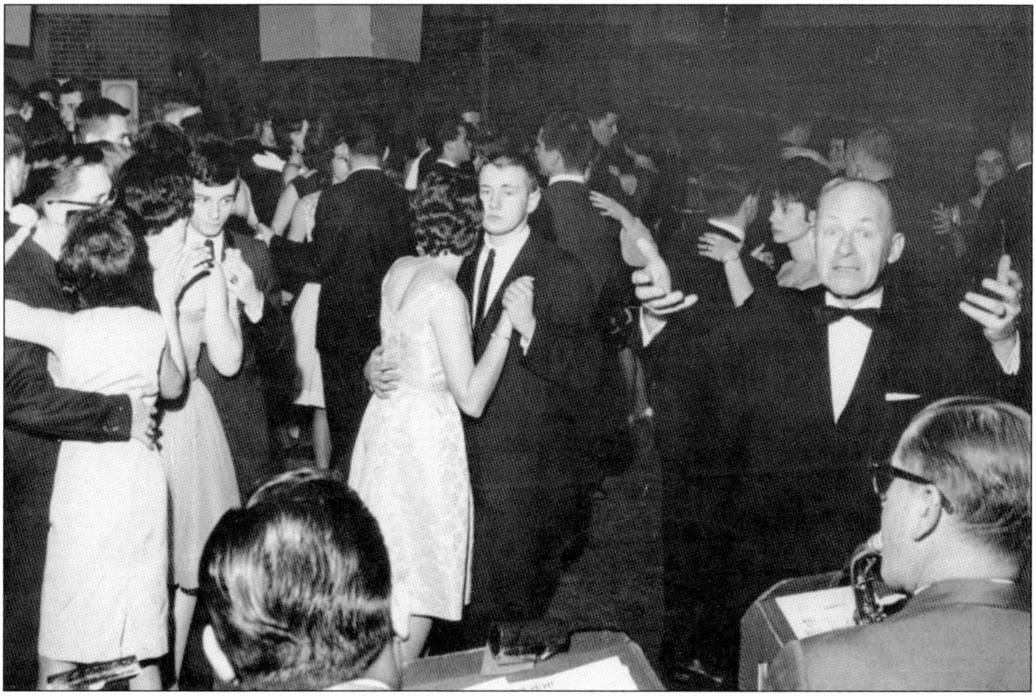

There were also dances for homecoming, which often included bands, and semiformals (below). Of particular importance in these images is the age difference among attendees because even in the 1960s, Worcester State had a solid commitment to educating traditional-age students along with older students.

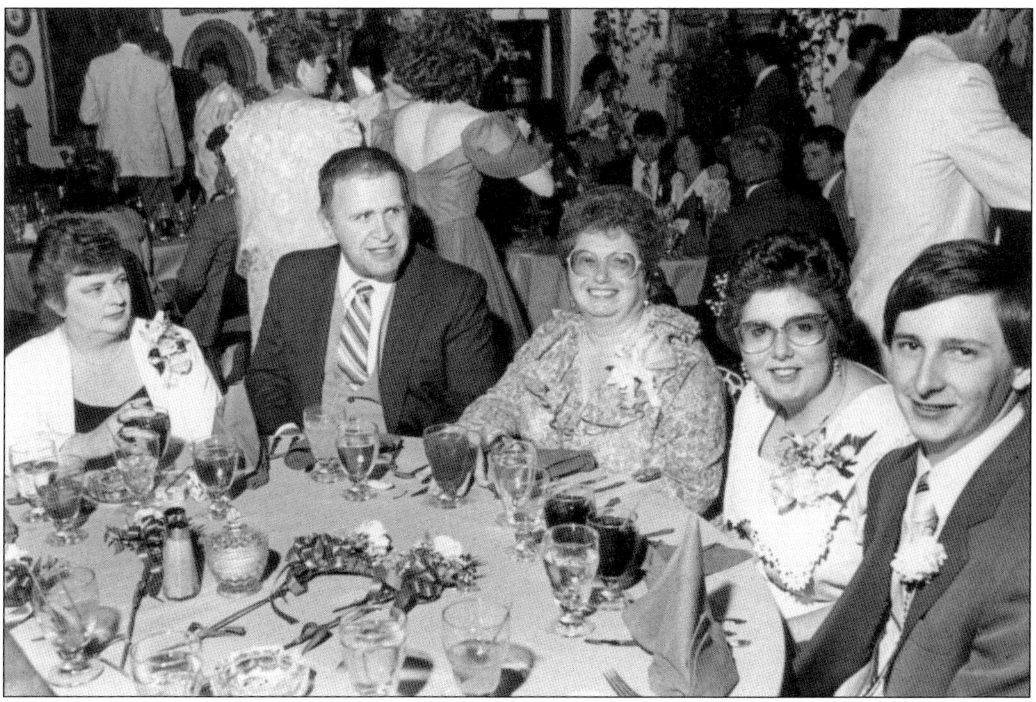

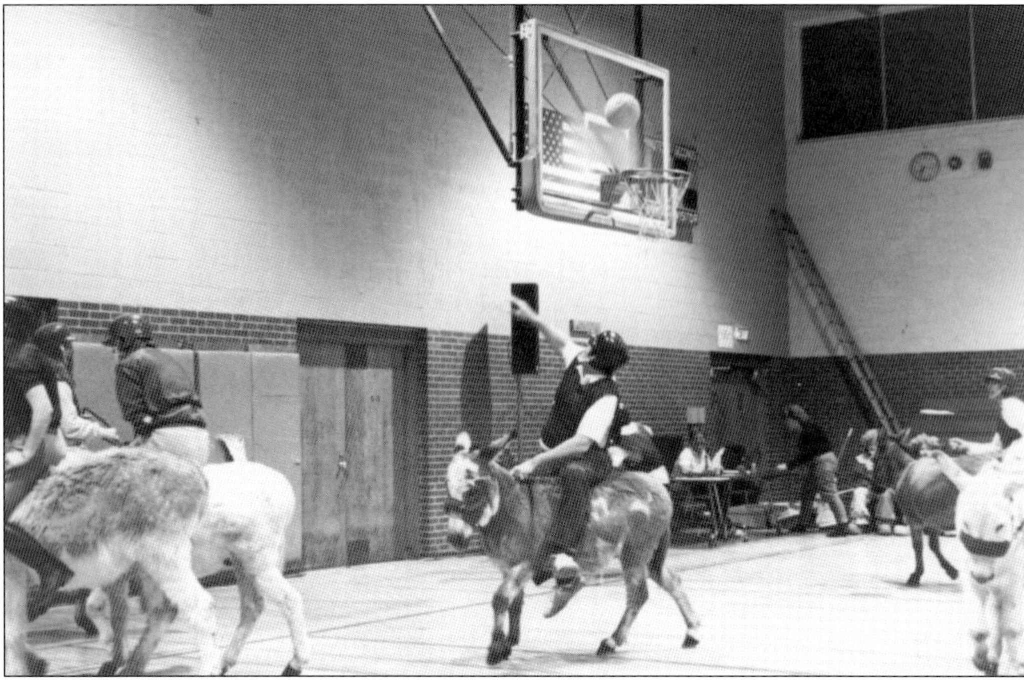

Donkey basketball had once been a popular event in many organizations, particularly around fundraising initiatives. This image comes from such an event in the "old gym," but it appears not to have been a regular event. For perhaps obvious reasons, such forms of entertainment have diminished while animal rights concerns have risen. (WSU Athletic Department.)

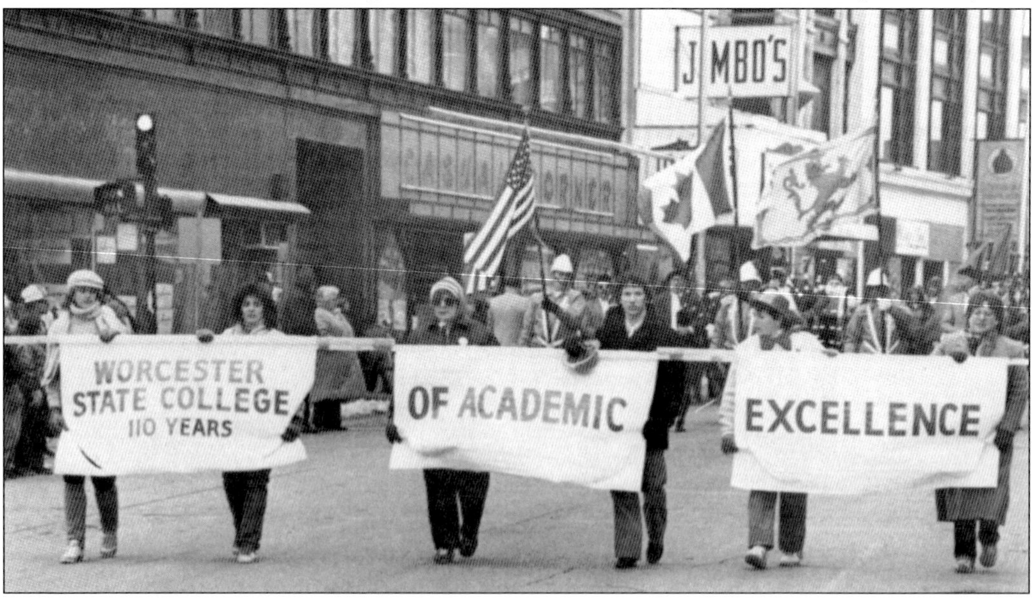

Parades in Worcester were moments to display school pride and engage with the city. Organized by student activities staff, this 1984 Main Street parade entry celebrated the 110th anniversary of Worcester State. Other parades in which students engaged were the St. Patrick's Day parade and the Columbus Day parade, each with its own ethnic flavor. (WSU Student Involvement and Leadership Development Collection.)

In the 1970s and 1980s, Halloween yielded often elaborate evenings with parties, costume contests, and holiday-appropriate revelry. This image features a costume dress made from copies of the student newspaper, the *Student Voice*.

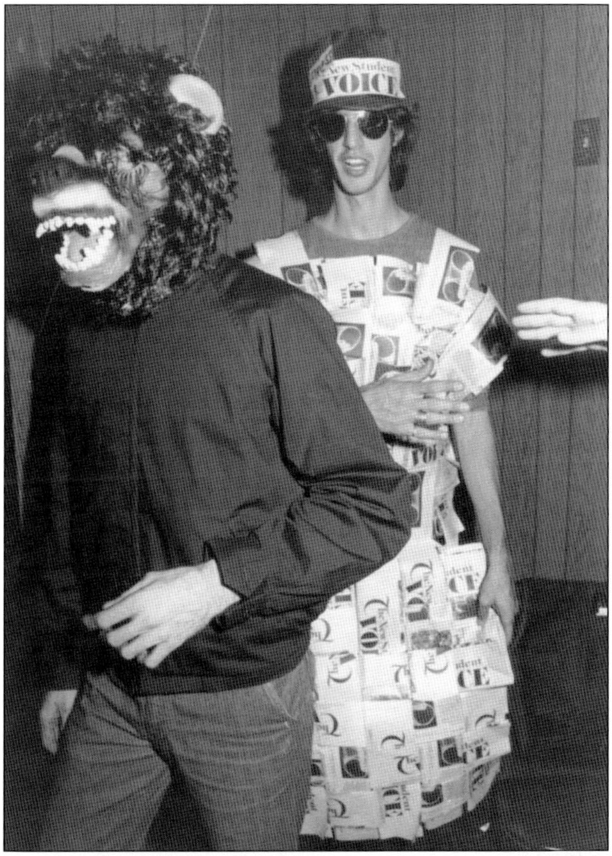

This Student Center cookout occurred in April 1982. Students are hanging out on the lawn between the Student Center and Learning Resource Center (pictured in background). In the center of the picture is a small child holding a guitar, again underscoring the multigenerational reality that has long been a part of campus life. (WSU Student Involvement and Leadership Development Collection.)

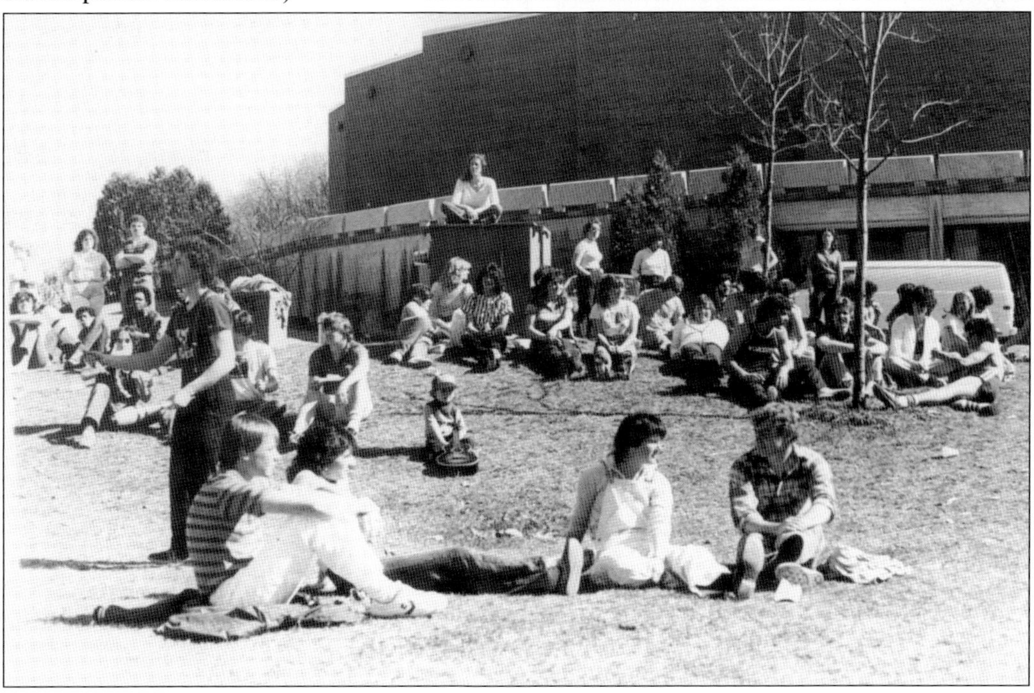

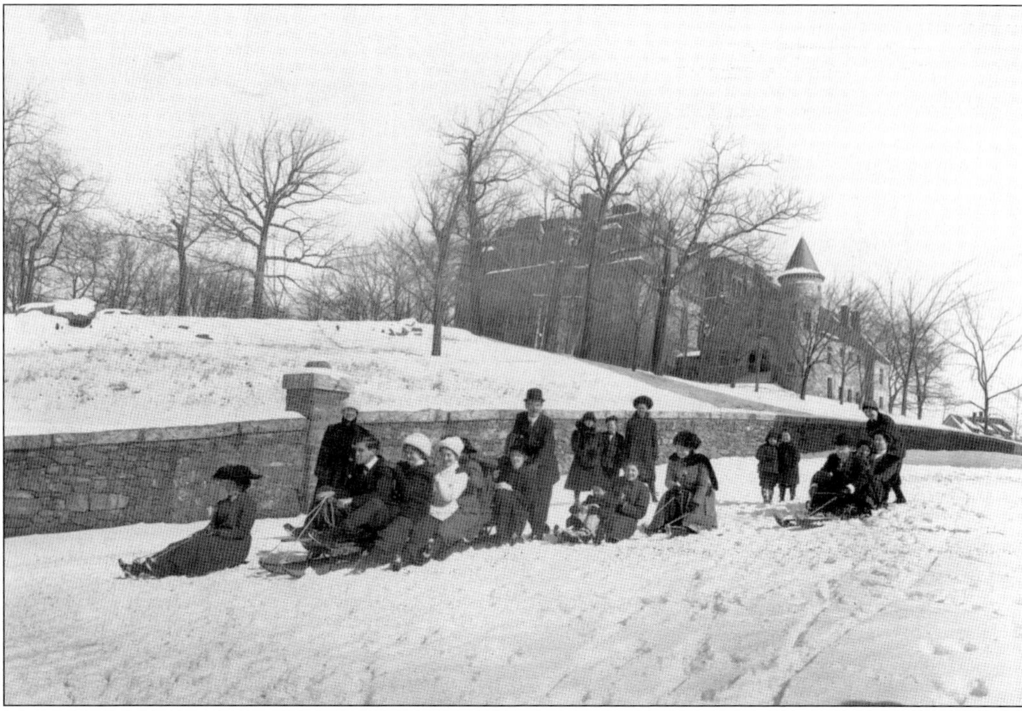

While students and principals alike complained about the elevation of the normal school, this classic image from the school's first home shows that there were advantages to being on a relatively lonely hill. It might also serve as a reminder that having fun at college was not just a late-20th-century device.

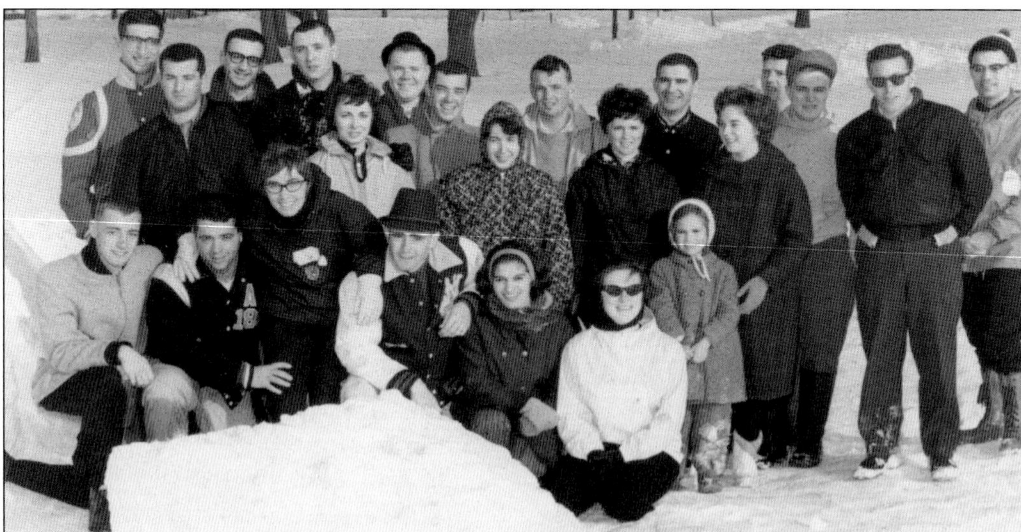

From the 1960s to the 1980s, students engaged in a variety of events under the banner of winter carnival. They competed in obstacle courses, broomball games, ice-sculpture making, and tugs-of-war, to name a few events. There were often accompanying dances and parties, too. (WSU Student Involvement and Leadership Development Collection.)

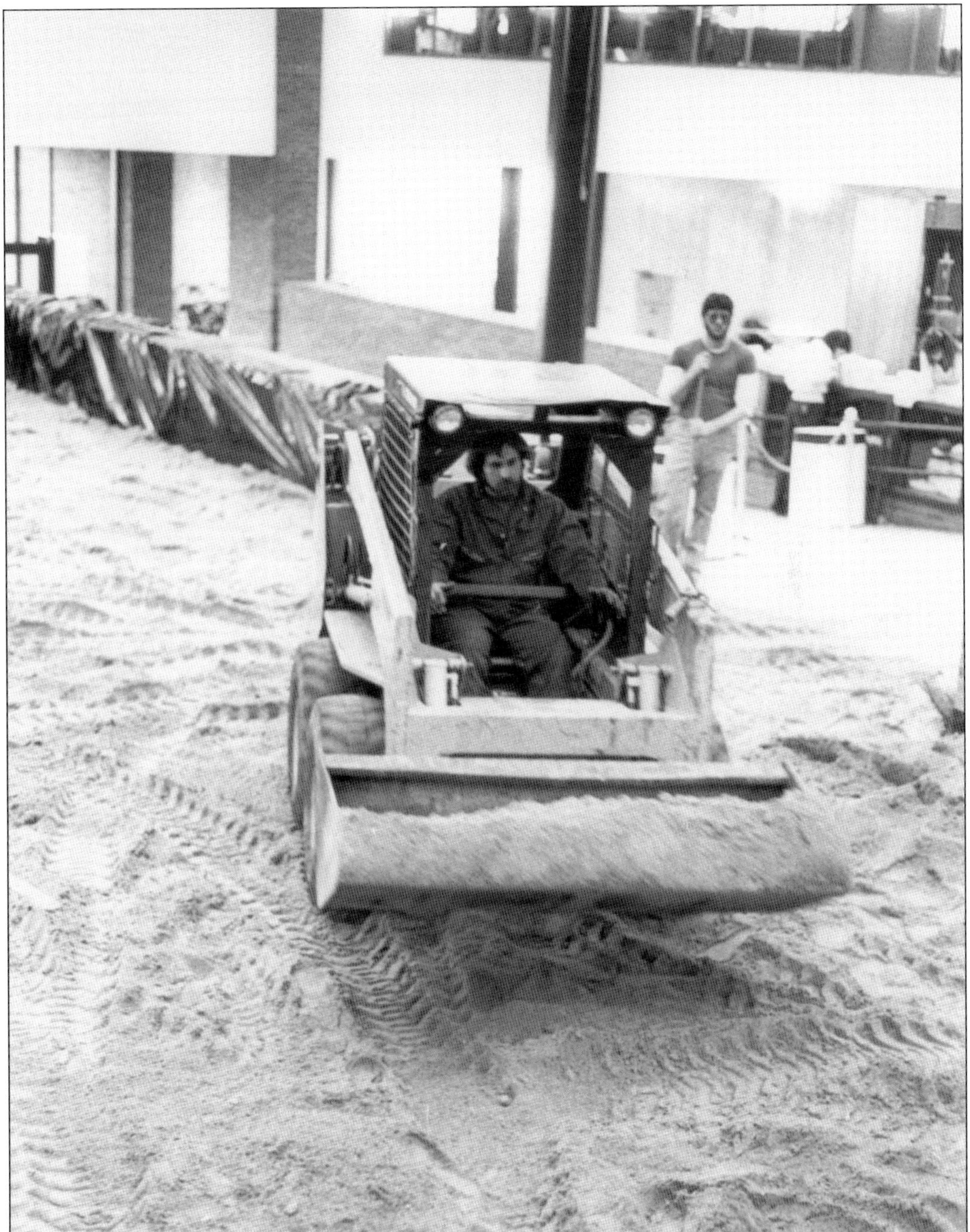

Winter carnivals in the 1980s were especially grandiose. For the 1986 "Go Hawaiian" theme, student activities and facilities staff created a beach scene in the Student Center's exhibit hall area by bringing in sand and building a two-story waterfall. (WSU Student Involvement and Leadership Development Collection.)

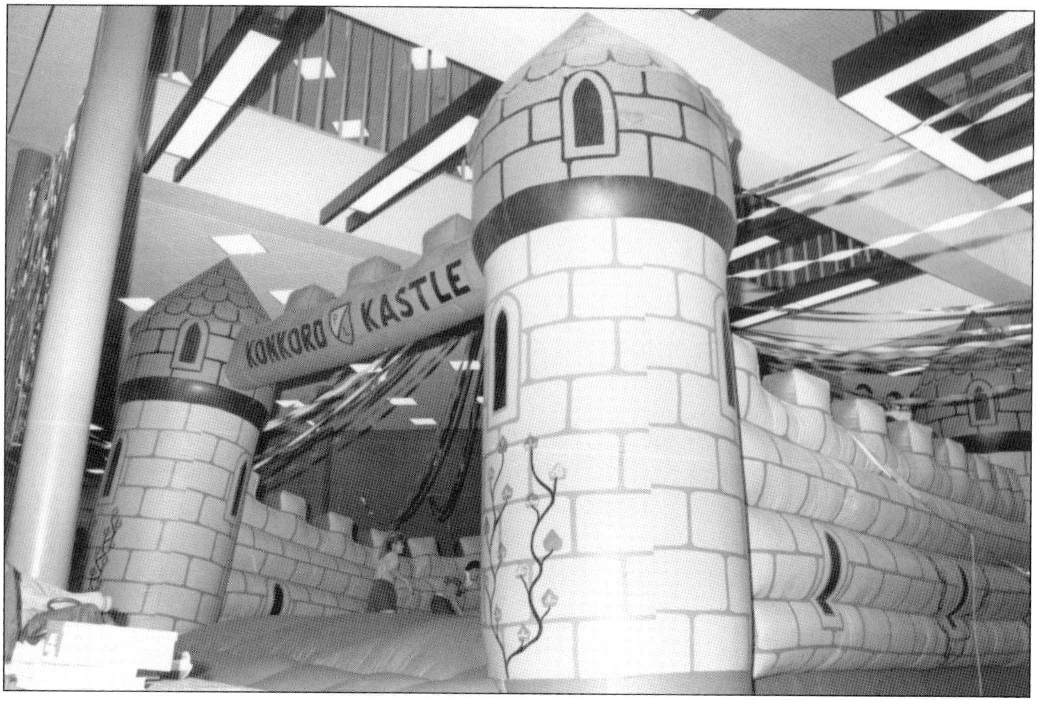

Some winter carnivals involved dunk tanks and inflatables for their inside events, such as this "Konkord Kastle" in the Student Center exhibit area (above). Outside offerings were more weather specific. If there was snow on the ground, outside events made use of it; if not, there were other competitions, sometimes interclass ones, that could happen. Tug-of-war (below) was particularly popular. (Both, WSU Student Involvement and Leadership Development Collection.)

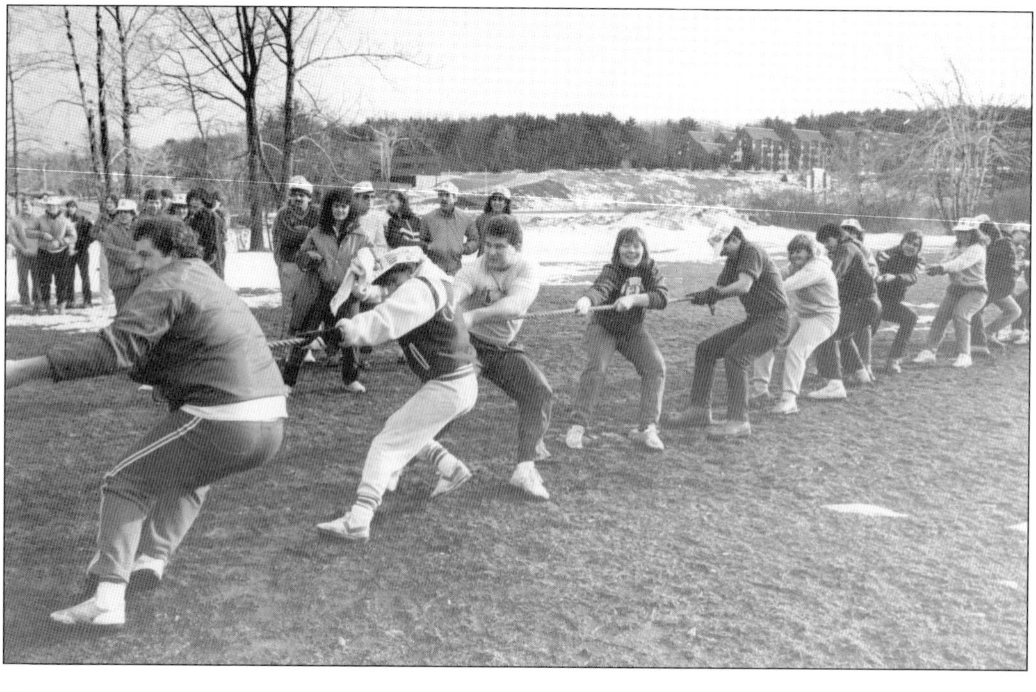

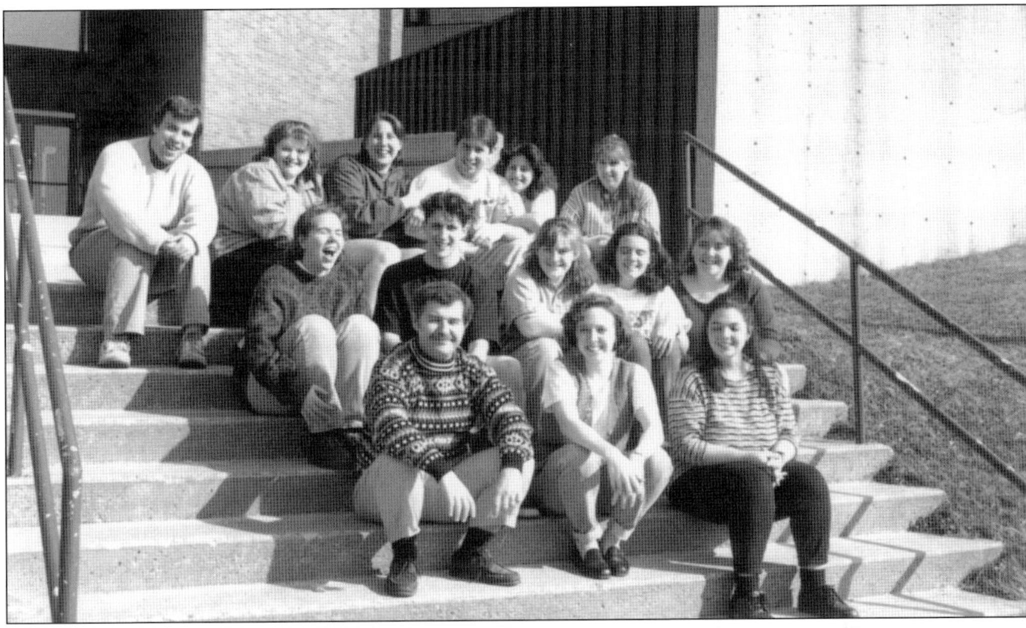

The student events committee was often the group behind the scenes planning campus events. Students and Worcester State staff worked together on the committee, and both are in the picture. (WSU Student Involvement and Leadership Development Collection.)

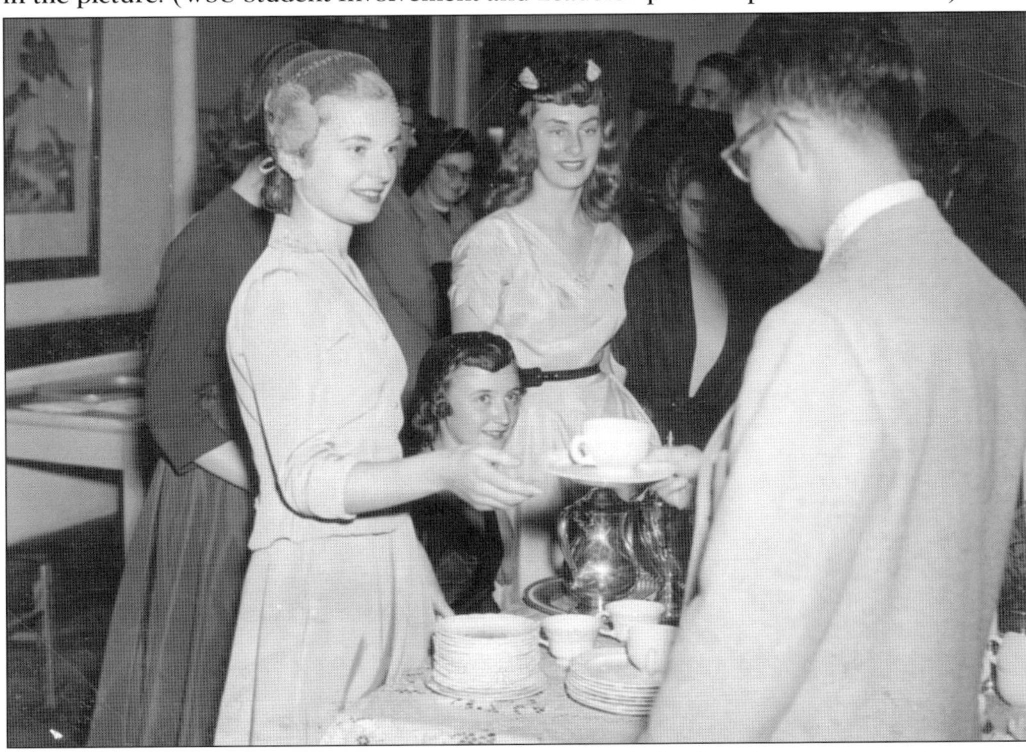

Teas were events held for a few different reasons. A Scholarship Tea remains an important university advancement event, but there were teas hosted by presidents and teas welcoming new classes in Worcester State's past.

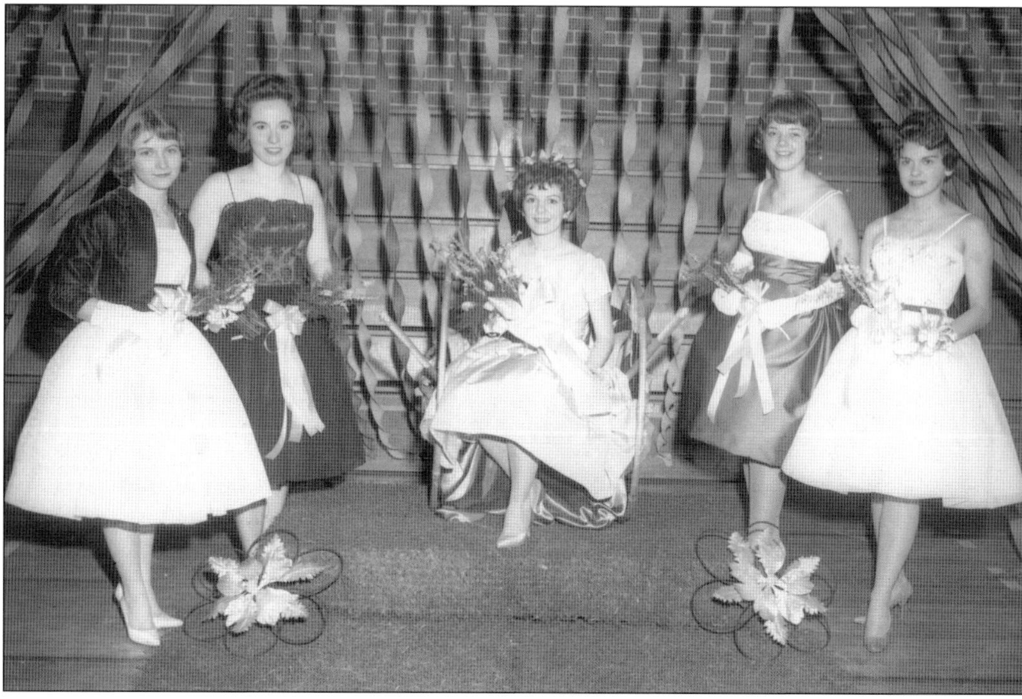

Some elements of homecoming have changed dramatically over time. Sports events and socializing provided backdrops for graduates to return to campus and reconnect with each other. However, homecoming courts have by and large not made it into the 21st century. (Below, WSU Student Involvement and Leadership Development Collection.)

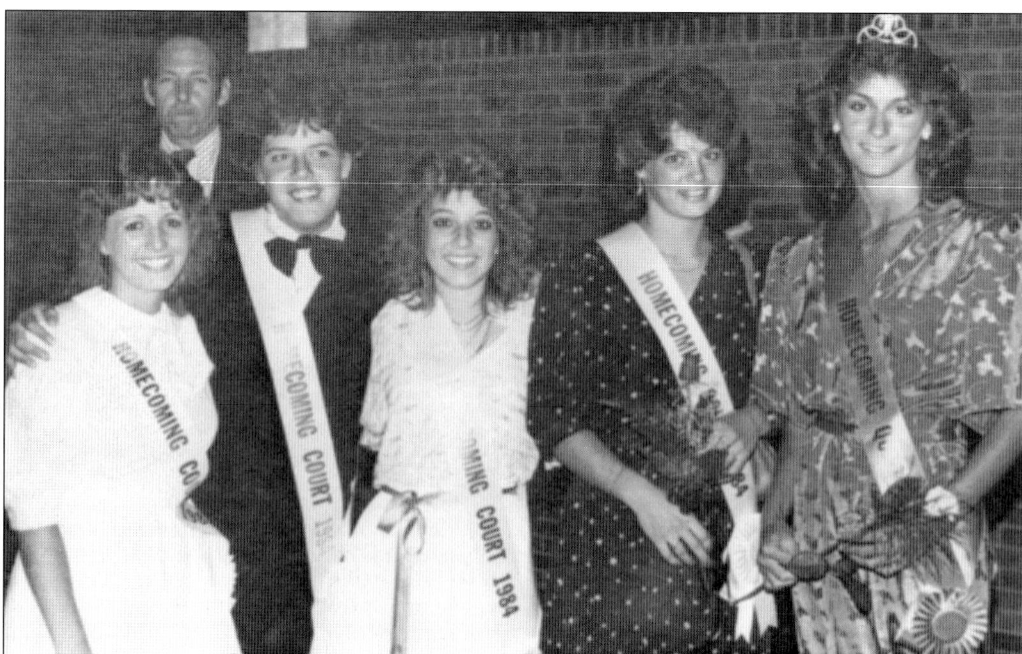

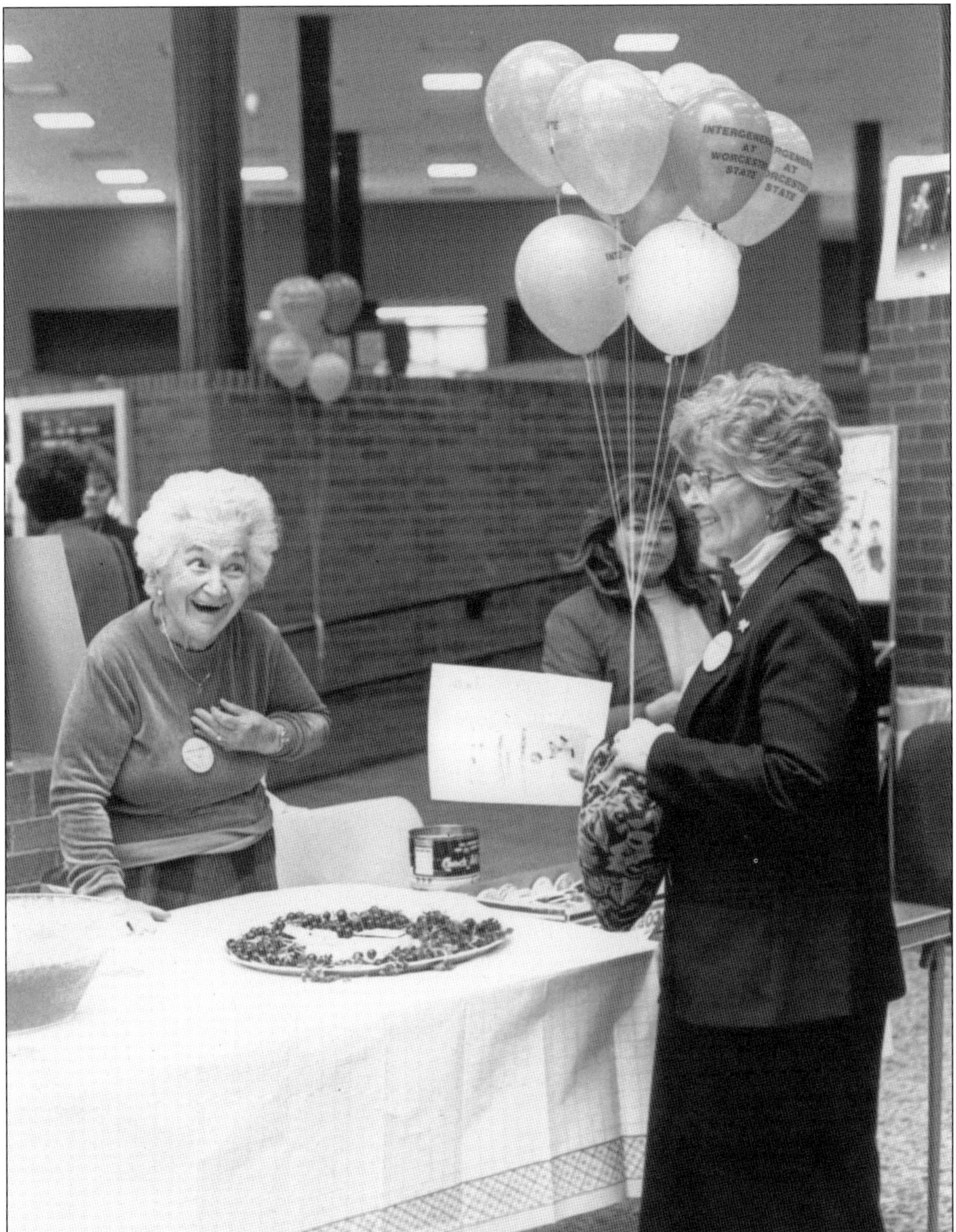

While nontraditional students have long been welcome at Worcester State, it has been officially designated as an "age-integrated" campus since the late 1970s. In this picture, older students interact with the campus community in the Student Center. The balloons read, "Intergenerate at Worcester State." Years later, the college created the Intergenerational Urban Institute, which became the Urban Action Institute to incorporate both intergenerational and intercultural action-based initiatives.

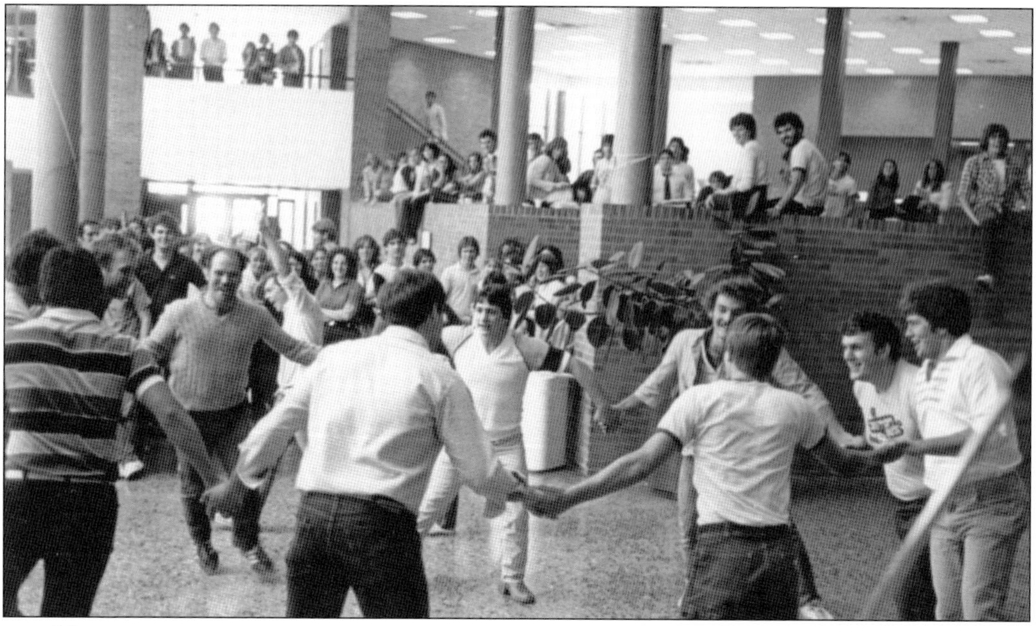

In addition to hosting events, some of which were multi-day programs, the Student Center was host to large-format Twister games and a variety of participatory activities enjoyed by groups and clubs as well as spectators.

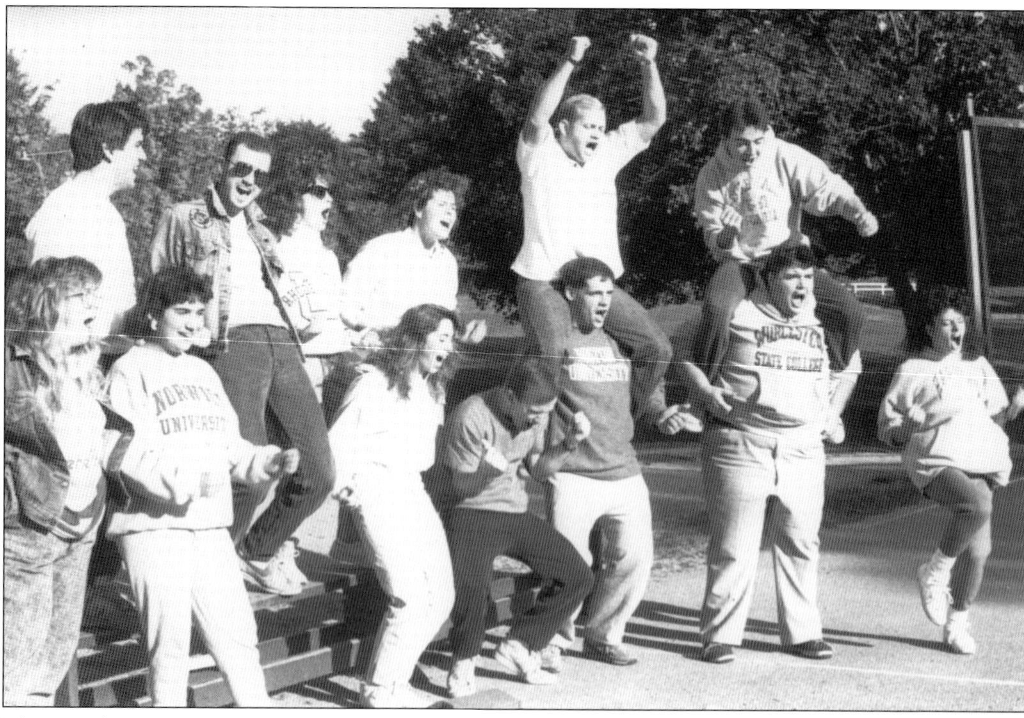

The Student Involvement and Leadership Development Office oversaw and worked with student clubs and programs. The Student Events Committee was among them. In this picture, students participate in a student leadership workshop that helped develop student group leaders. (WSU Student Involvement and Leadership Development Collection.)

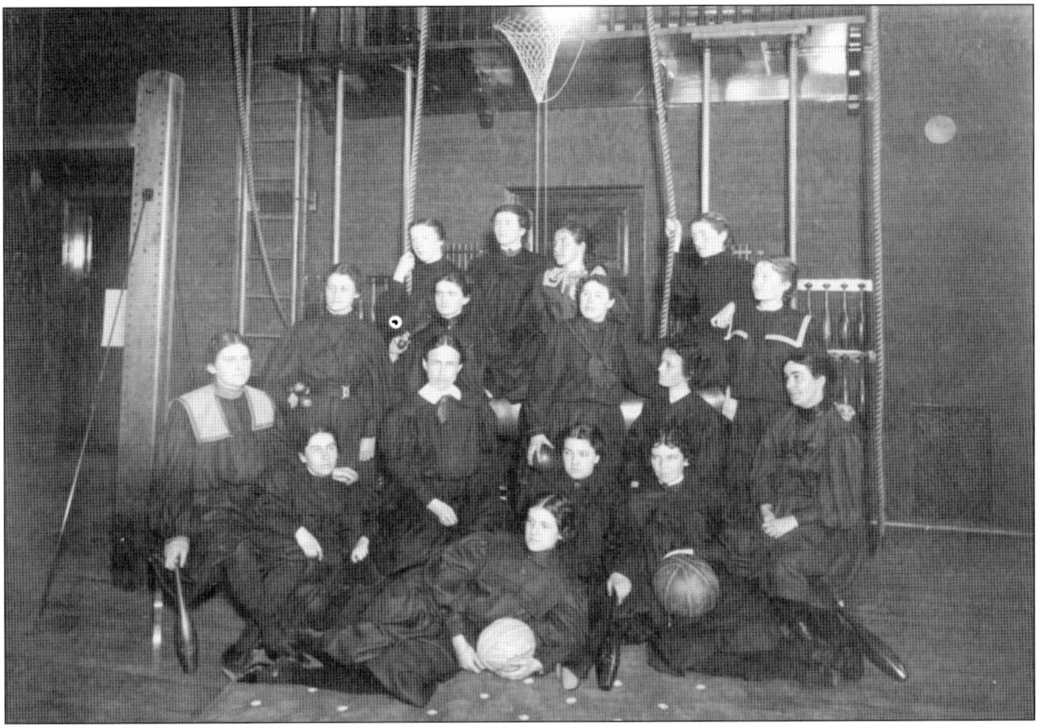

Recreational sports, an important aspect of student life, are distinguished from varsity sports. Even at the original campus, recreational sports existed, as suggested in this picture, taken at the first gym, with students holding a variety of gear and sitting under a new basketball hoop.

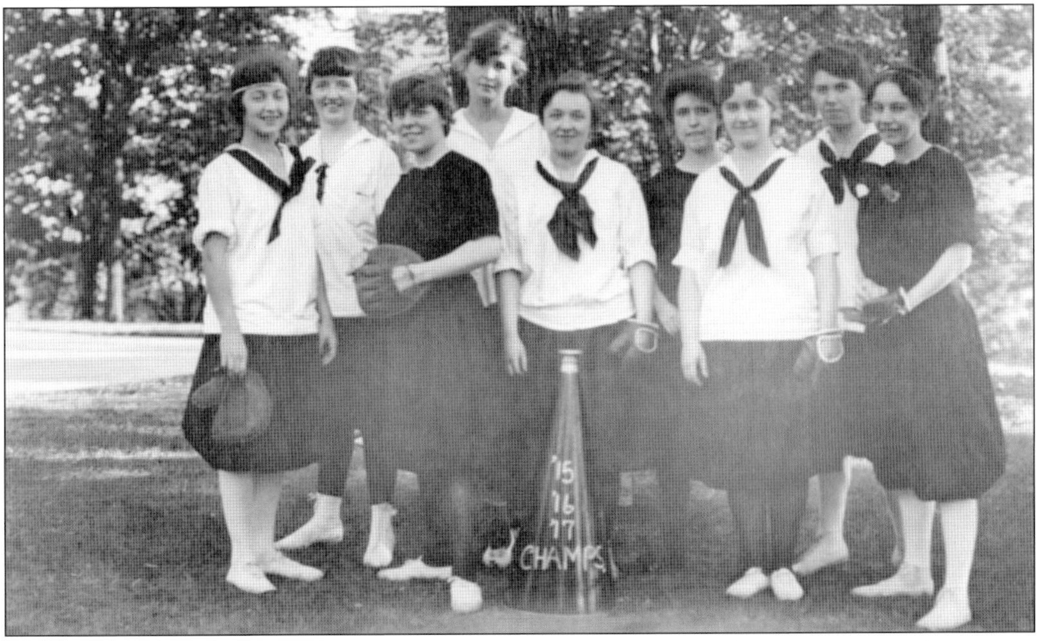

Varsity sports began at Worcester State in the mid-20th century. These 1915–1917 champions played in intramurals and club-sport systems. These systems, which pitted class years against each other internally and schools against schools externally, continued for decades.

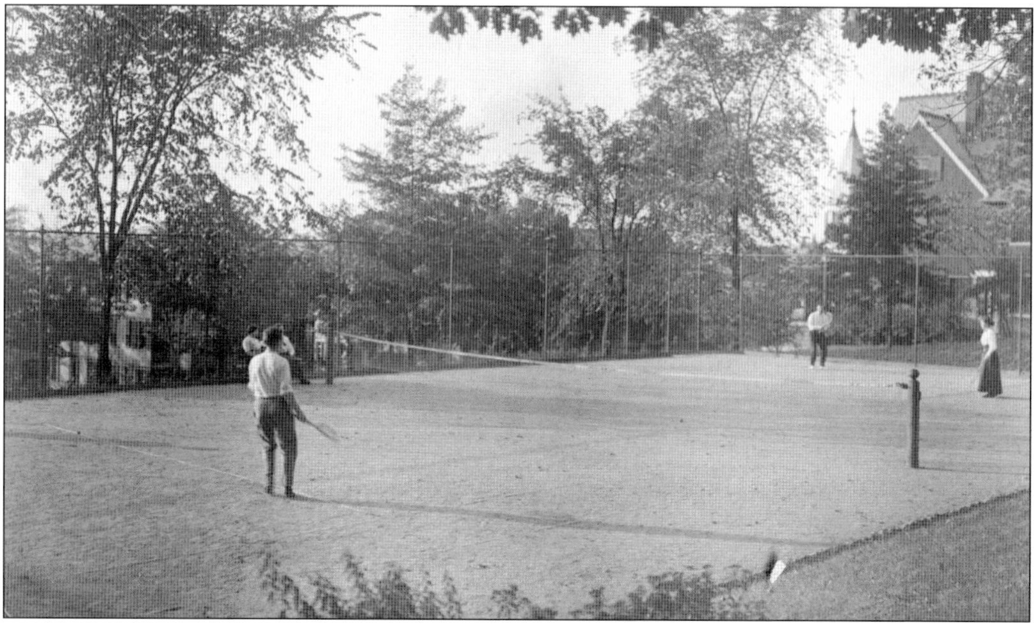

In addition to a gymnasium, students at the normal school also had use of this tennis court after its installation in 1904. It was located outside of Stoddard Terrace and available to students and faculty members. The court could also be converted for volleyball, which in 1904 was a decade old.

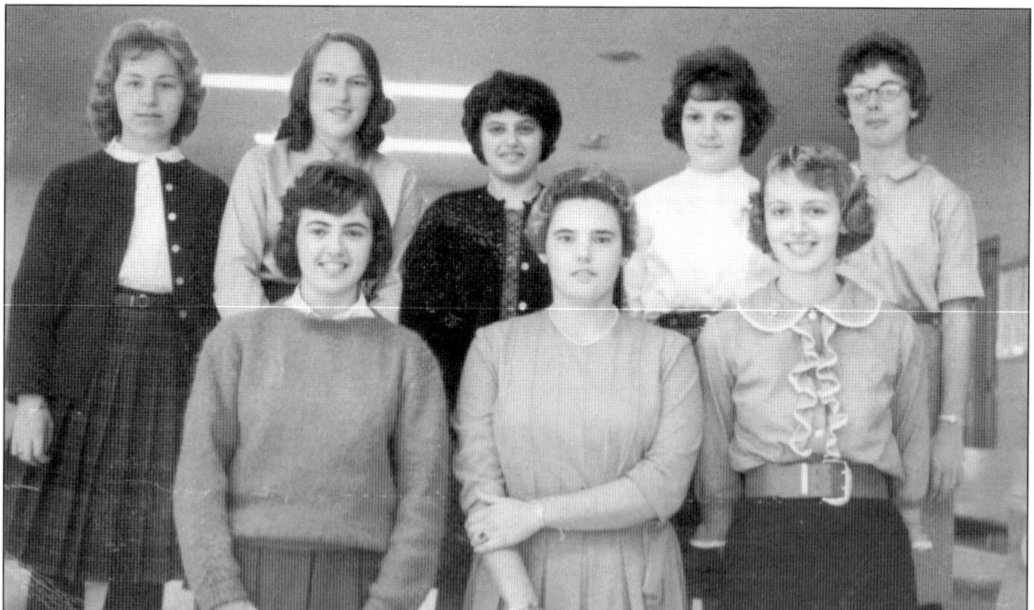

This image shows the Women's Athletic Association in 1961. At this point, this student club had been around for 20 years—a year before the Men's Athletic Association formed. In 1941, its inaugural year, the women's committee oversaw the "Blue and Gold Teams," competitive sports, basketball, Ping-Pong, soccer, field hockey, a conference at Bridgewater, "modern dance get together in the auditorium," and Sports Day. (WSU Student Involvement and Leadership Development Collection.)

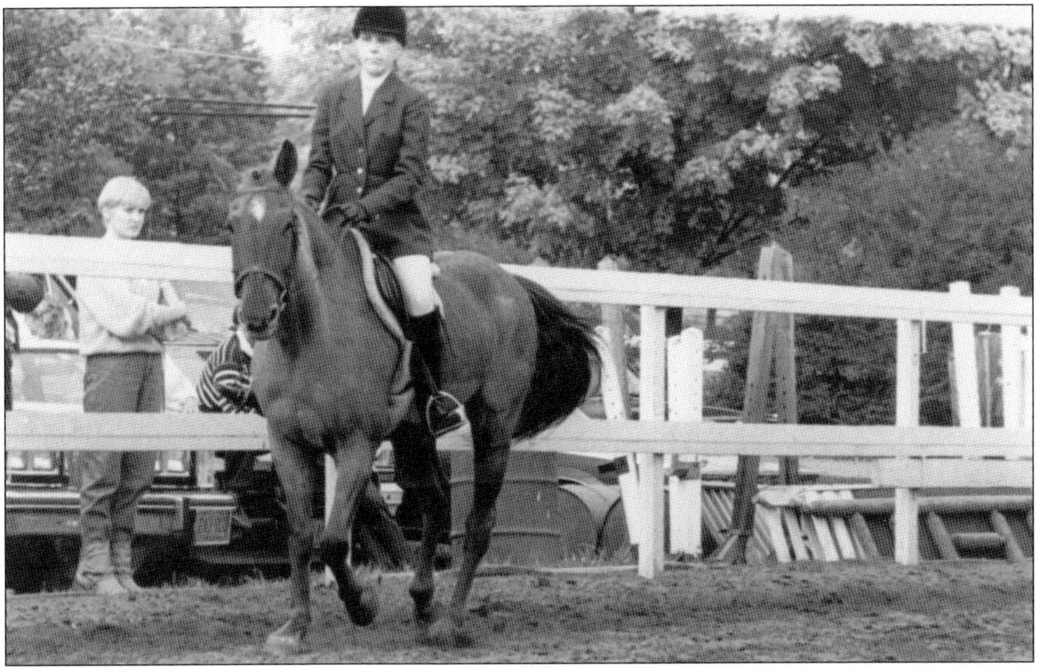

Equestrian teams compete as a club sport at Worcester State and, as such, are not involved in the varsity sports structure. While they receive some university support as a student club, they have also raised money for their activities. They remain quite active, unlike the rugby team (seen below), which was also once a club sport on campus. (Both, WSU Athletic Department.)

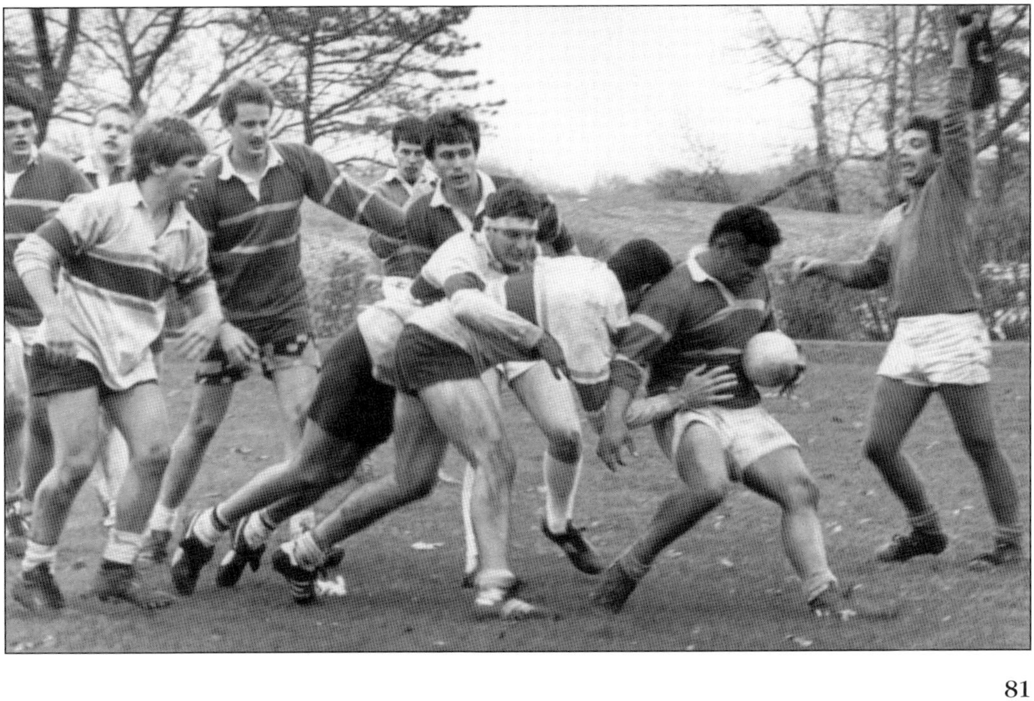

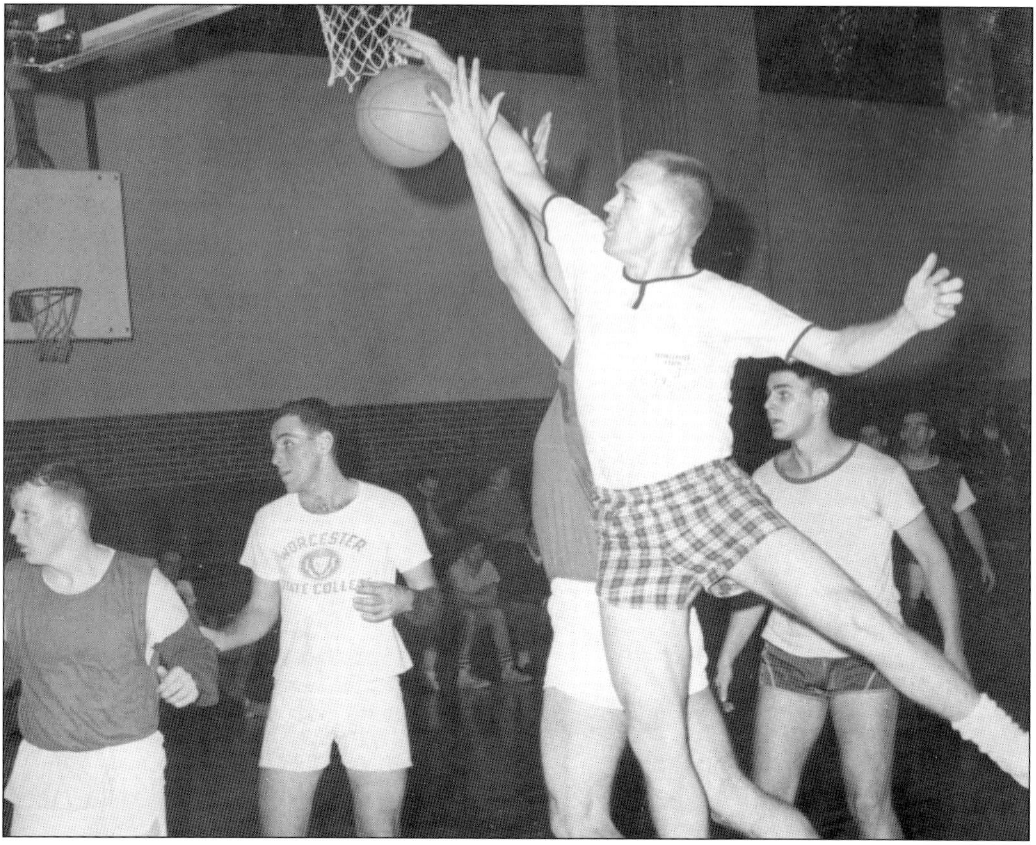

Basketball intramurals have long been part of the student experience at Worcester State. Class teams played each other at the normal school, Worcester State Teachers College had teams that played other schools, and winter carnivals had robust intramural games such as the one from 1965, pictured above. Unlike basketball, which also became a varsity sport, crew remained a club sport with both men's and women's teams. Below, the men's crew team rows on Lake Quinsigamond. (Above, WSU Student Involvement and Leadership Development Collection; below, WSU Athletic Department.)

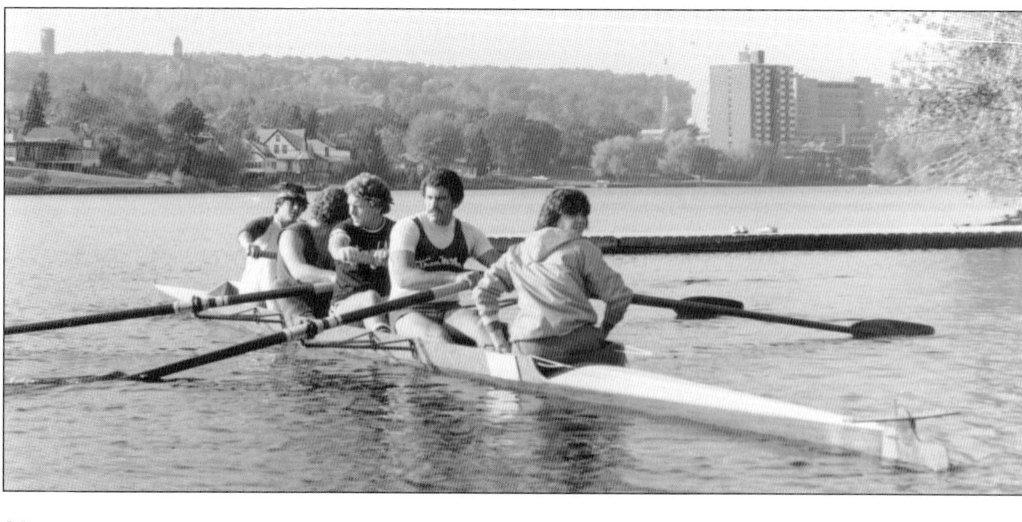

Six

Athletics

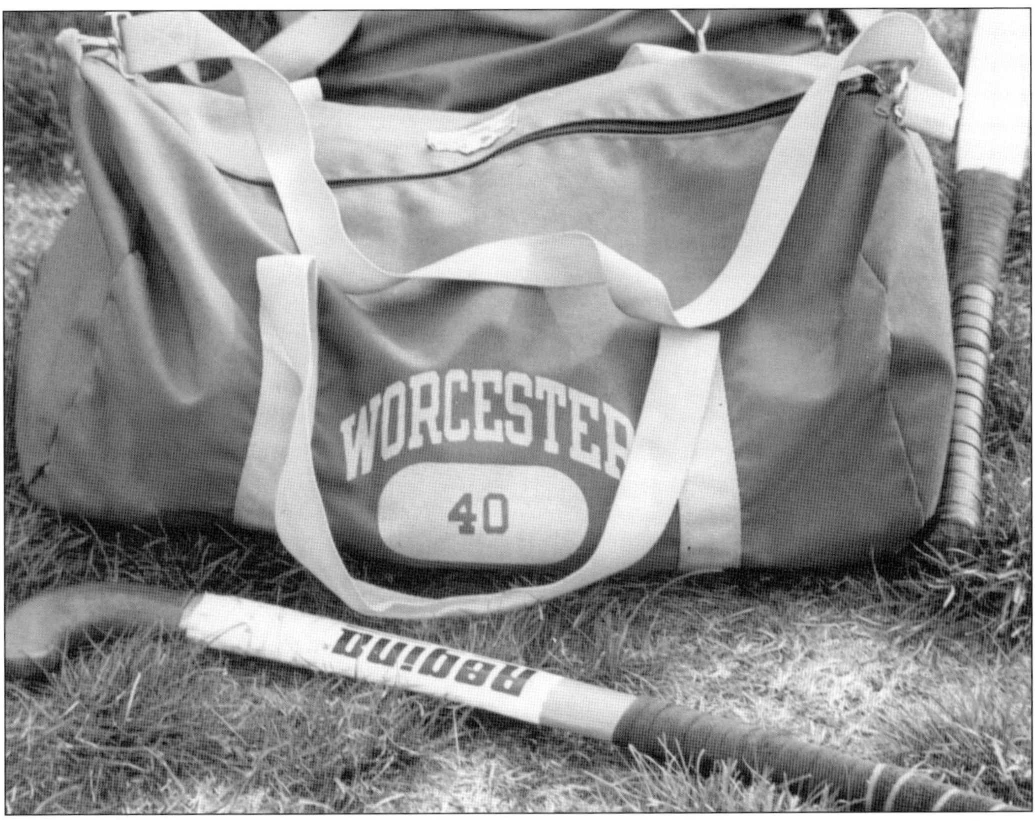

The Worcester State University Department of Athletics has 20 Division III varsity athletic teams as of this writing. There are 9 men's and 11 women's teams. This chapter provides a brief survey of the university's varsity sports history. (WSU Athletic Department.)

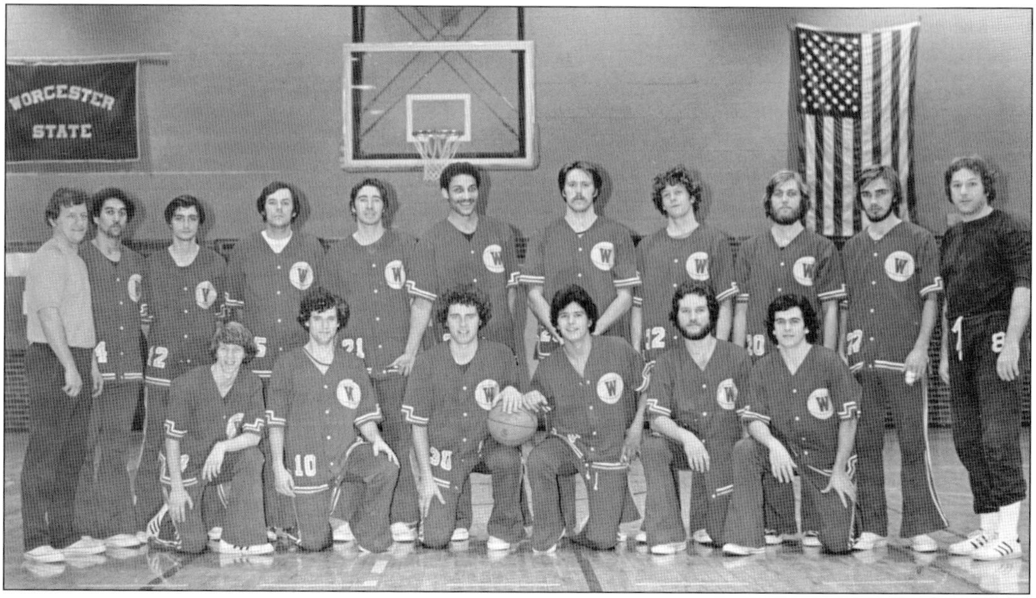

During the 1950–1951 academic year, both men's basketball and baseball began as the university's first varsity sports. But given that the basketball season occurs in the winter and baseball occurs in the spring, men's basketball holds the distinction of being the oldest varsity sport at Worcester State University. Above is an early team photograph; the image below is from a 1963 game against a team from Boston State College (later UMass Boston). (Both, WSU Athletic Department.)

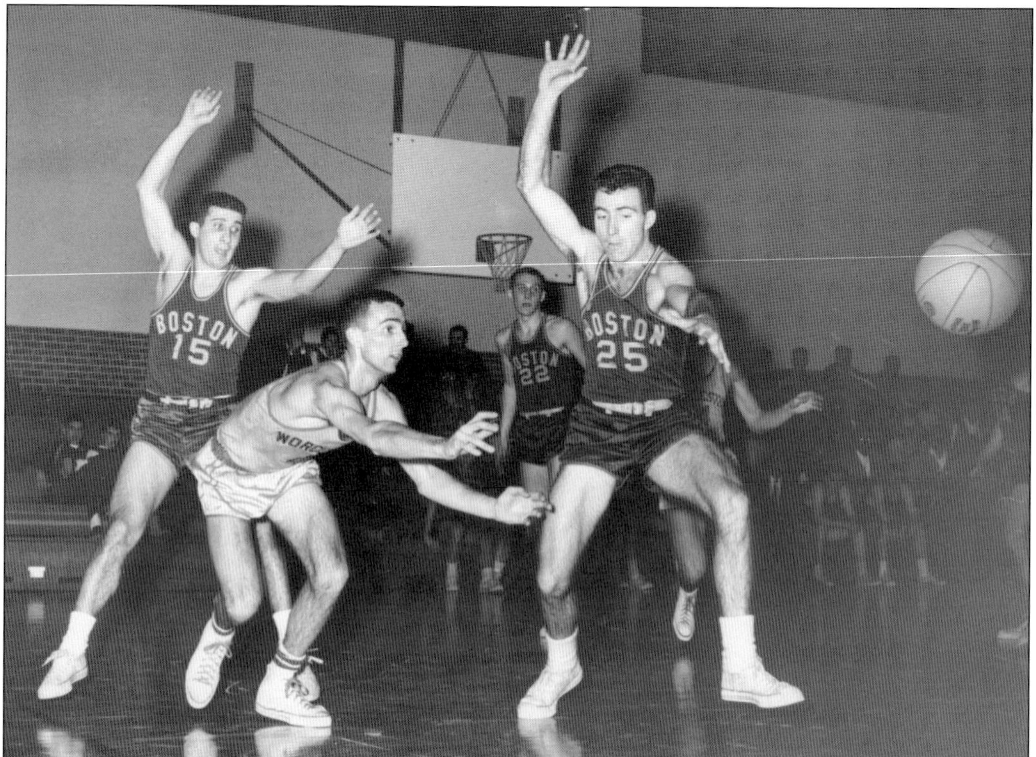

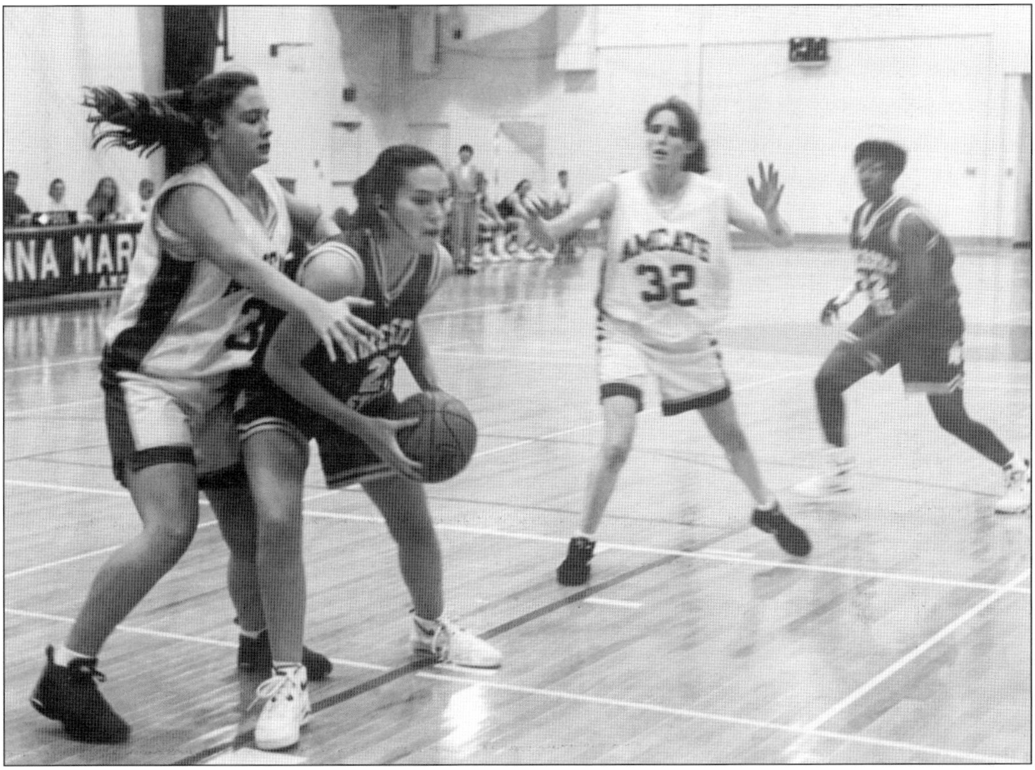

The women's basketball team had its first season in 1967–1968; it went undefeated that year. In 1980, the team won the AIAW National Basketball Championship. The image below shows the championship trophy with, from left to right, Celtics legend Bob Cousy, coach Donna Devlin, WSC president Joseph J. Orze, Massachusetts governor Edward King, Jackie Shaker, Kathy Westall, Joanne Medeiros, Mayor Jordan Levy, city manager Francis McGrath, and Denise Decorcy. (Both, WSU Athletic Department.)

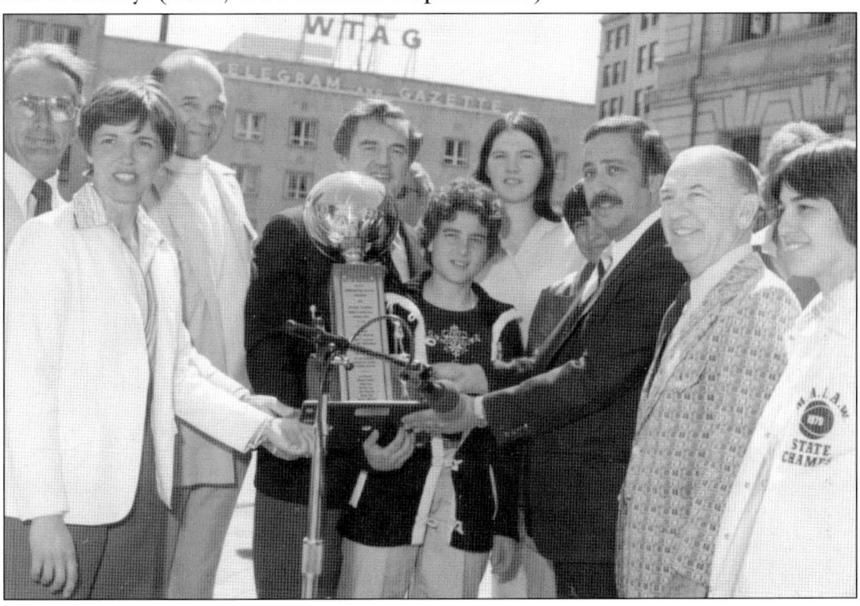

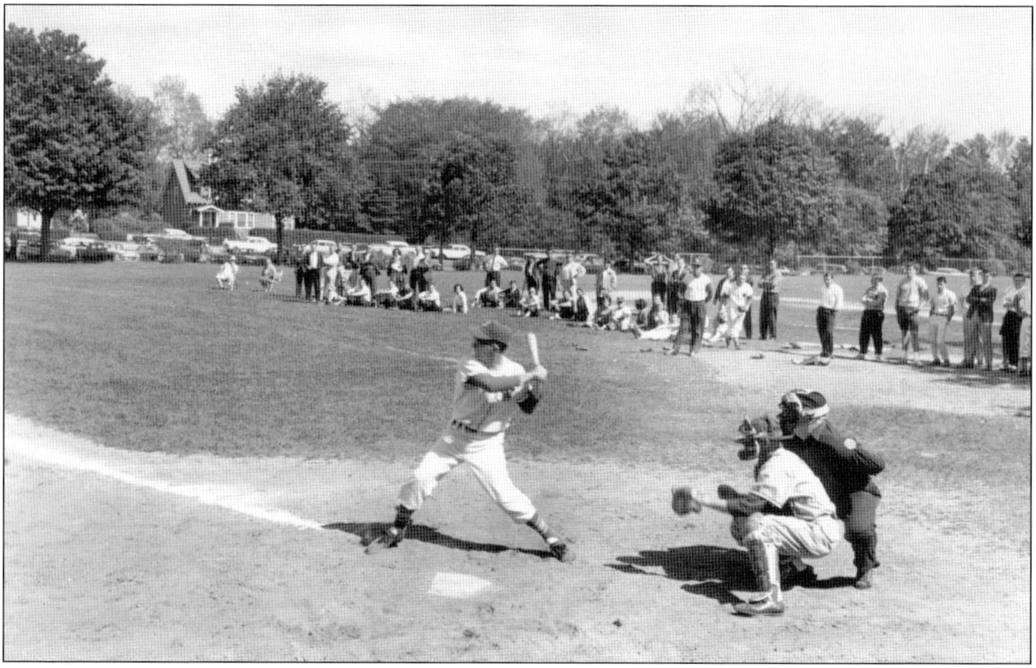

The first record of varsity baseball is from the spring of 1951. Baseball was played on a field behind the old gym (above) and moved to Rockwell Field much later. Teams that Worcester State played against varied over time. Early on, "State," as Worcester State was known, played "Tech" (Worcester Polytechnic Institute), Assumption, and "Agi" (University of Massachusetts [UMass] Amherst). Below, a Worcester State player tries to run through the UMass catcher. (Below, WSU Athletic Department.)

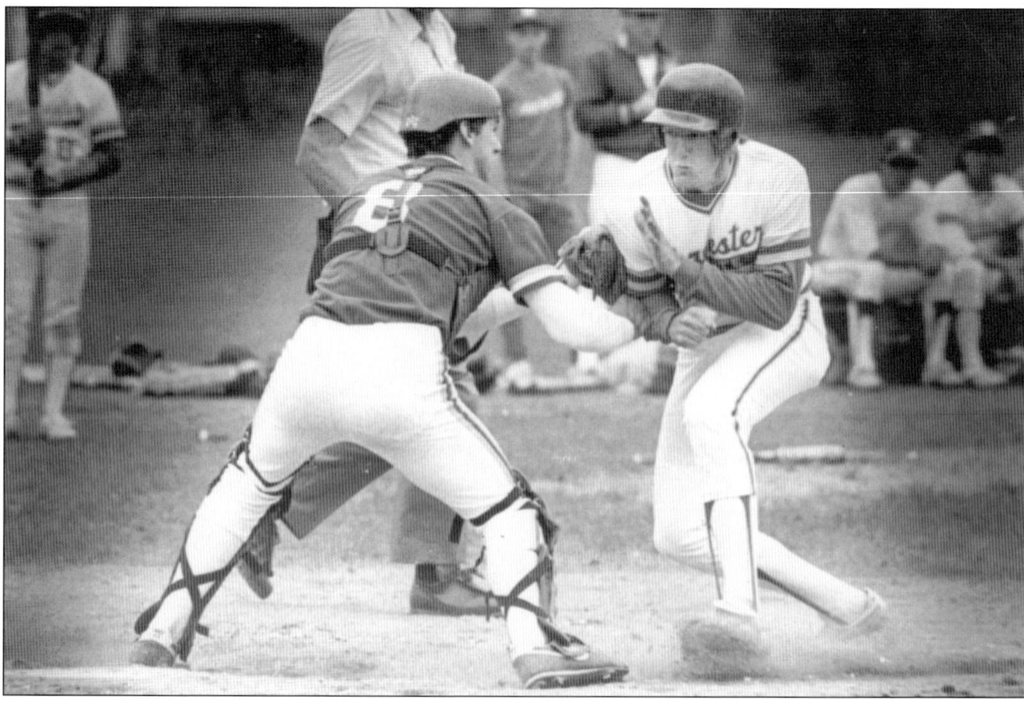

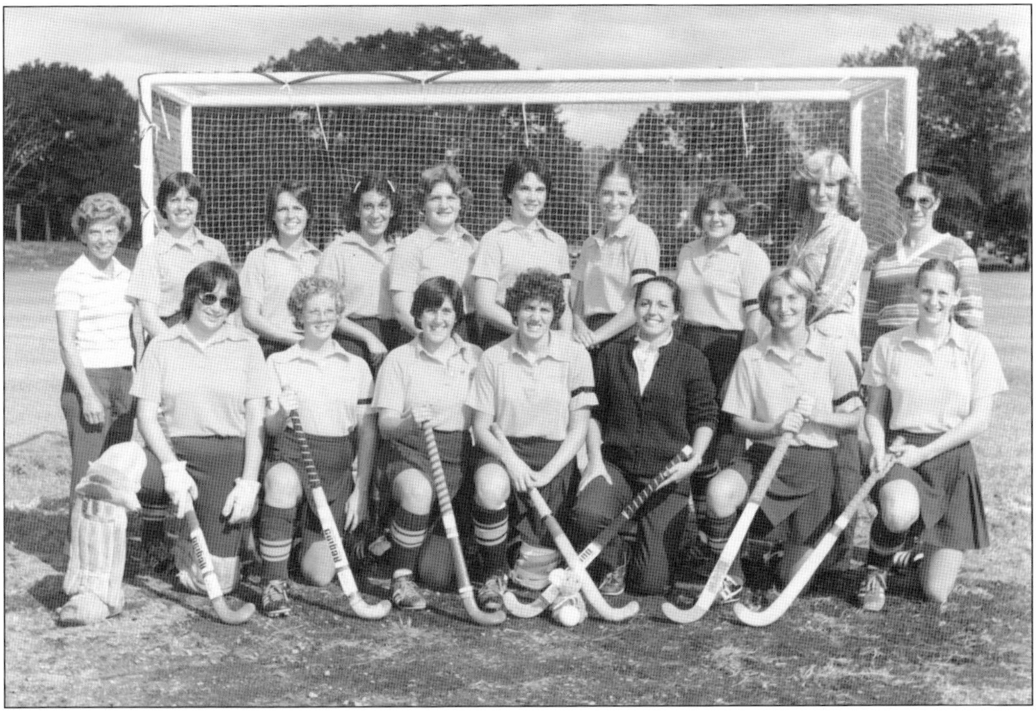

Women played field hockey at Worcester State first as a club sport. The first records of it being a varsity sport were in 1970. The above team picture is from 1980–1981. The game photograph below shows where field hockey games were played on campus: where the Ghosh Science & Technology Center is now. Chandler Magnet School, once Chandler Street Junior High School, can be seen across the street. (Above, WSU Athletic Department.)

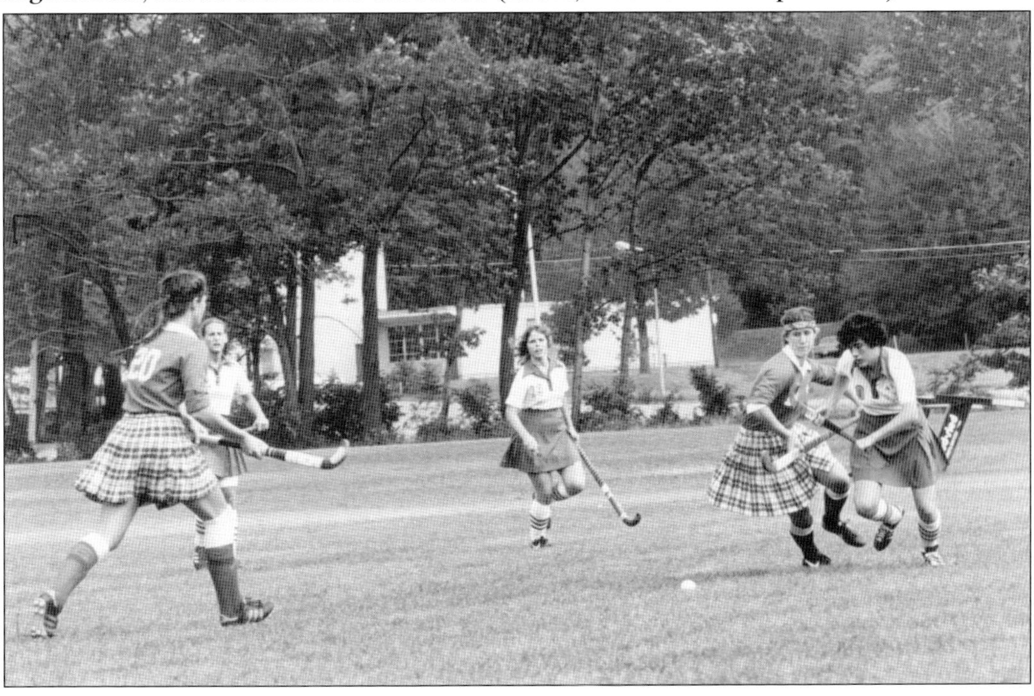

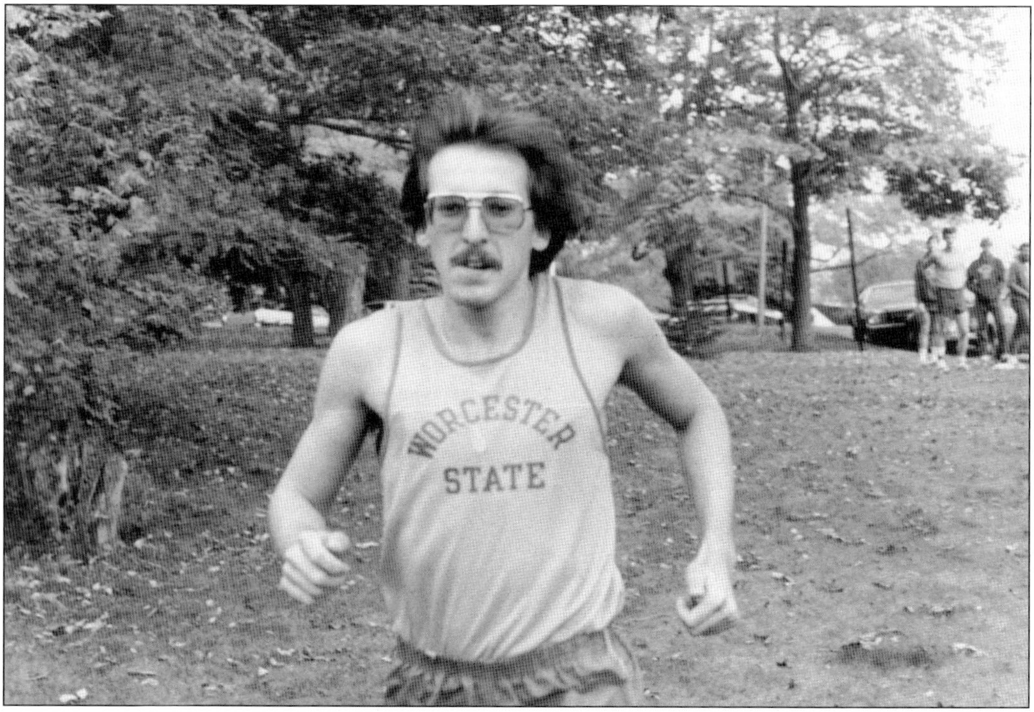

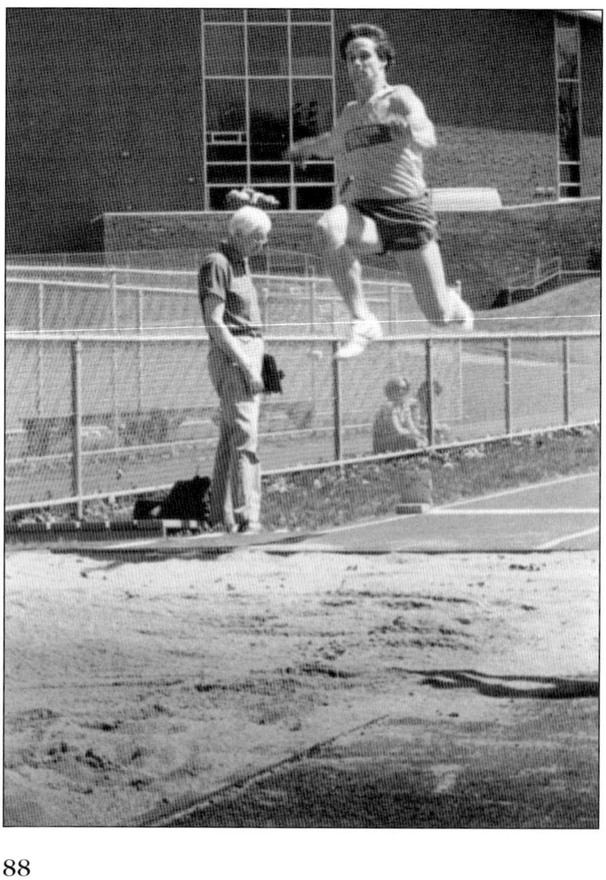

Track and field and cross-country have slightly different histories despite their related natures. Men's indoor and outdoor track and field began as varsity sports in the winter of 1968–1969. Women's outdoor track and field began in the early/mid-1970s and became a varsity sport later, while women's varsity indoor track and field began in 1992. (Left, WSU Athletic Department.)

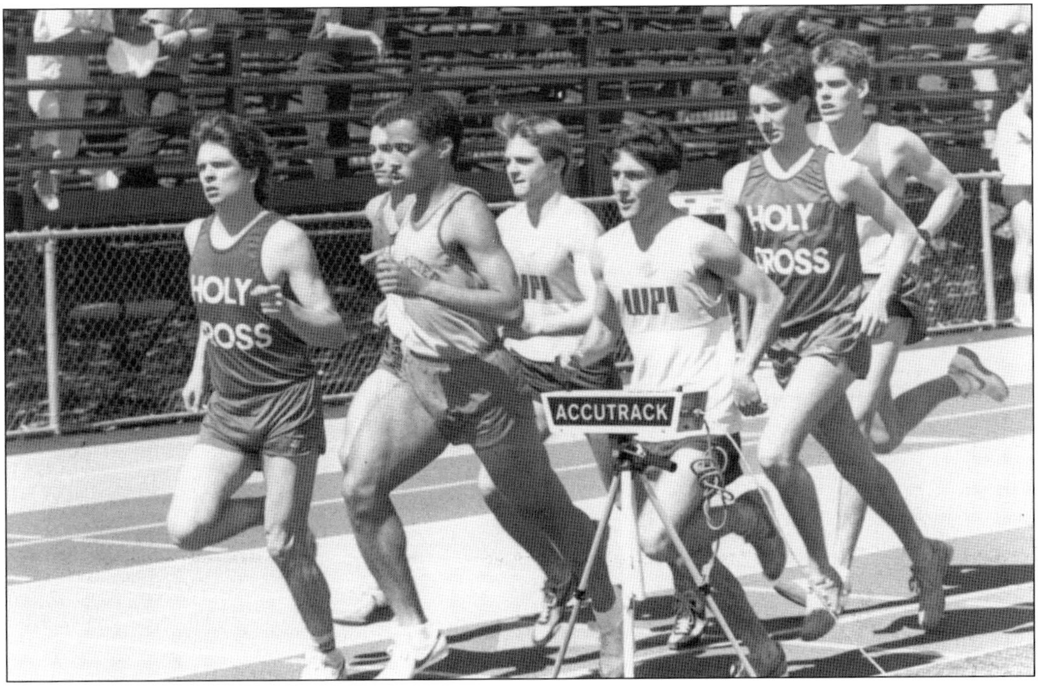

Yearbooks in the 1960s show a men's cross-country team as a sport, but it was likely a club sport at first. By the late 1960s, it was a varsity sport. Women's cross-country began in the early/mid-1970s, around the same time as track and field. (Both, WSU Athletic Department.)

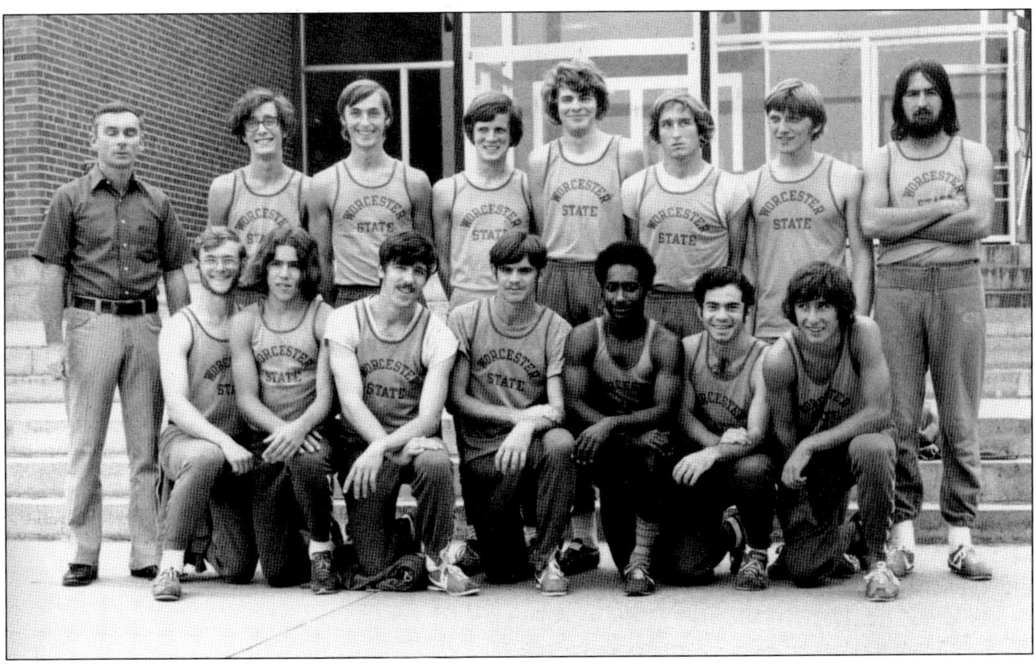

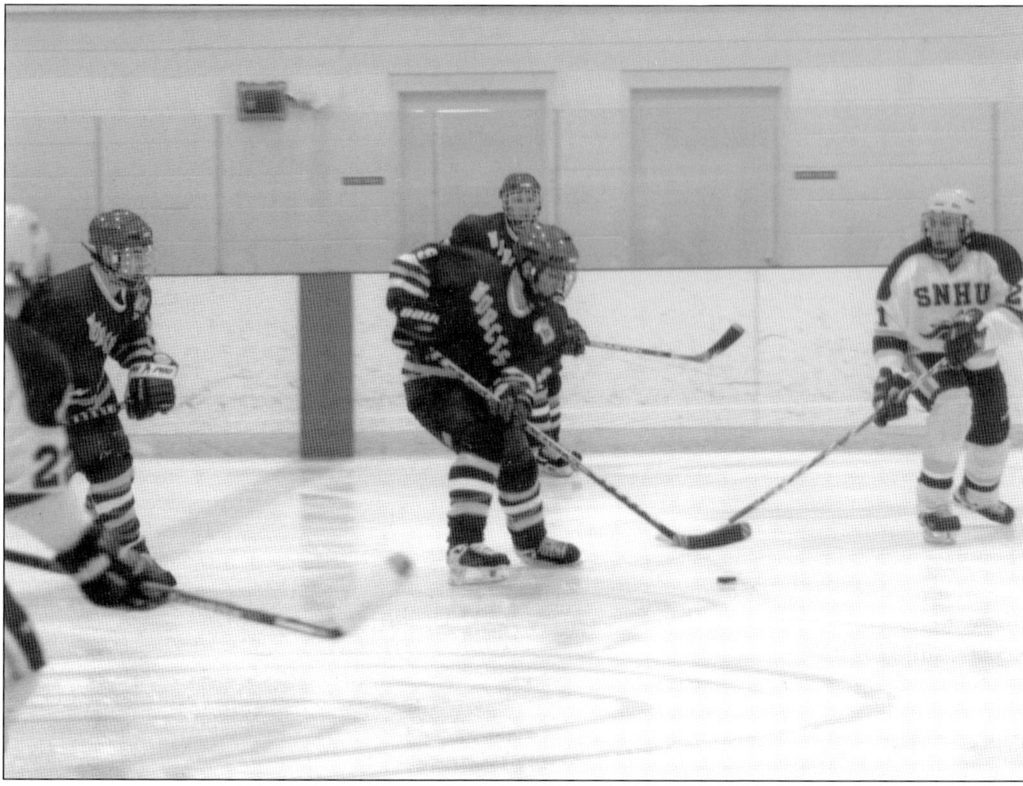

Ice hockey was first played as a varsity sport in the 1966–1967 season. Home games were frequently played at the Webster Square Arena and at the Hart Center at Holy Cross. The coach for the first 20 years was John Coughlin Sr., second from the right in the second row (below). (Both, WSU Athletic Department.)

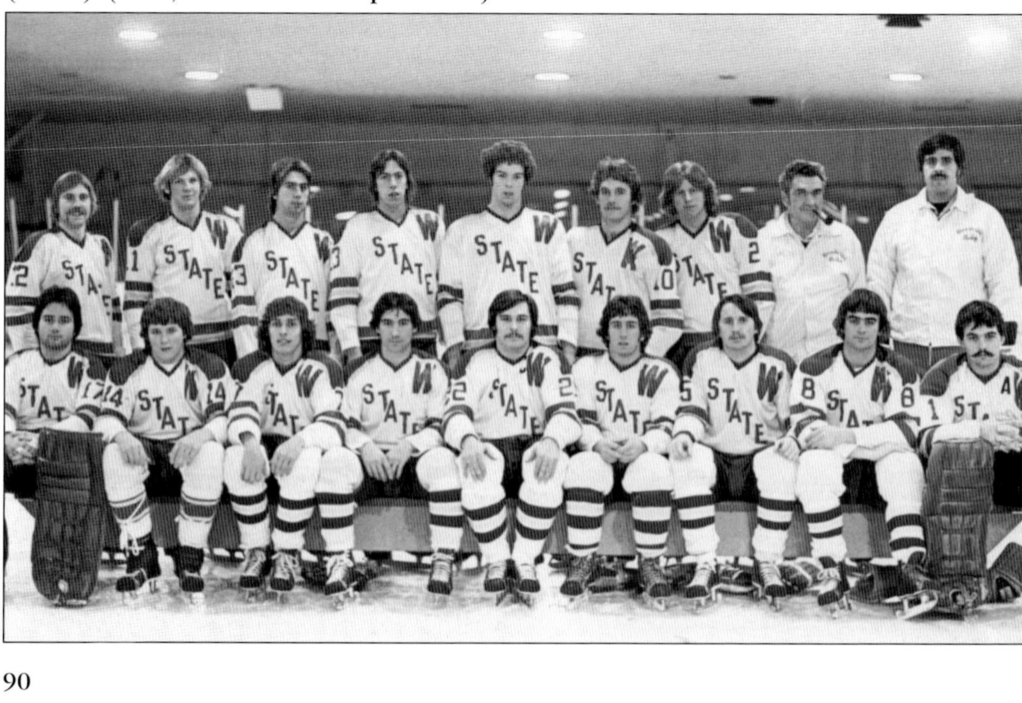

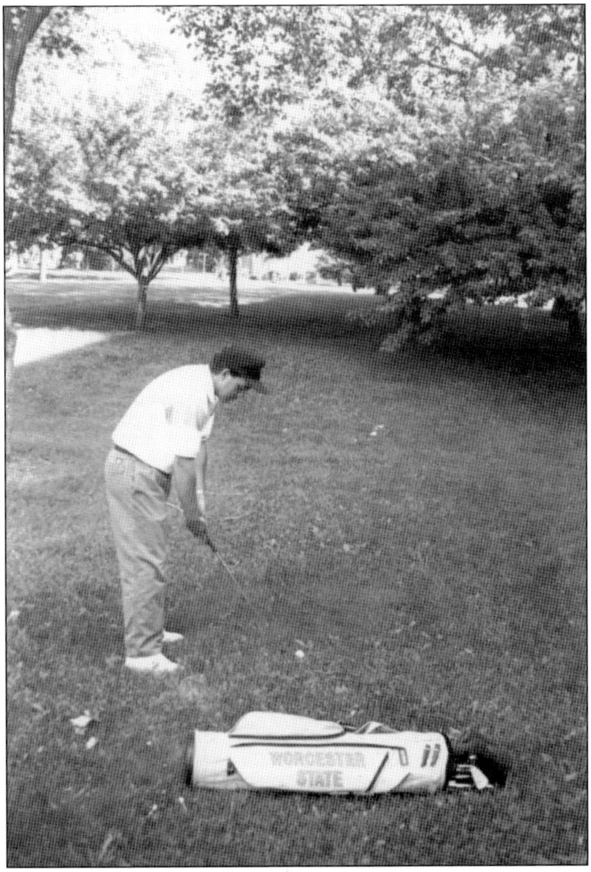

The first records for men's golf suggest it is a varsity sport played at least since 1980. But as with other sports, evidence of it being played shows up as early as the 1960s in yearbooks—suggesting it, too, was once a club sport. A women's golf varsity team began in the 2017–2018 season. (Both, WSU Athletic Department.)

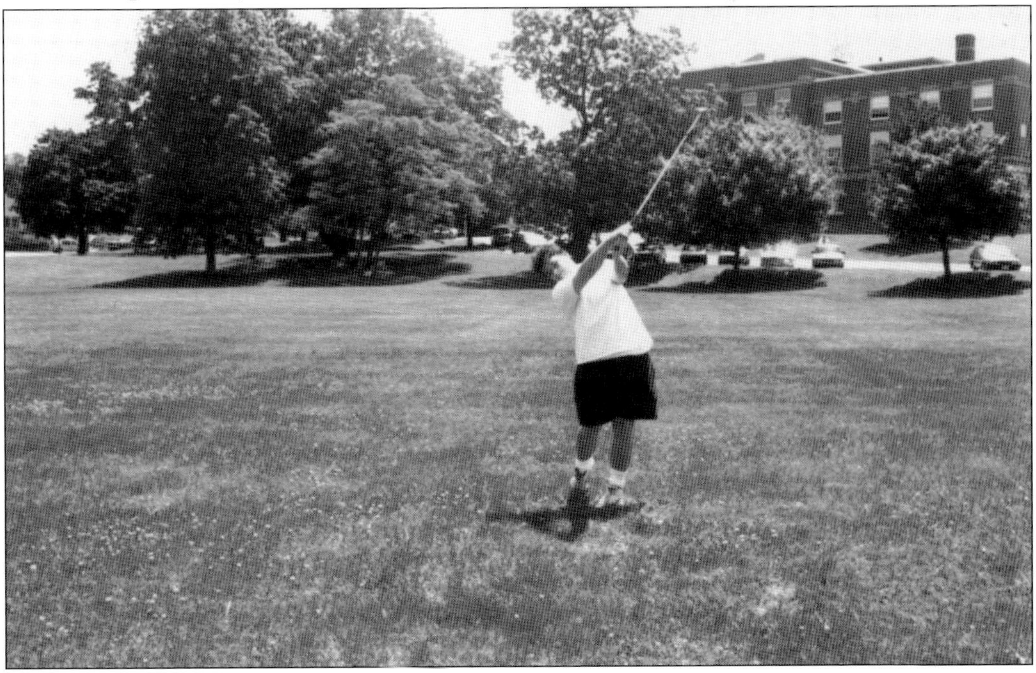

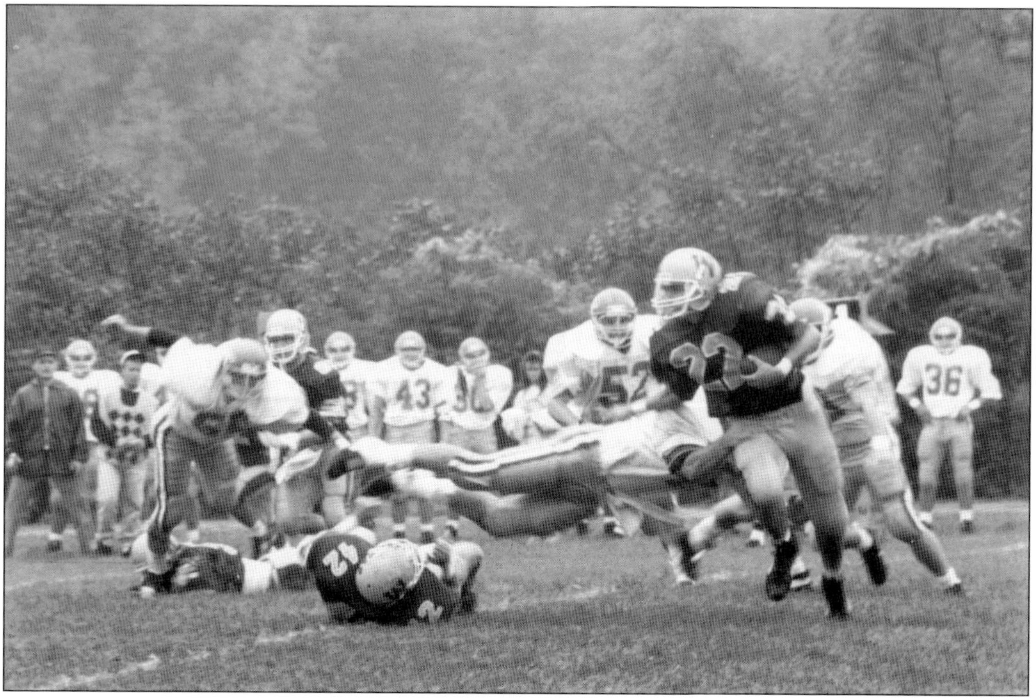

Although Worcester State College had an active team for at least a few years before 1985, athletic department records show it being a varsity sport beginning in that year. In fact, the team won the 1984 National Club Championship. While Worcester State football teams formerly played in an unremarkable field next to the Student Center, the team now plays in Coughlin Field—sharing time with soccer, field hockey, lacrosse, and track and field. (Both, WSU Athletic Department.)

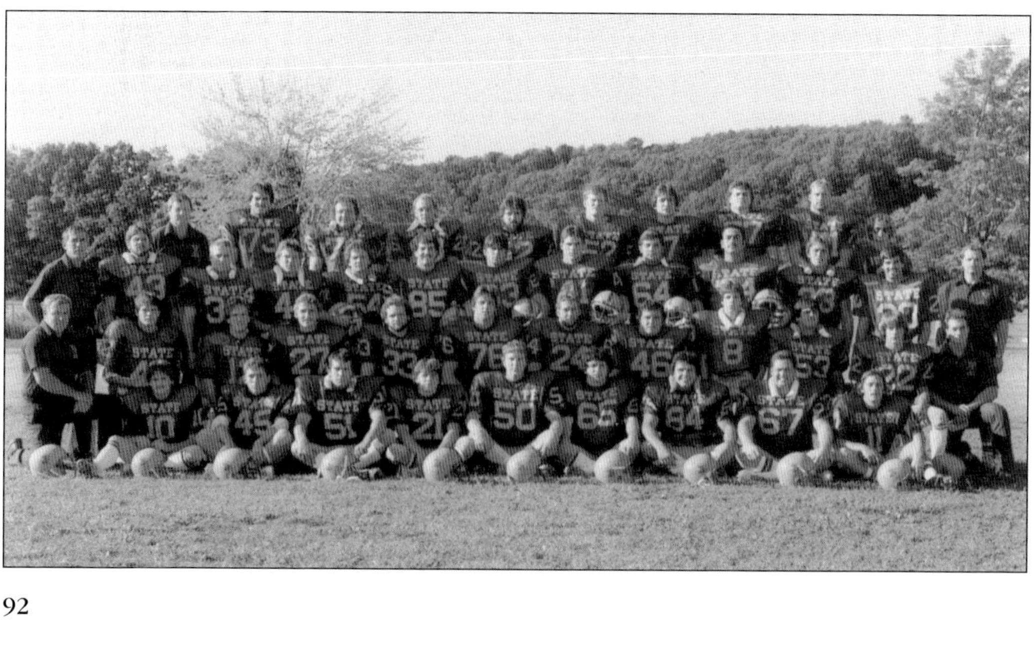

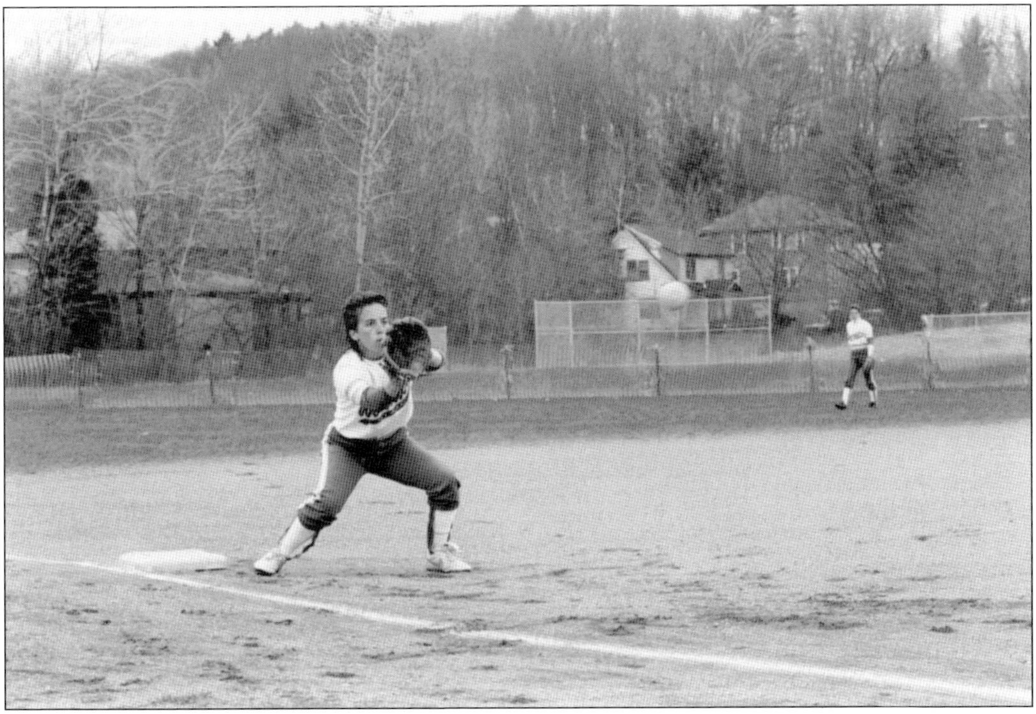

The first varsity softball season was in 1971. It was the fourth women's varsity team on campus following basketball, field hockey, and tennis. (Both, WSU Athletic Department.)

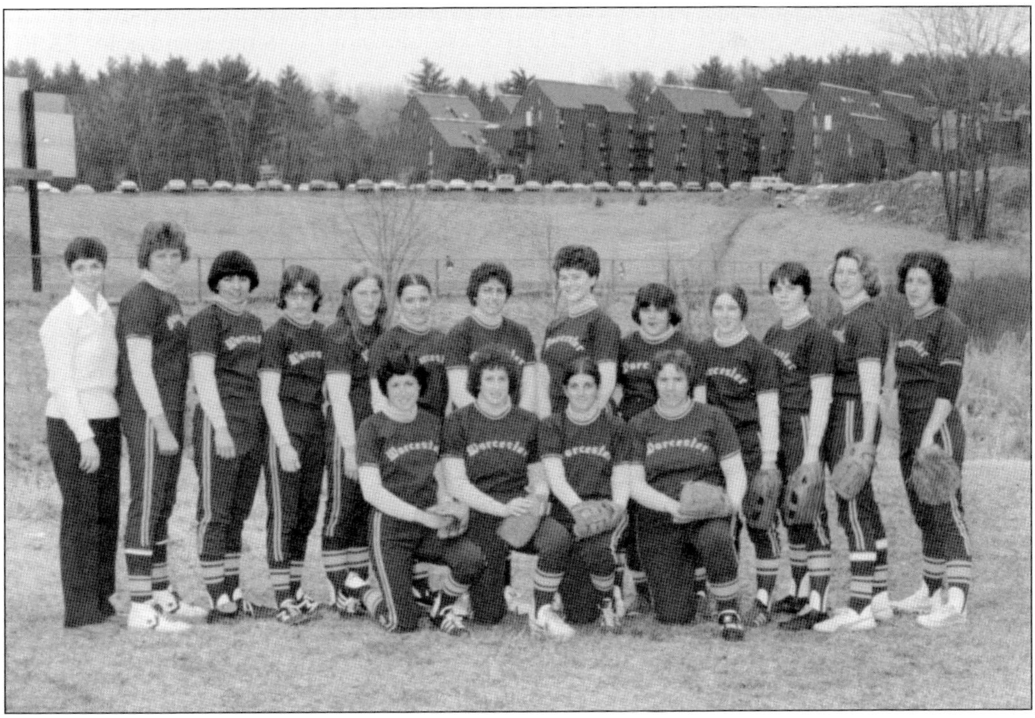

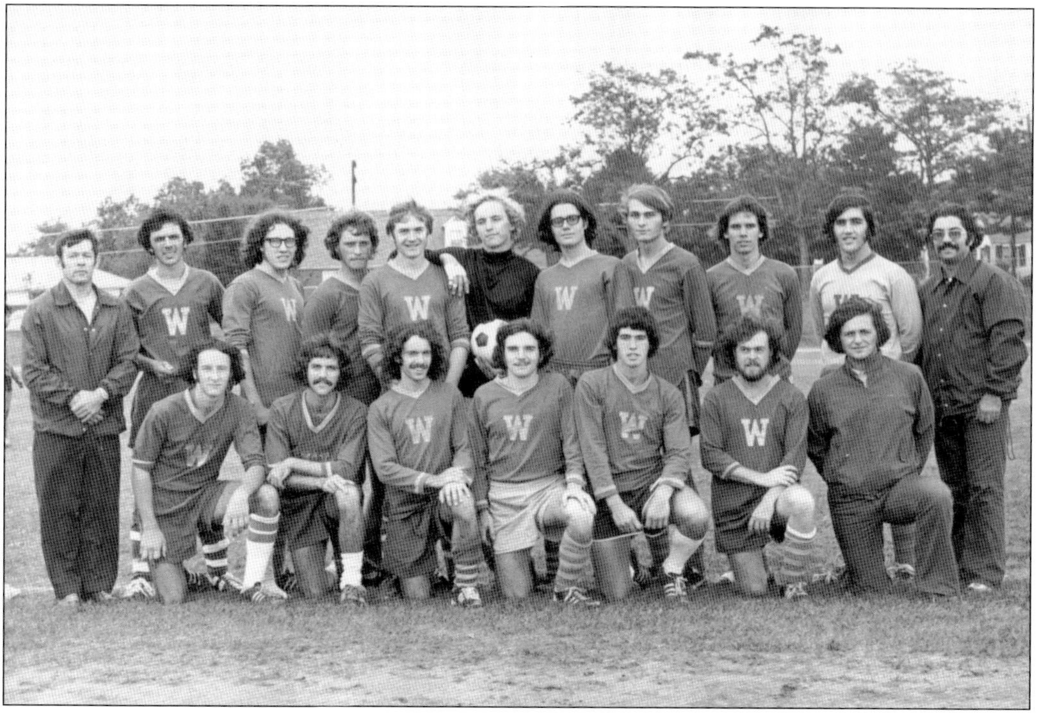

The first men's varsity soccer team played in 1968. The team is shown here in an early team photograph (above) and in a later image (below) from a game. (Both, WSU Athletic Department.)

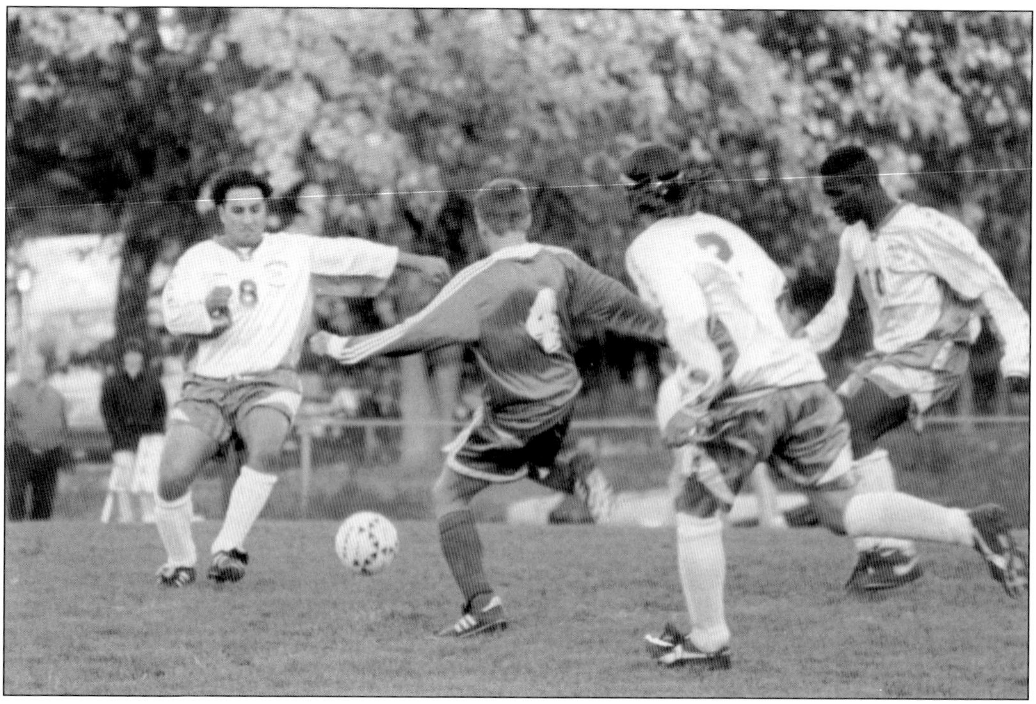

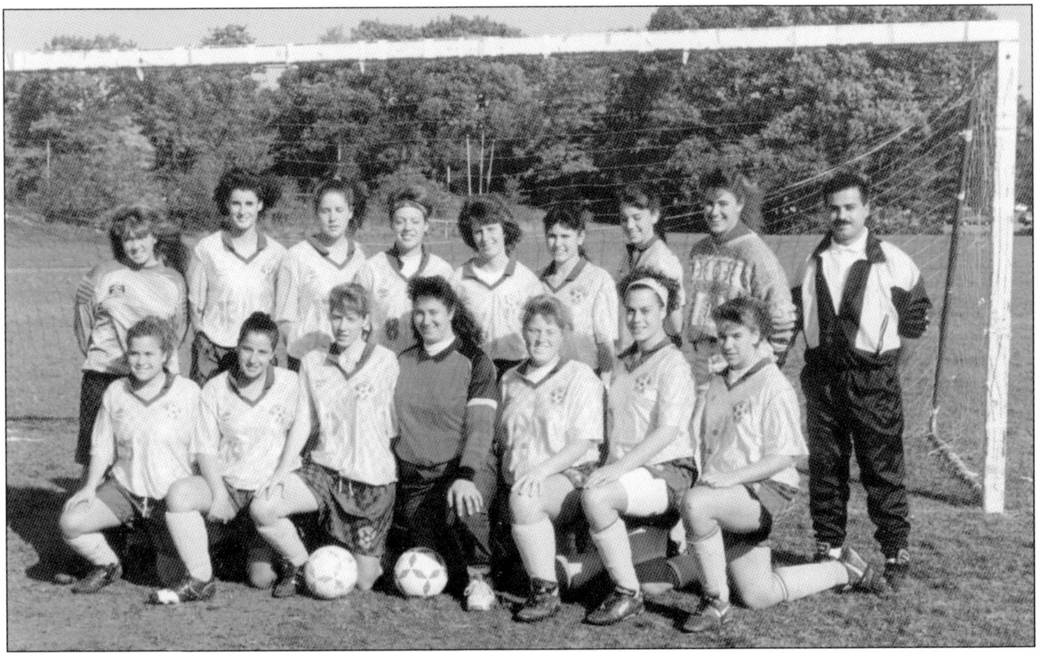

Women's soccer was first played as a varsity sport in 1991. It was played on the unremarkable field that predated Coughlin Field, which can be seen in these images. The team photograph above was taken on the land that would become the site of the Ghosh Science & Technology Building and north parking lot. (Both, WSU Athletic Department.)

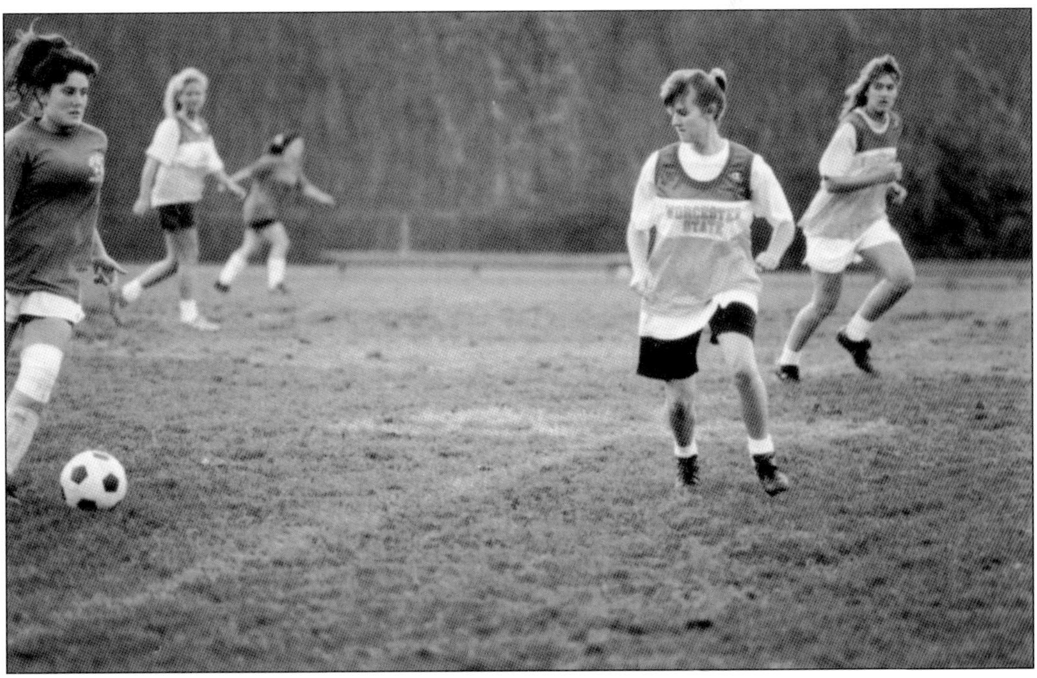

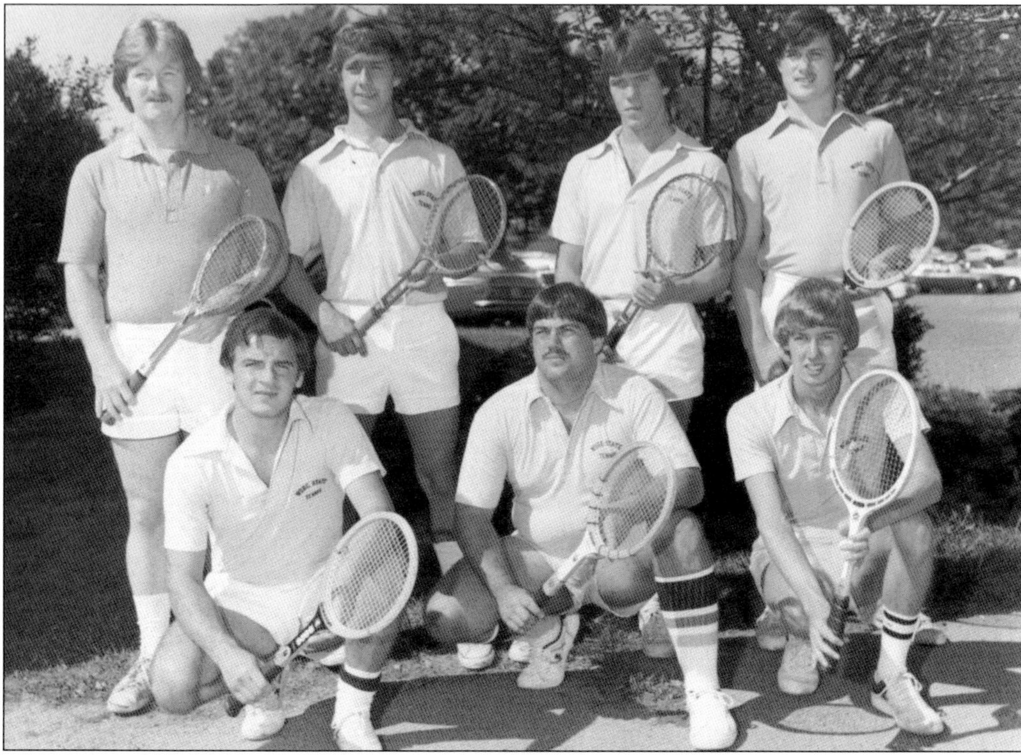

While tennis had been played on campus since before the move to Chandler Street, it became a varsity sport for men in 1969 and for women in 1970. Both pictures show 1980–1981 teams. (Both, WSU Athletic Department.)

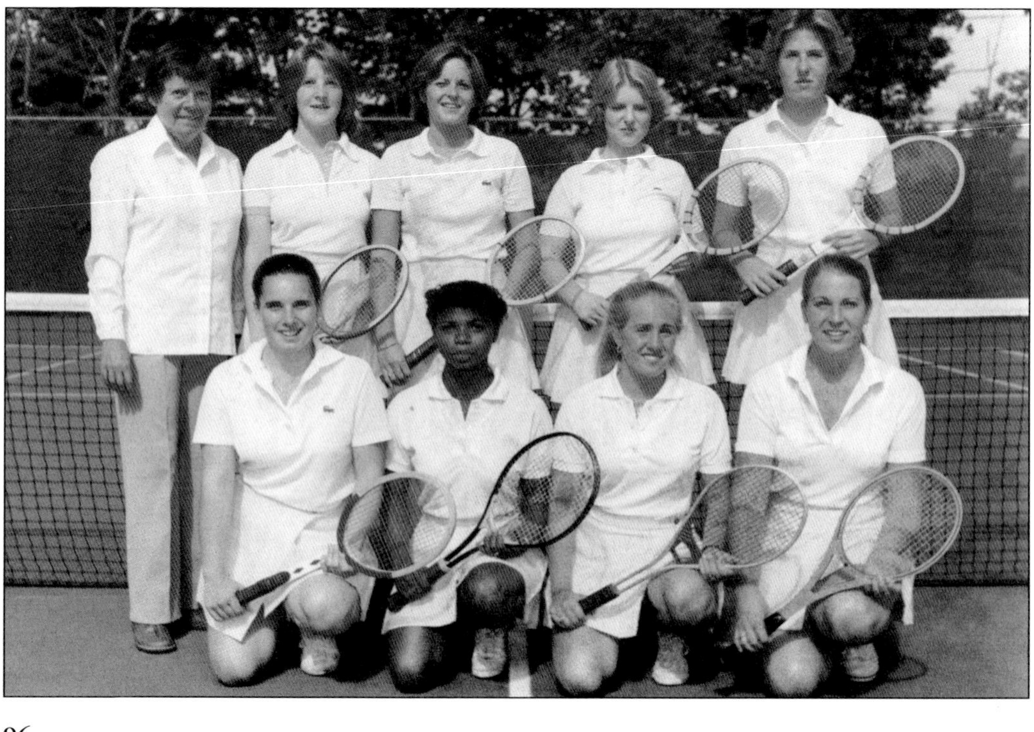

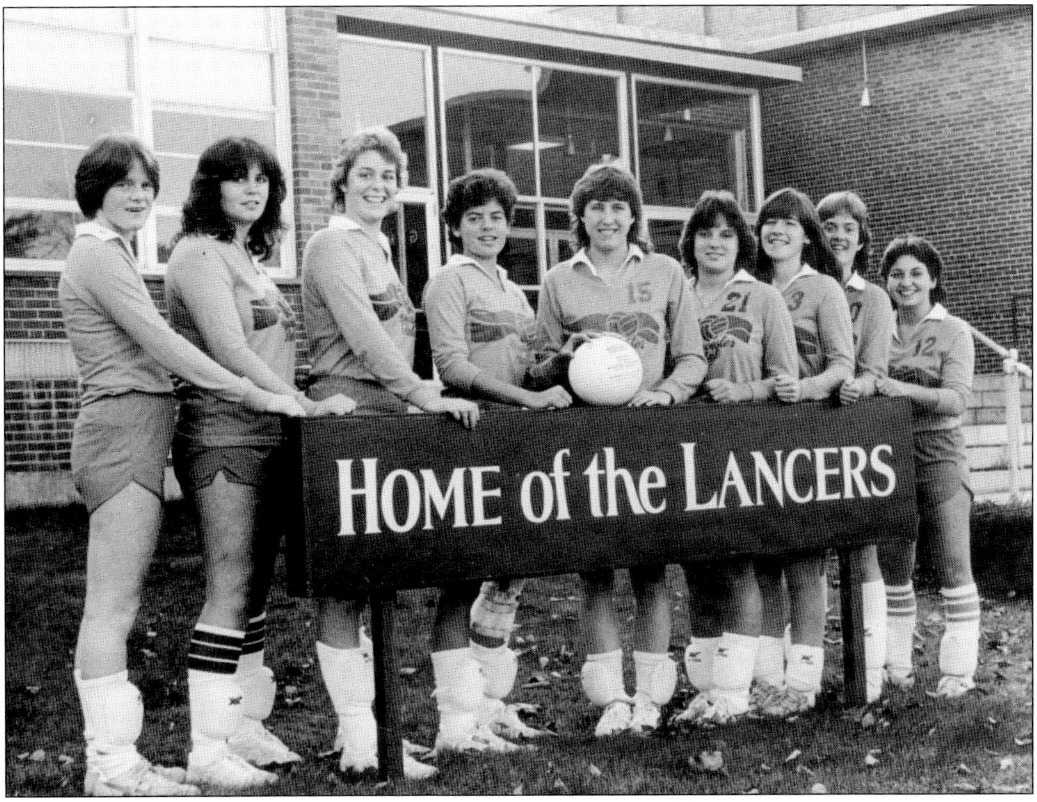

While men played volleyball on campus, they did not have a varsity team. The women's varsity volleyball team started in 1983 and captured the Massachusetts State College Class C Championship the following year with the team shown above. It played indoors in the old gym (below) until games moved into the Wellness Center in 2016. (Both, WSU Athletic Department.)

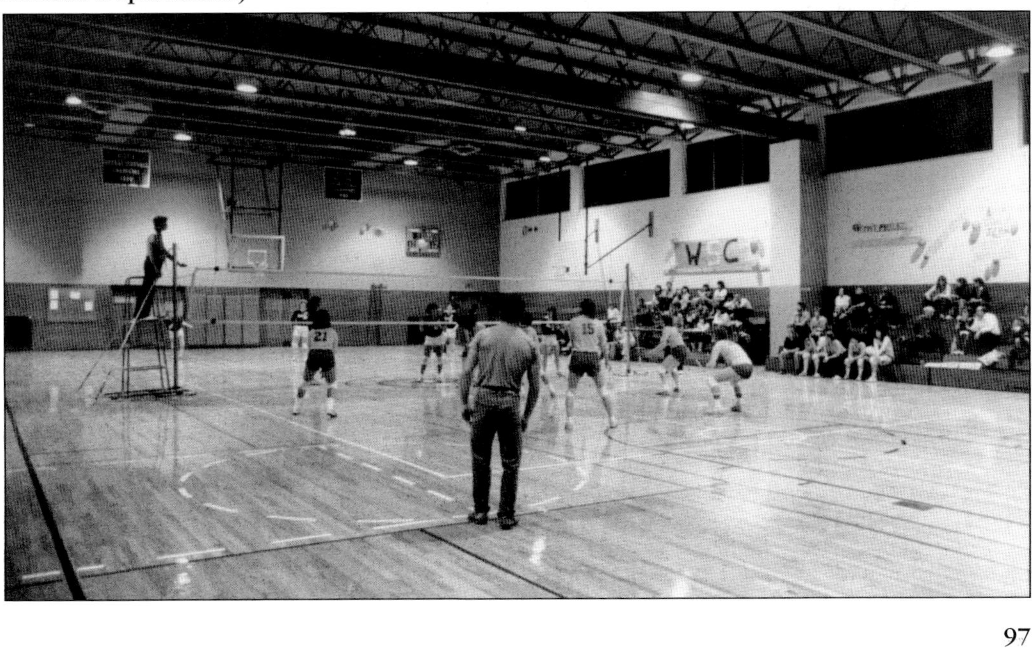

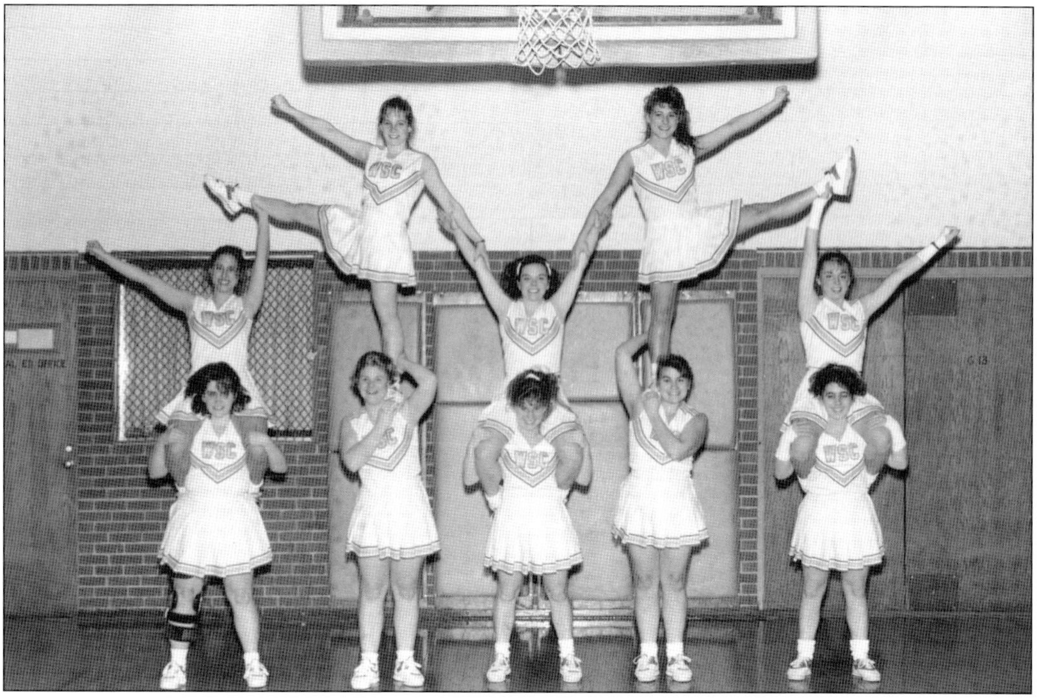

Cheerleading is actually a club sport, not a varsity sport. But it is included in this section because cheerleading is mainly practiced in the context of varsity sports. Use of the name Lancerettes, for the squad seen in the 1978 photograph below, was short-lived. (Both, WSU Athletic Department.)

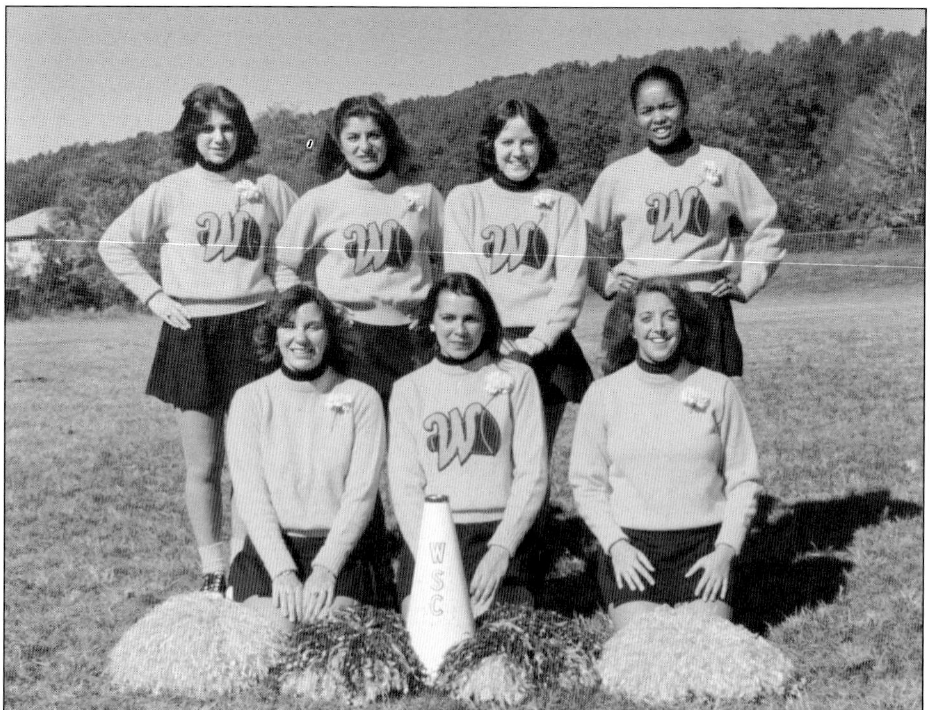

Seven

The Arts on Campus

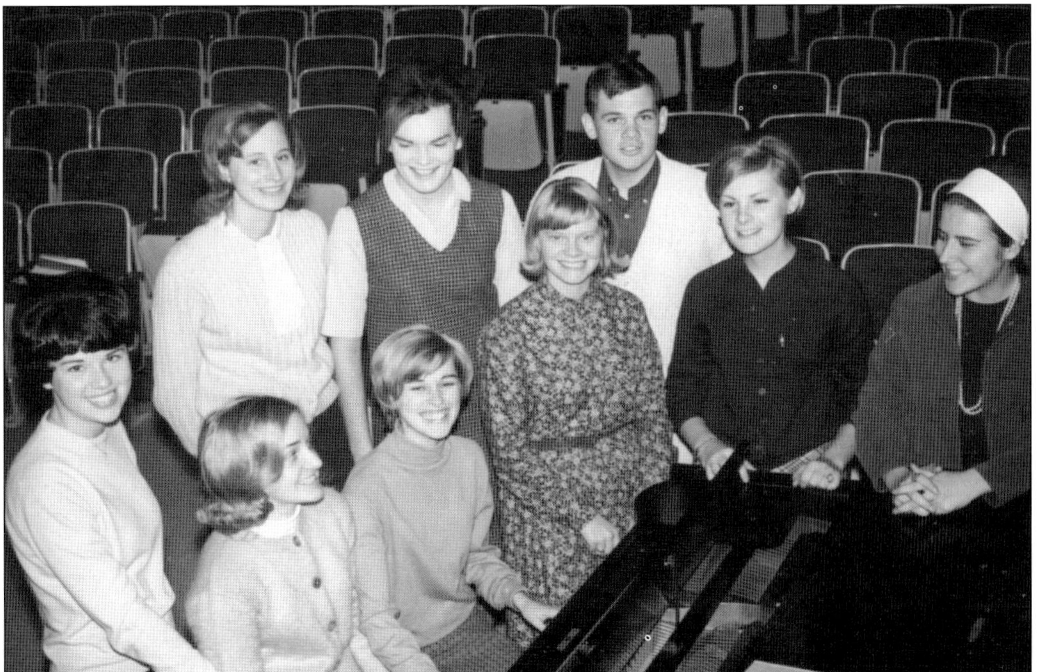

This group of students is practicing singing in the Sullivan Auditorium. The arts have long had a place in the curricular and recreational lives of Worcester State students. This chapter focuses on some of those moments throughout the university's history.

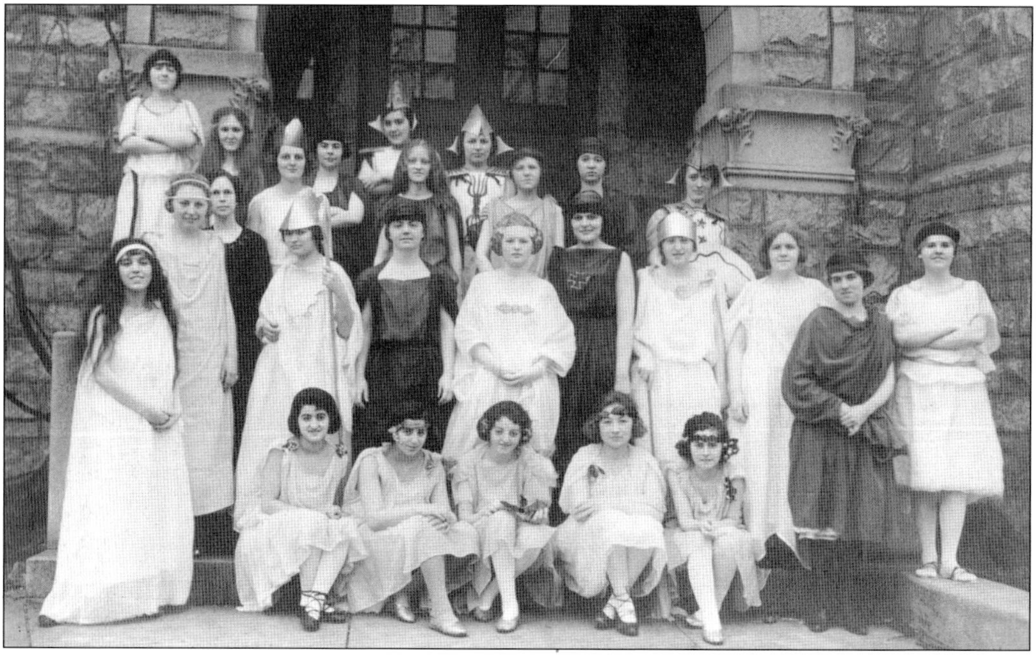

Students at the normal school commonly engaged in visual arts course work (sculpture, drawing, and painting) as well as performing arts in class or through student clubs. Posing here outside the gym, these students were likely involved in a pageant production, which became popular during the Colonial Revival movement and remained so for years.

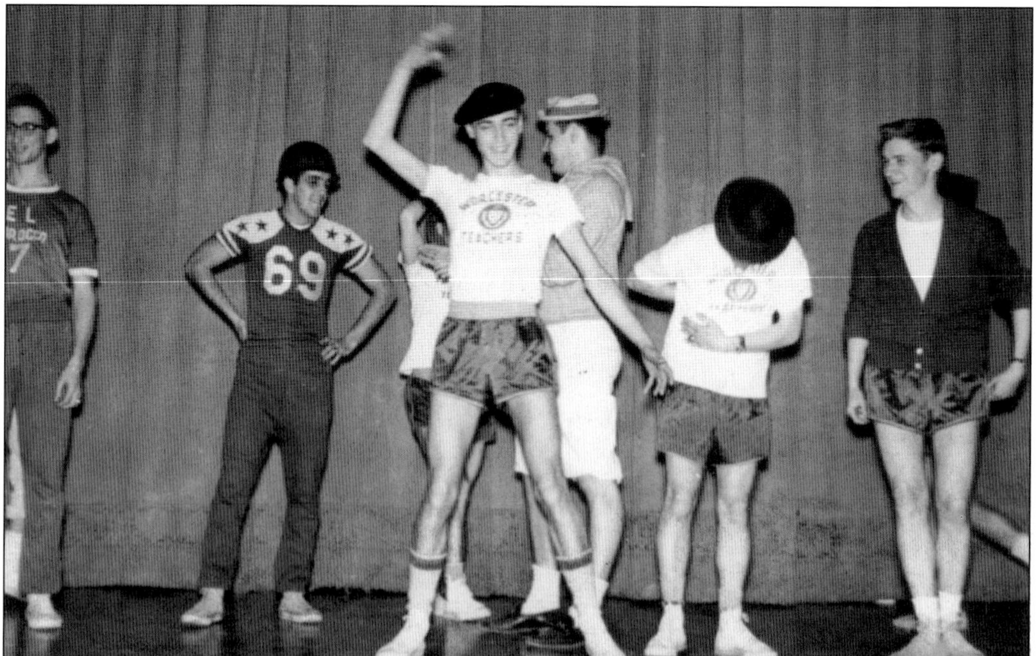

Skits often accompanied larger events. For example, this skit was part of the 1961 winter carnival. What they lacked in production value they made up for in satire, as skits were designed to poke fun at fellow students, faculty, or situations on and off campus.

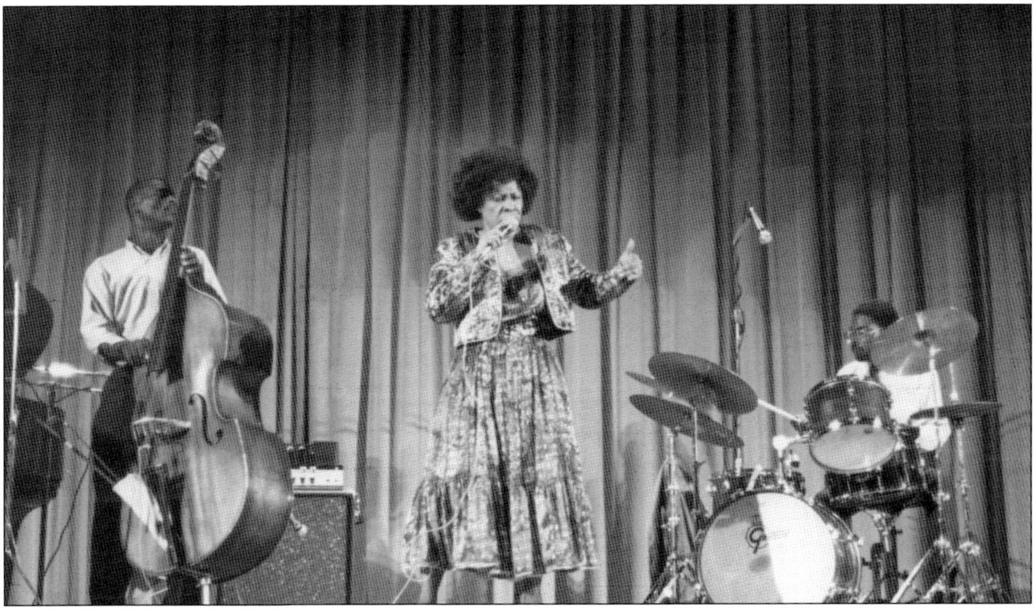

Especially in the 1950s–1990s, it was common to bring musical acts and performers to campus. These included big bands for dances as well as ensembles, comedians, rock bands, and solo performers who were headline acts. Above, a jazz ensemble performs in Fuller Auditorium; below, the band Orleans performs in Sullivan Auditorium.

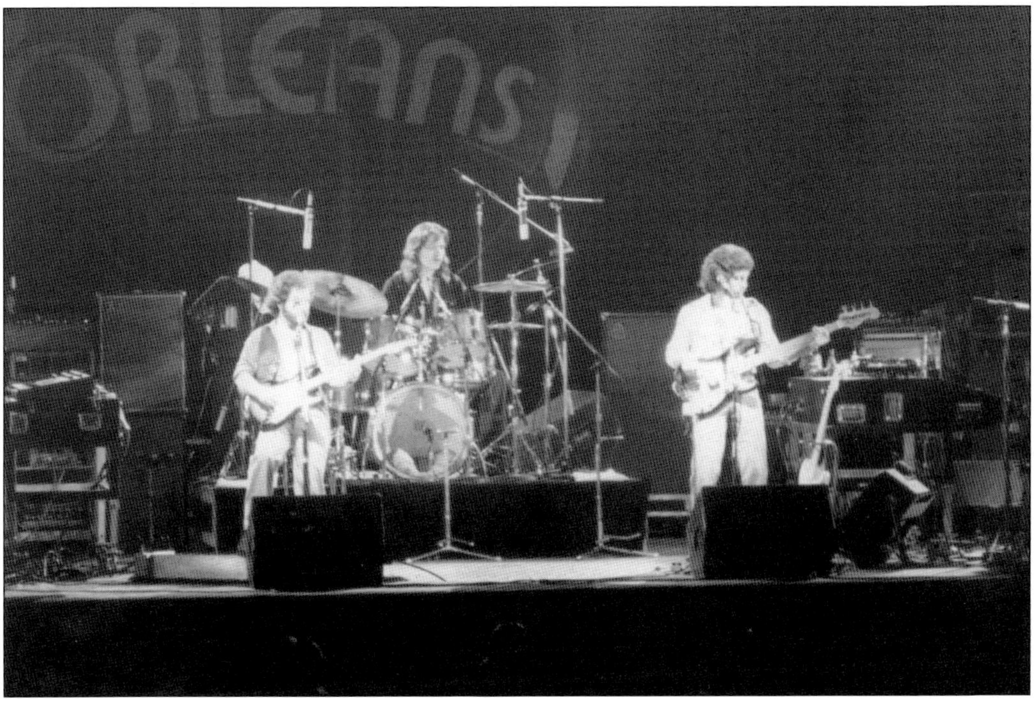

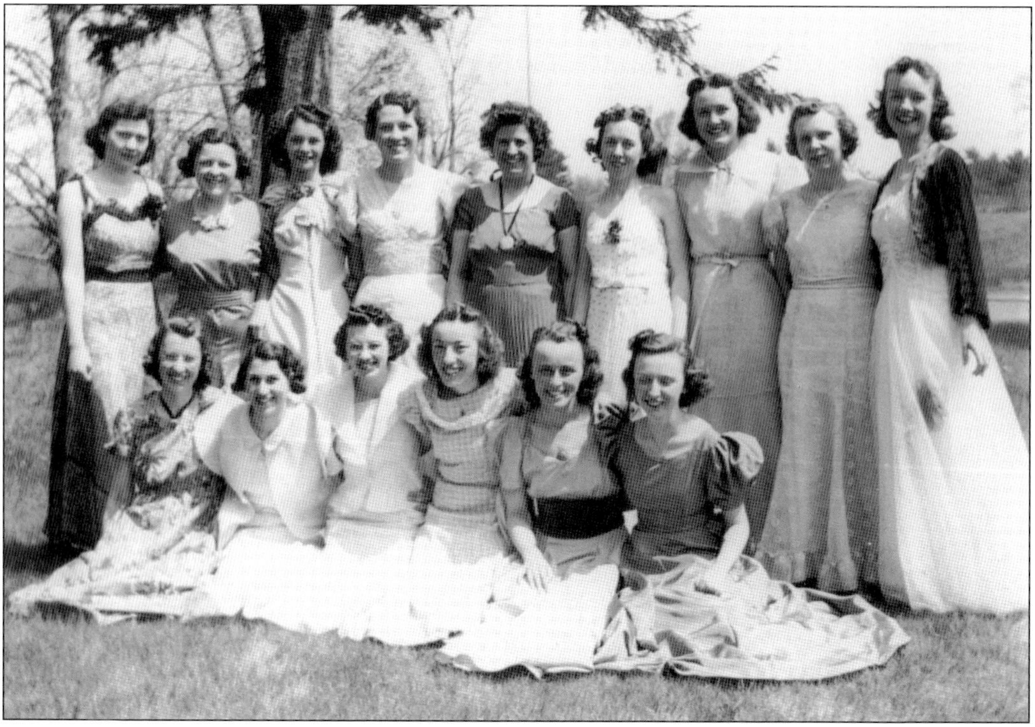

Music was an integral part of the curriculum in the normal school because teachers were expected to teach it when they got into their classrooms as professional educators. That ideal remained at the Chandler Street campus, and it spawned the desire to perform outside of class. The picture above shows the college glee club's senior choir, all members of the class of 1939. Below is a picture of the Worcester State University Chorale during a performance in Europe. (Below, WSU Office of Marketing.)

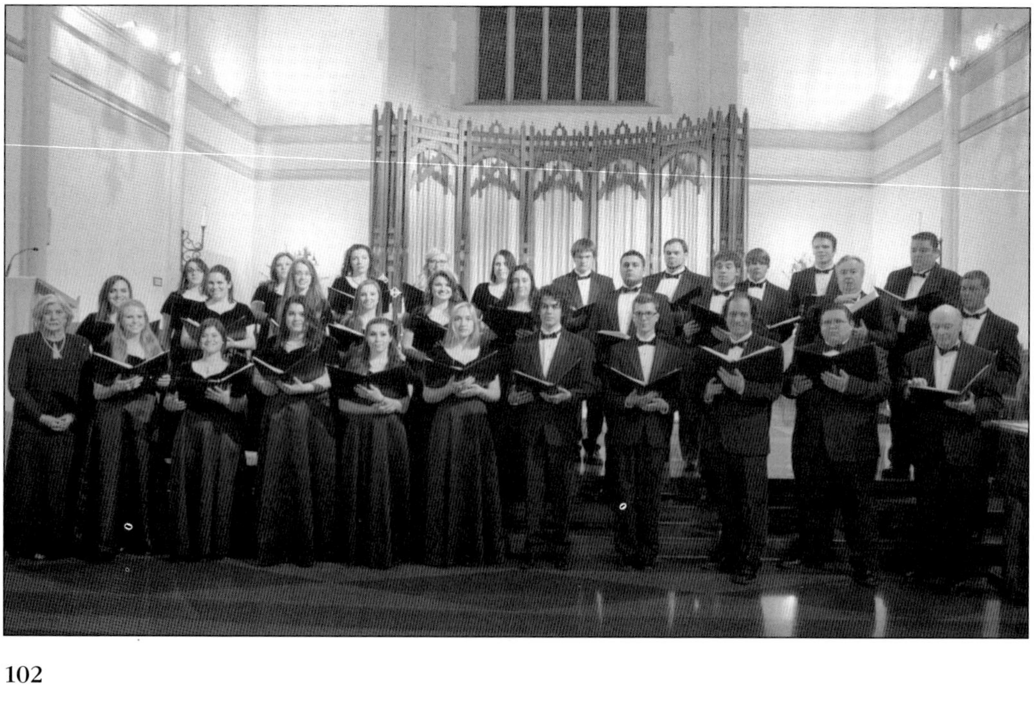

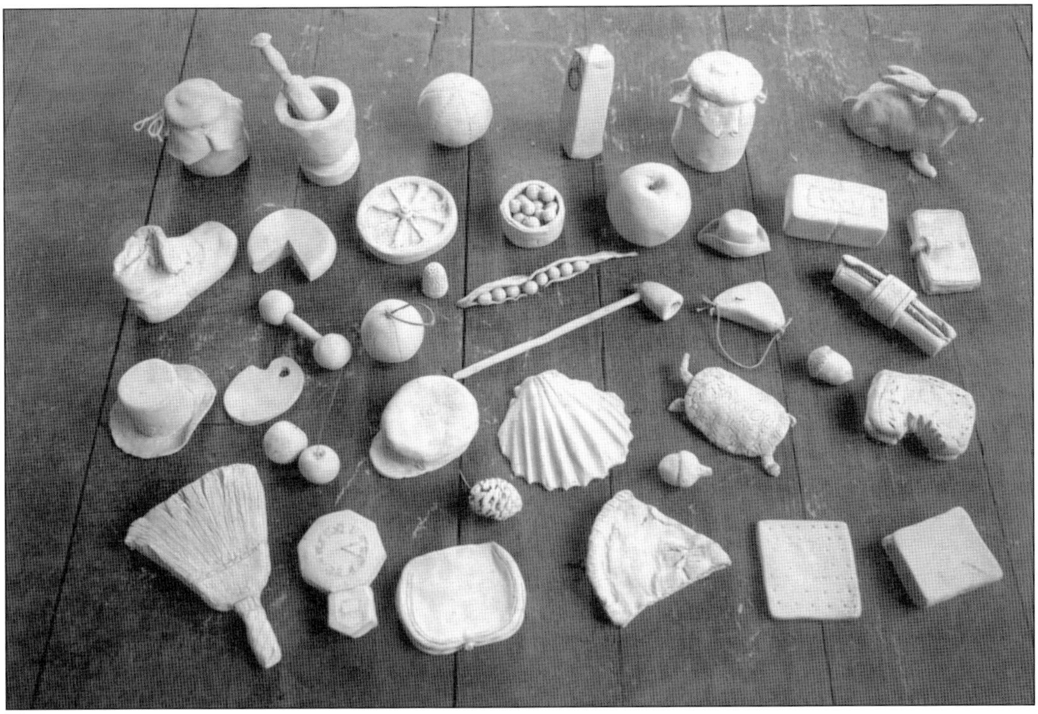

The normal school curriculum included lessons in clay sculpting, again because graduates would be required to teach it in schools. The early-1890s image above shows what was termed "everyday classwork" in art class, the best of which was displayed in cases. Today, the work of visual and performing arts students is displayed in the Mary Cosgrove Dolphin Gallery, seen below, and includes two-dimensional and three-dimensional visual art. (Below, WSU Office of Marketing.)

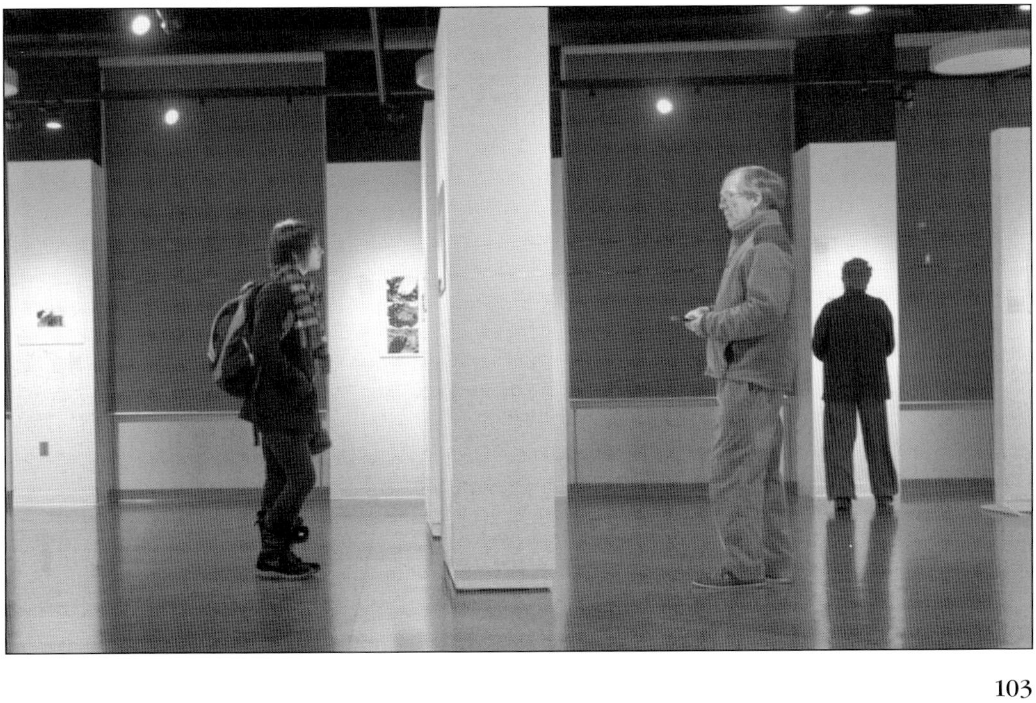

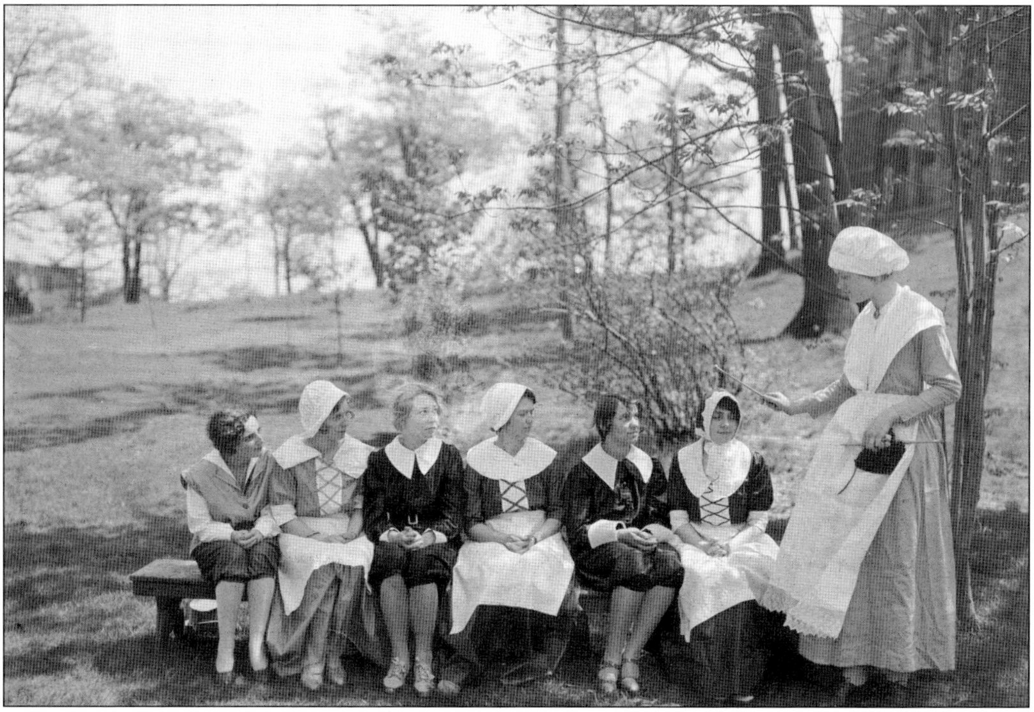

Pageant performances lasted at least until the move from Normal Hill to Chandler Street. In the above picture from 1930, a group of students is dressed in what were viewed at the time as typical colonial costumes. But it was the drama club, a student organization that first brought theater performances to Worcester State. The club in 1935, seen below, was particularly well-attended and would stage shows mainly in the Fuller Auditorium. (Below, WSU Office of University Advancement.)

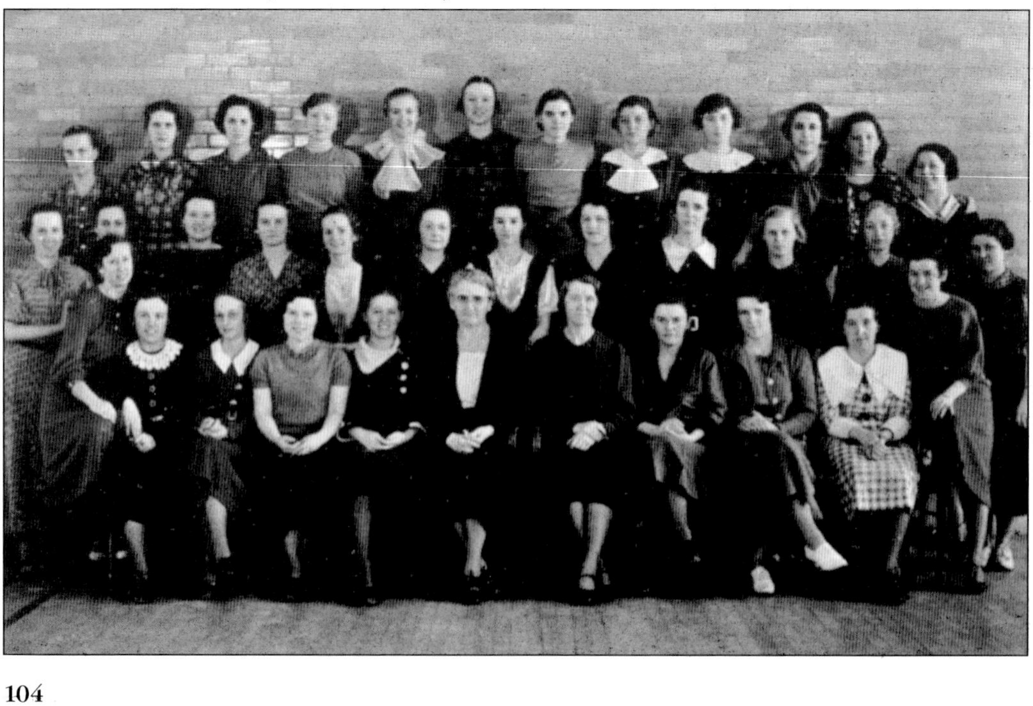

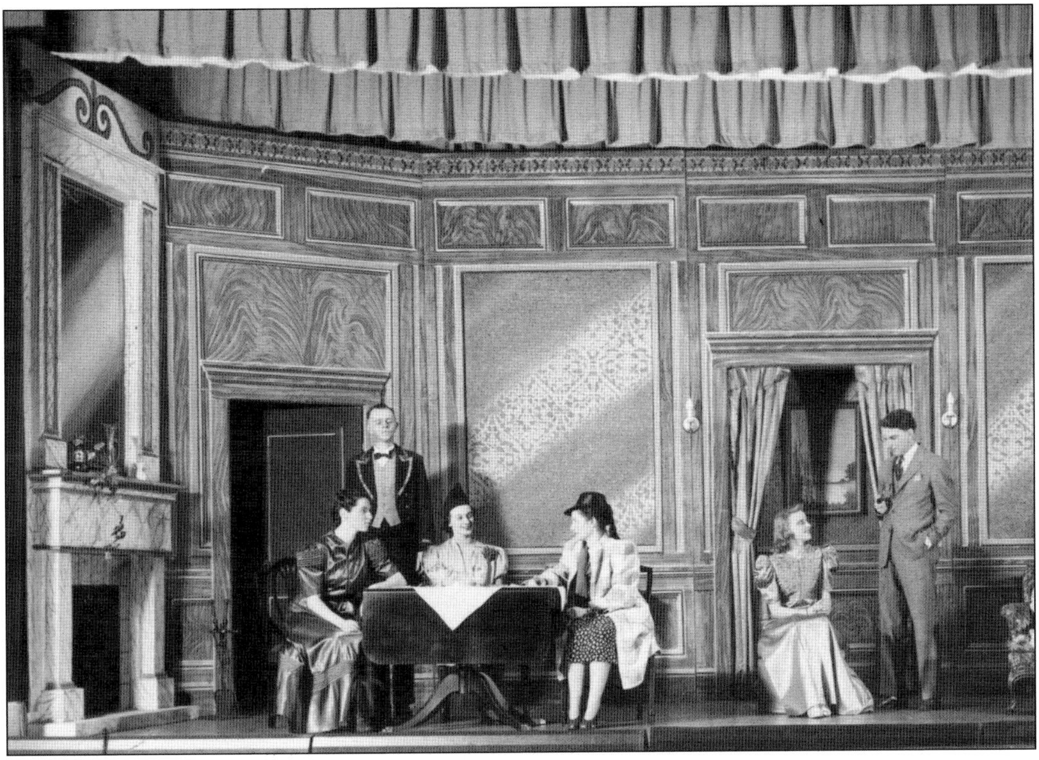

The drama club was formed in 1928 and membership had to be limited to 50 students. It presented scenes and series of scenes, as when it presented portions of *Alice in Wonderland*, but it also presented fully staged shows (above). In the 1960s, another club, formed under the name Sock & Buskin, also presented theatrical works. Over time, the presentation of theater became the provenance of theater professors, notably Anne Marie Shea, and the Visual and Performing Arts Department.

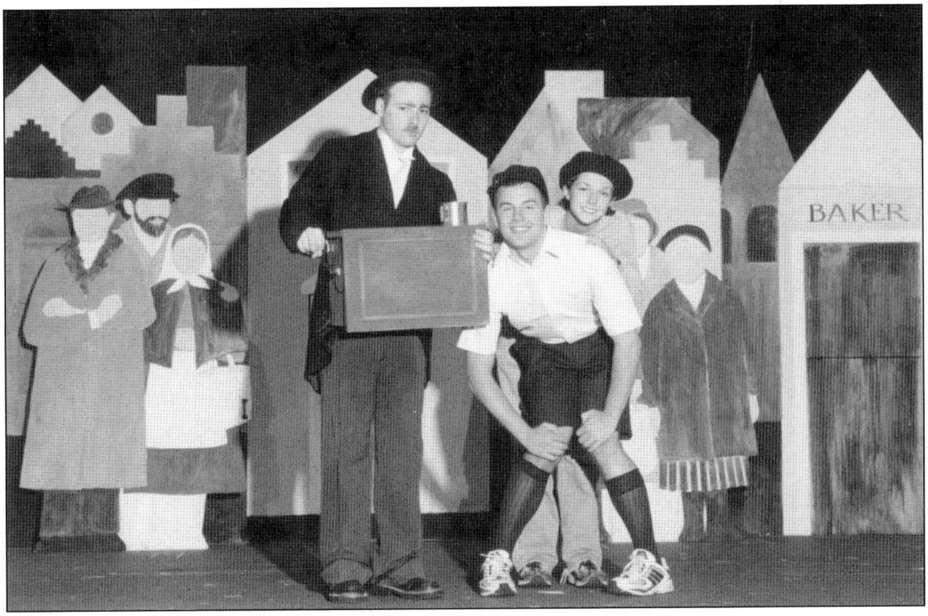

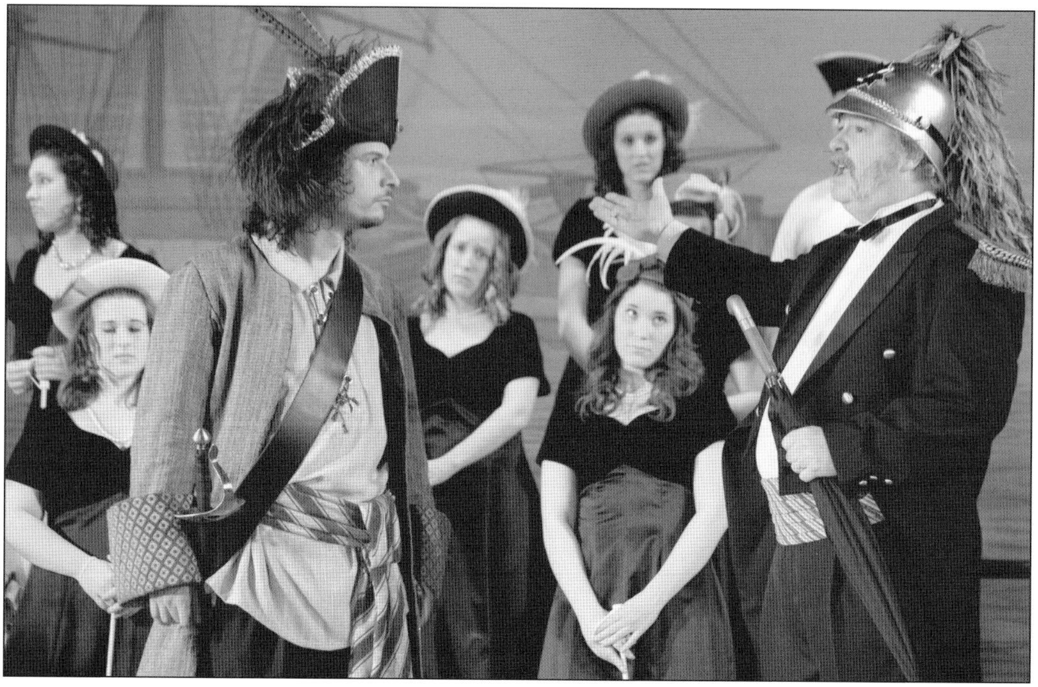

The interdisciplinary Visual and Performing Arts Department offers performances in music and musical theater, such as *The Pirates of Penzance* (above), and a full complement of drama and comedy, ranging from classics to more modern and original devised theater pieces, such as *War Children* and *CitySpeak* (below). (Both, WSU Office of Marketing.)

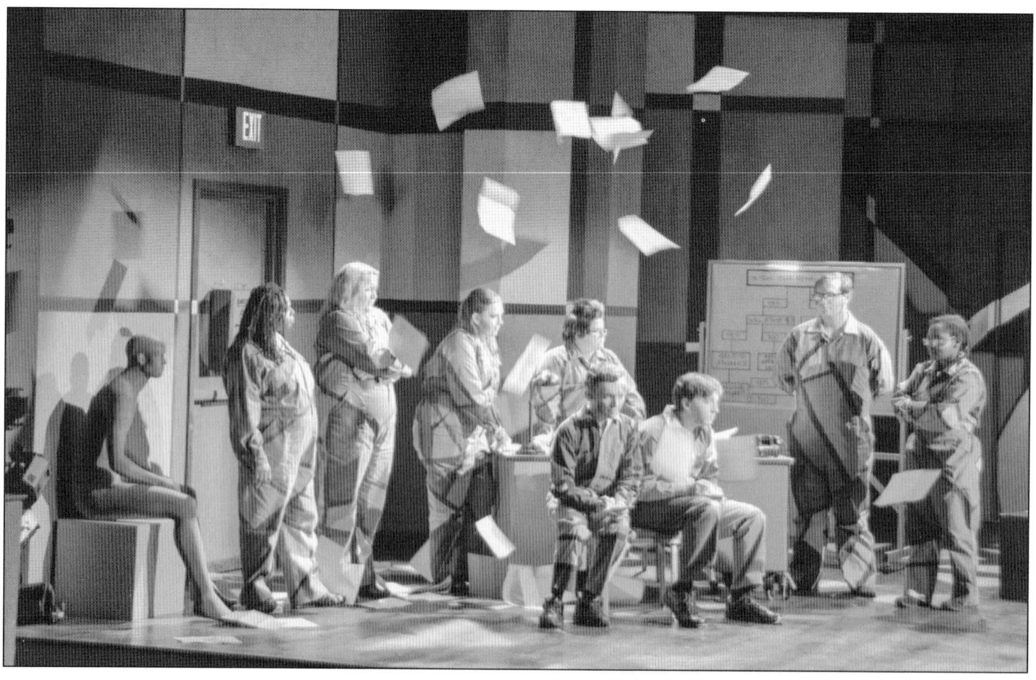

Eight

GRADUATIONS

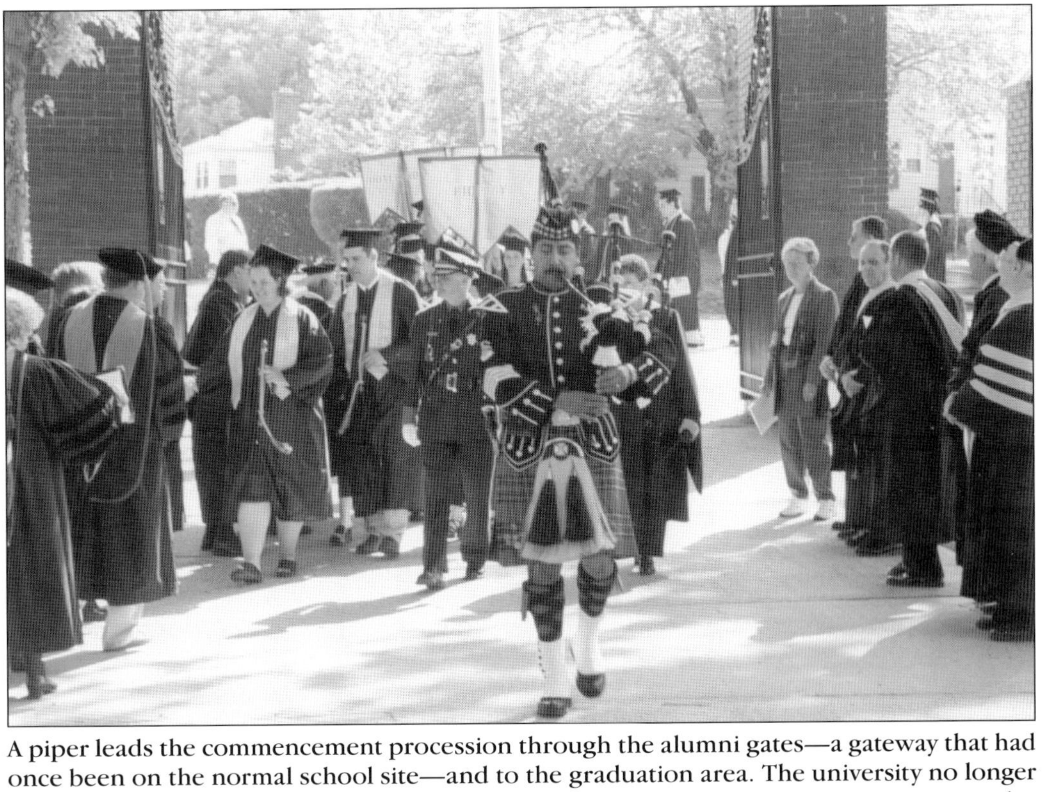

A piper leads the commencement procession through the alumni gates—a gateway that had once been on the normal school site—and to the graduation area. The university no longer holds graduation ceremonies on campus, but graduation remains the most important day of the academic year regardless of where the ceremony is held. This chapter looks at some of Worcester State's graduating classes, graduates, and commencement ceremonies.

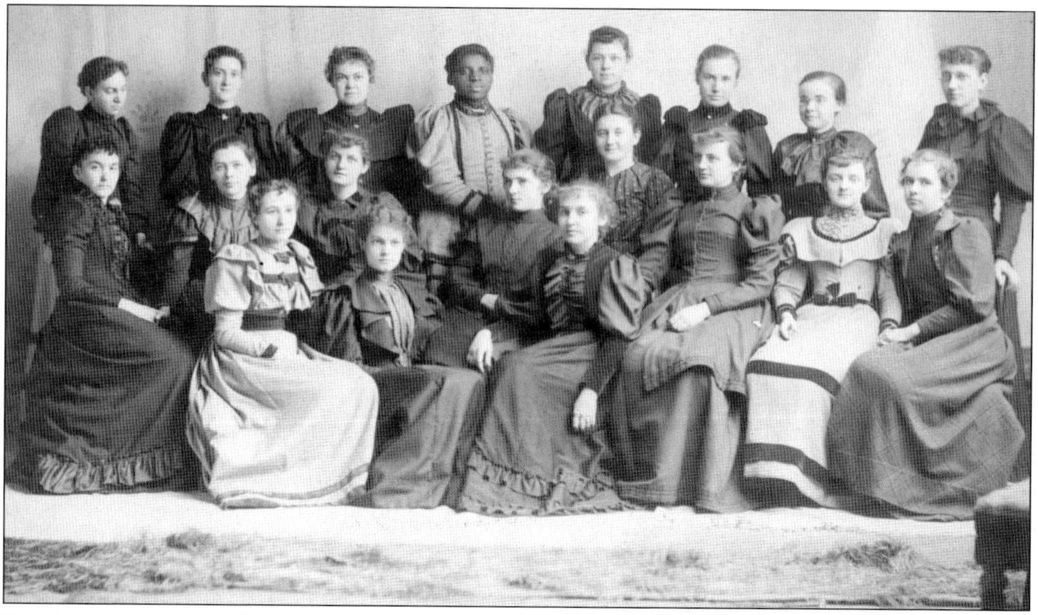

For the most part, graduation pictures in the normal school years consisted of class photographs that did not change that much from year to year. Fashions and faces changed, of course, but a couple of them will give the flavor of the times. Above is a picture from 1894, and among those graduating is Sarah Wilson, who was one of the school's first African American students who went on to teach. Below is a graduating class in the 1910s in academic regalia and likely pictured with all the year's normal school students.

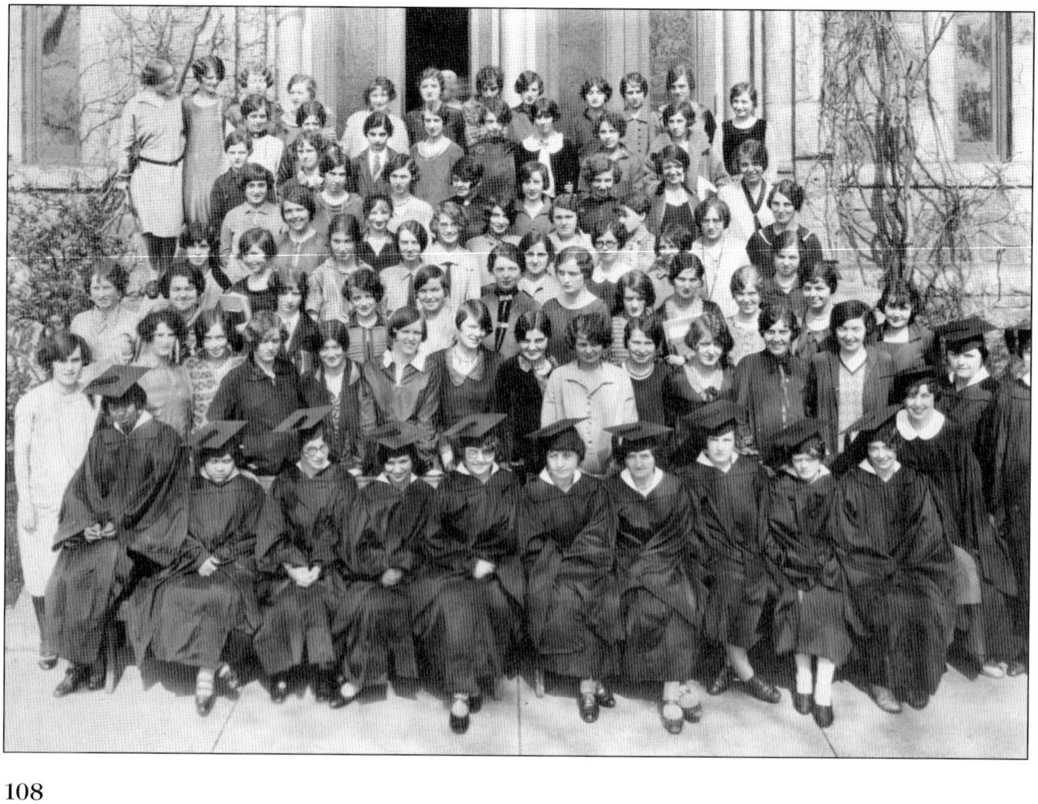

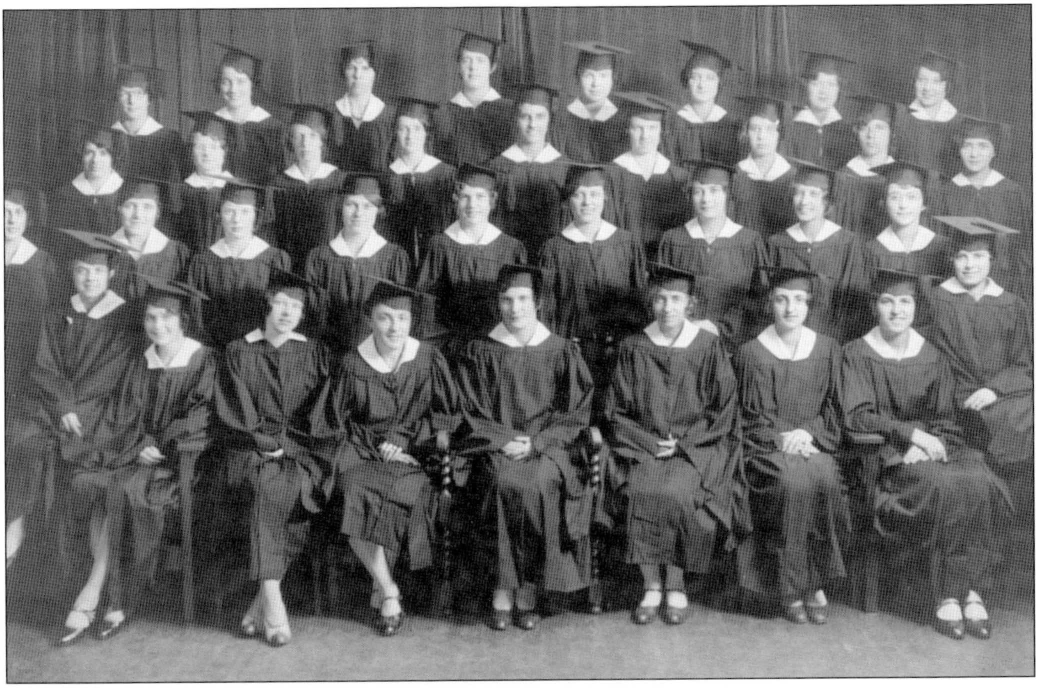

By 1930, the graduation pictures had become more formal and complete with regalia (above). This is one of the last classes to graduate from the original site. The class of 1935 (below) is made up of the last students to have begun their collegiate experiences at the original site. Graduates are pictured in front of the main building on Chandler Street (Shaughnessy Administration Building).

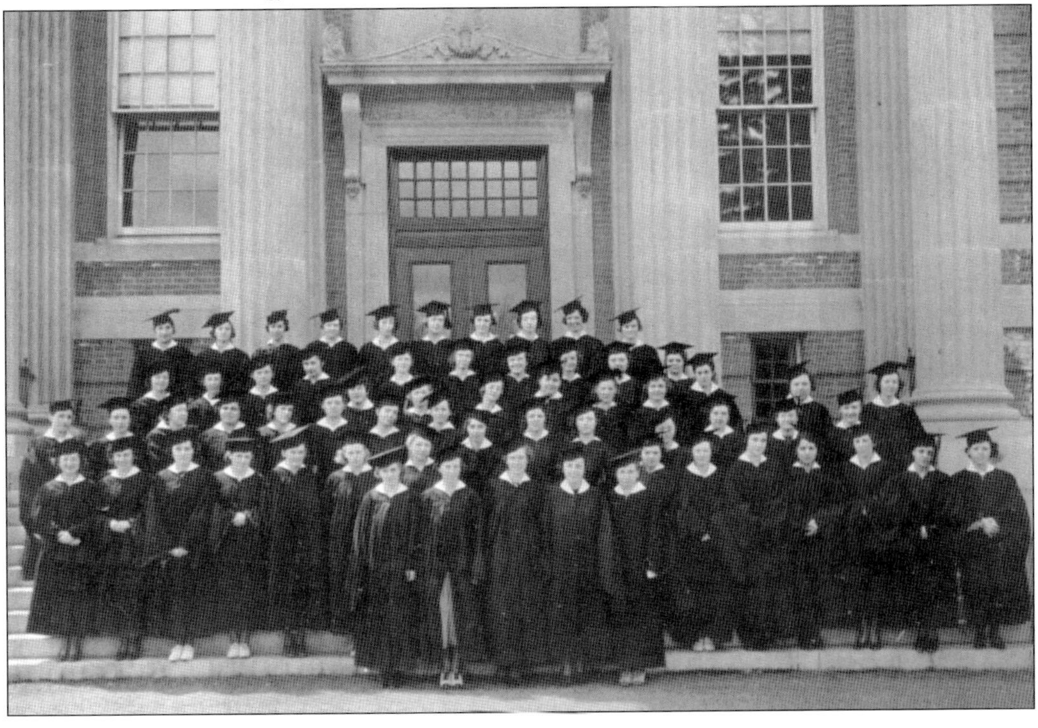

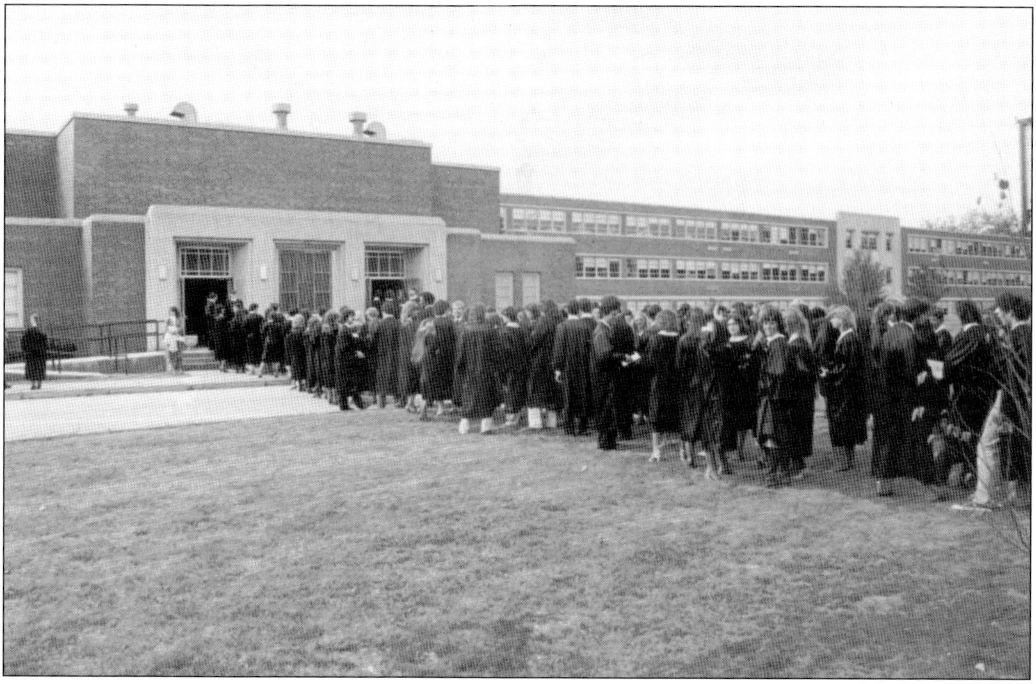

Before being moved downtown to Worcester's DCU Center, commencement was held at a number of sites on campus. Initially, commencement was in the main hall at the normal school, and upon the move to Chandler Street, it was held in the main building. The Sullivan Auditorium (above) hosted the commencement for many years and is still the location for the graduate hooding. There were also ample spaces to hold graduations outside (below).

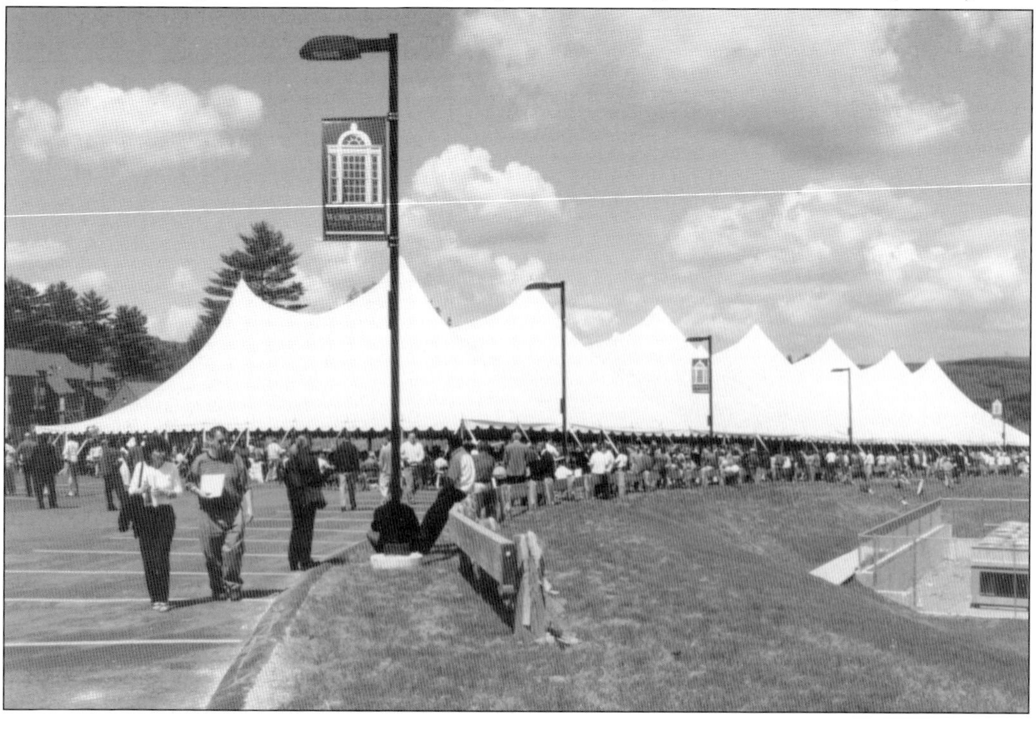

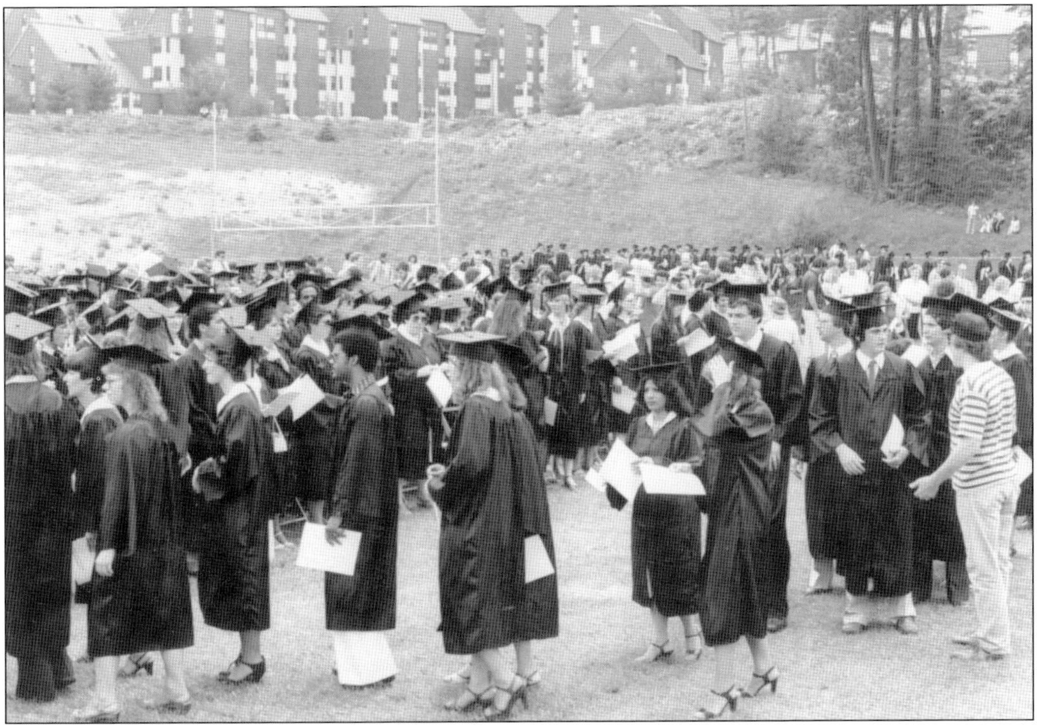

The outside commencement pictured above provides a good sense of the growth of Worcester State; gone are the days when the graduating class could neatly pose on the administration building's front stairs. Both this photograph and the one below, showing a particularly warm outside commencement, provide good views of Chandler Village and the old sports field.

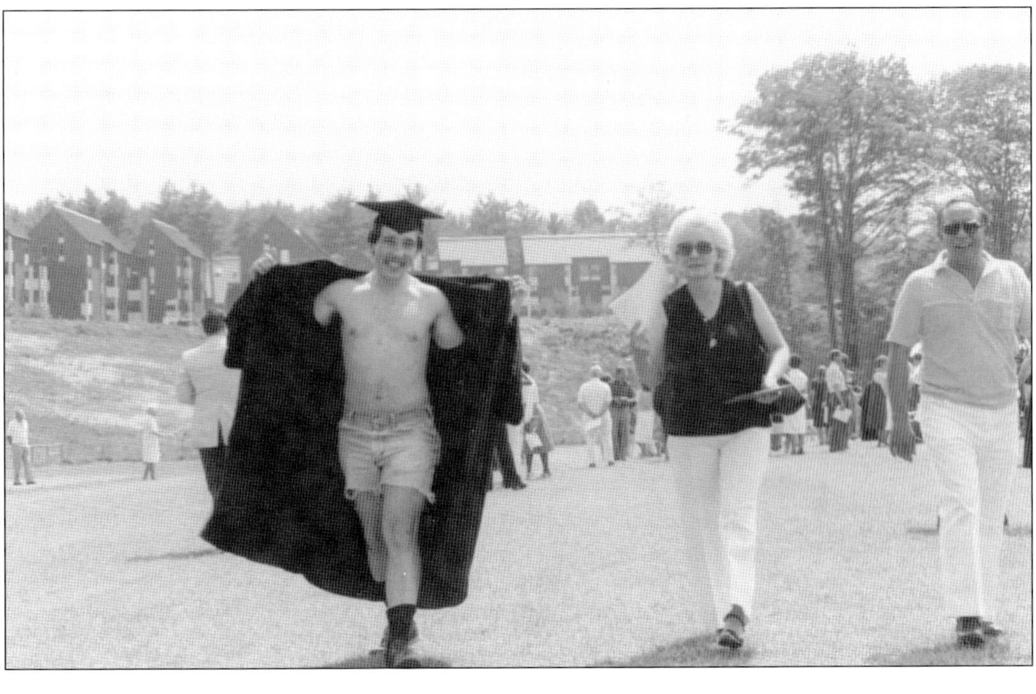

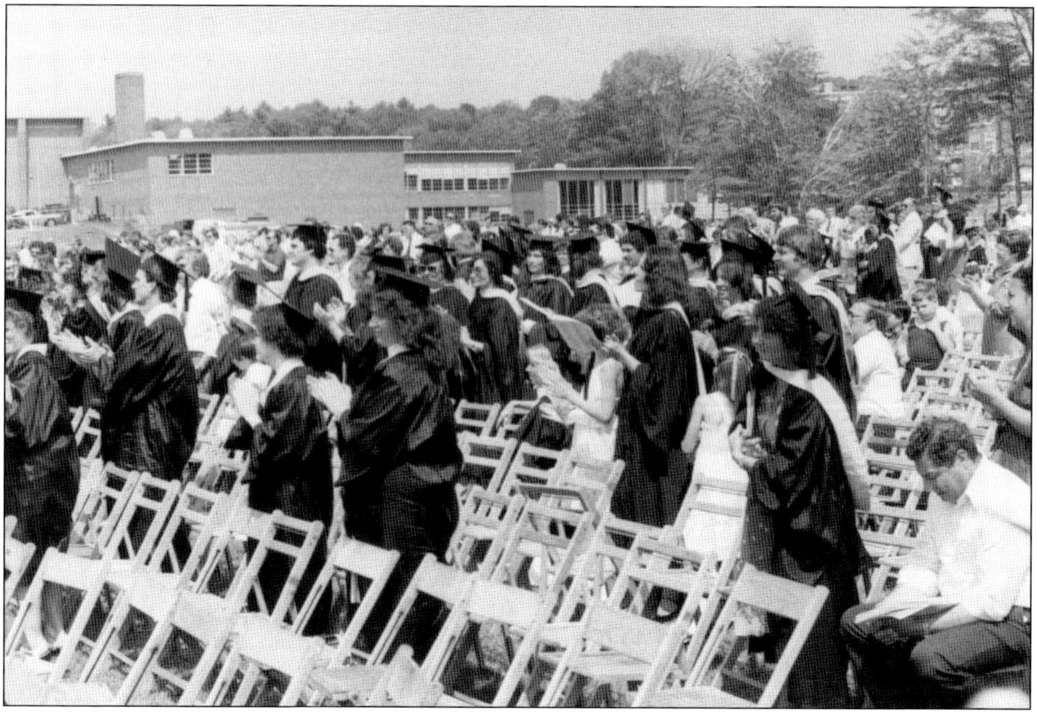

Finally, the basketball court in the old gym and the building's exterior were both locations for academic events including commencements and All College Days.

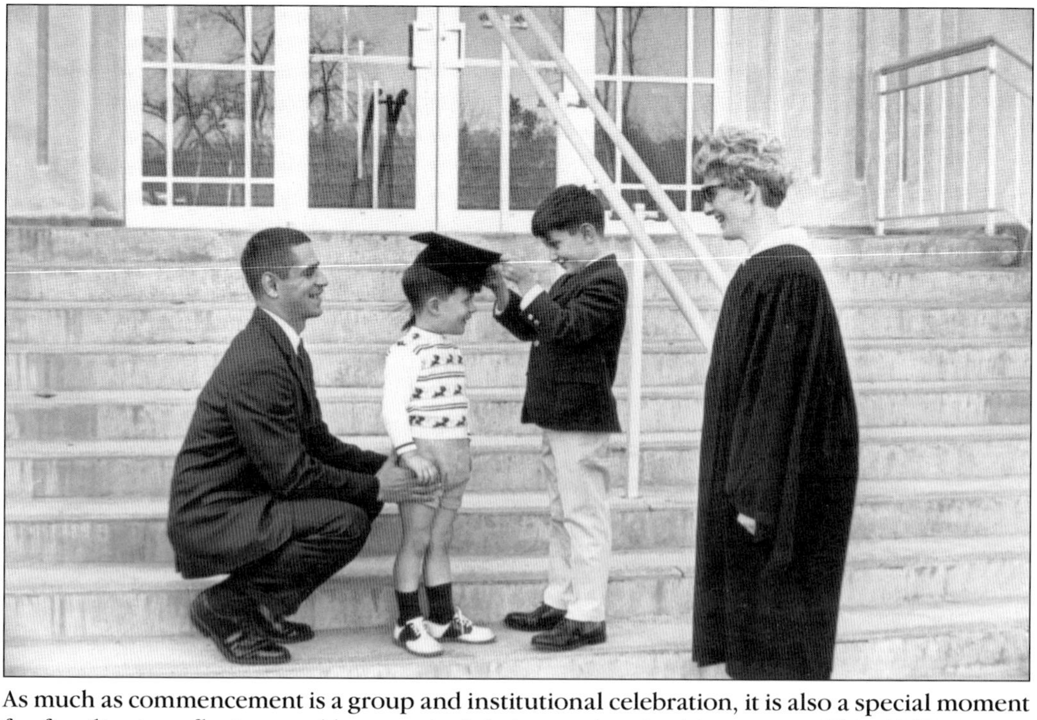

As much as commencement is a group and institutional celebration, it is also a special moment for families to reflect on and be proud of their members' achievements. This 1967 picture, perhaps, captures that spirit on the steps of the Sullivan Building.

Nine

Then and Now

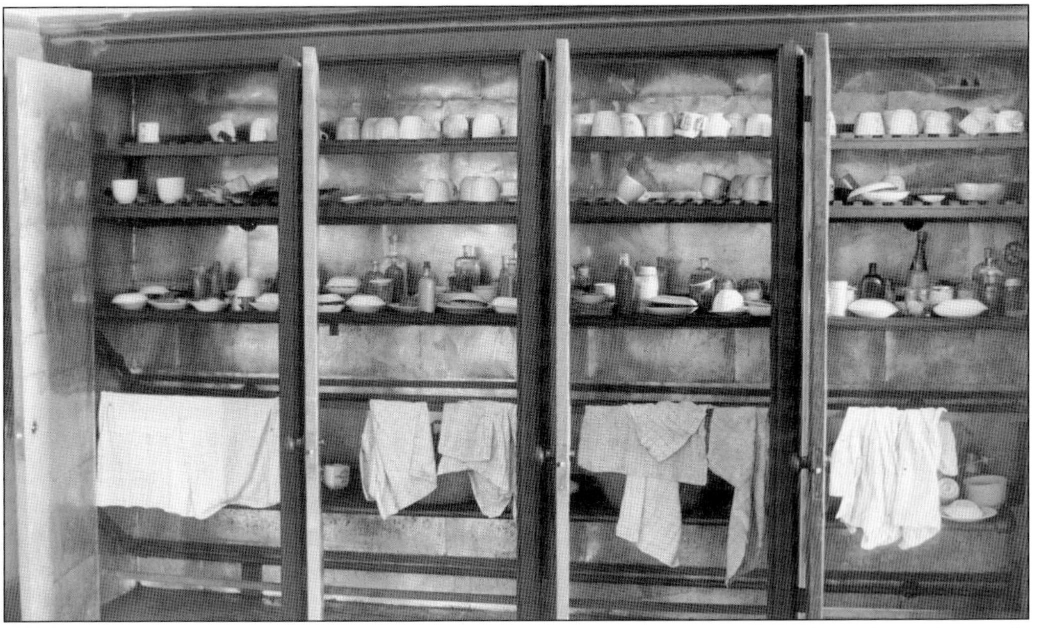

This is a meal warming closet from the normal school lunchroom. Students brought meals to school and kept them warm while they were in classes. Such things have not survived the years. This chapter looks at things that were once part of Worcester State University but no longer survive or have evolved into something else.

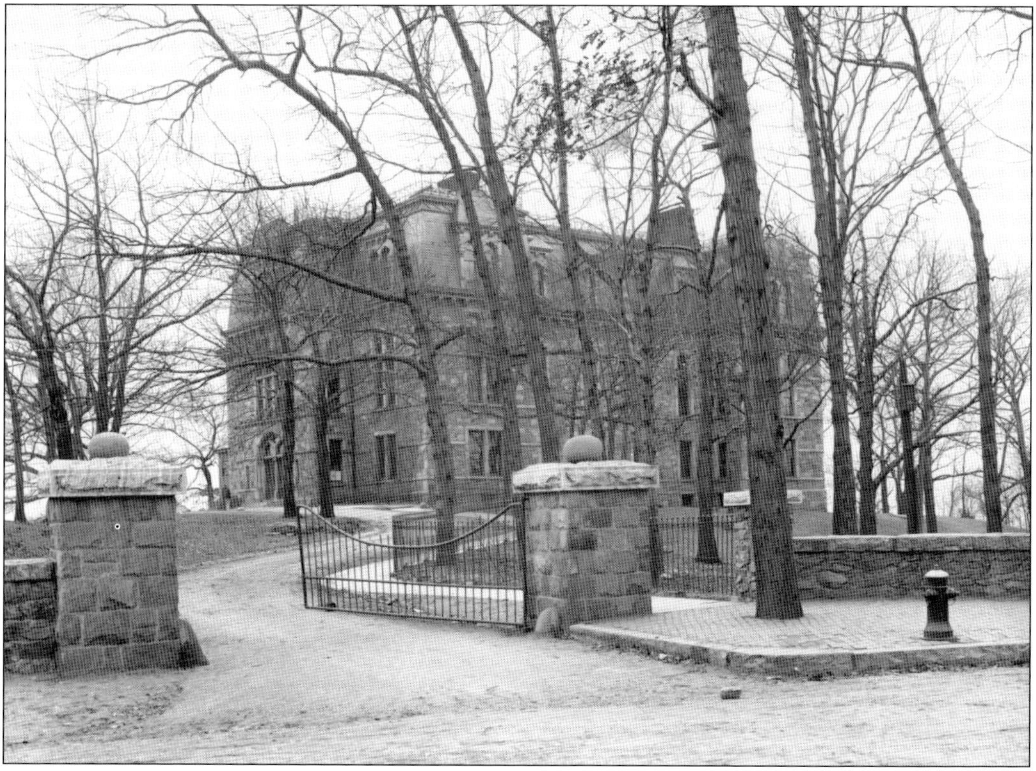

This view of the normal school as seen from Prospect Street shows the entrance and driveway to the main building (above). On the same site today is City View Elementary School (below), although some of the original elements of the surrounding wall remain. (Below, author's collection.)

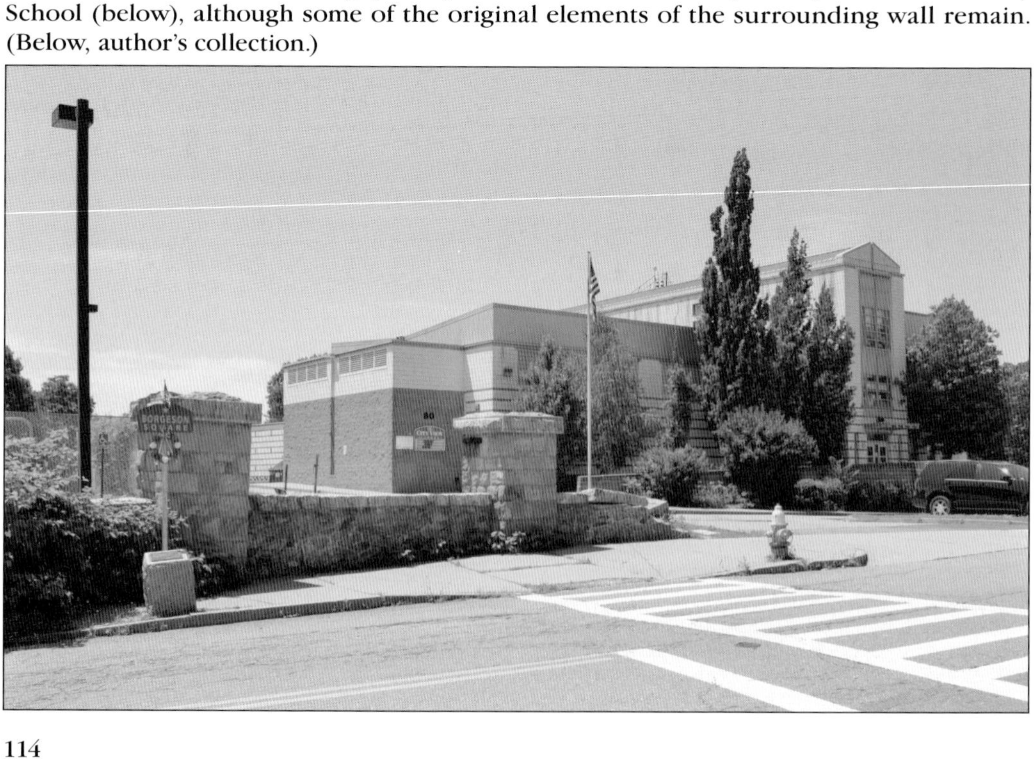

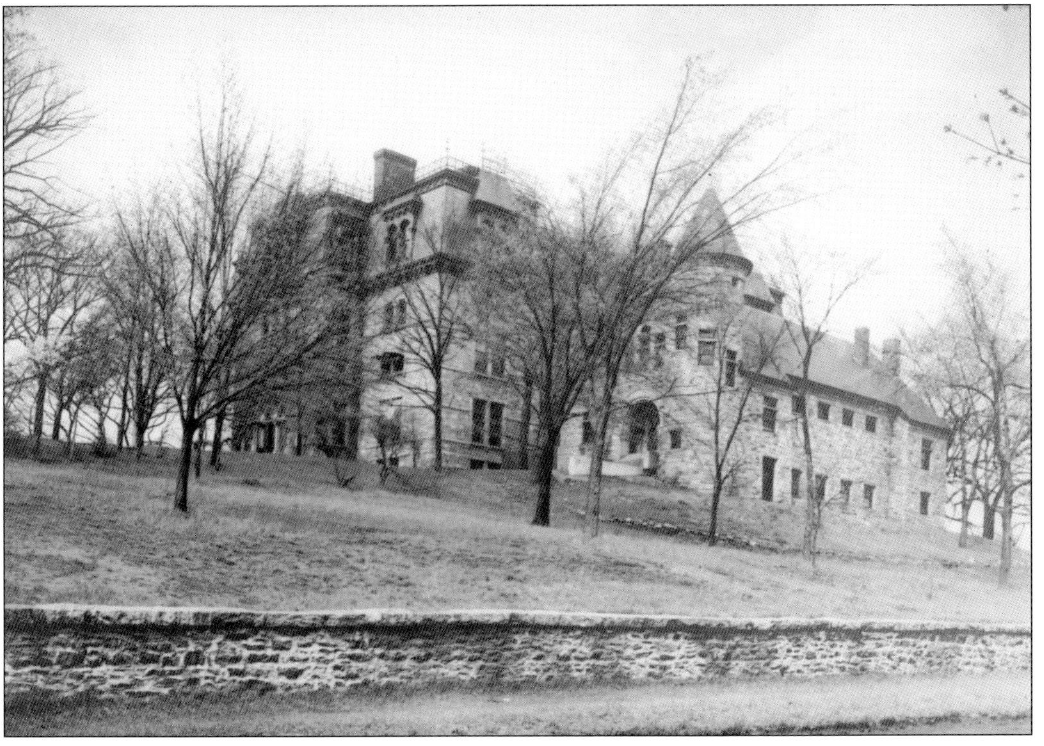

This picture of the normal school building with the gym from 1915 (above) shows little vegetation, well-groomed grounds, and the stone wall that surrounded the entire campus. In 2017, the original buildings are gone from this perspective and the grounds have overgrown, but the wall remains (below). (Below, author's collection.)

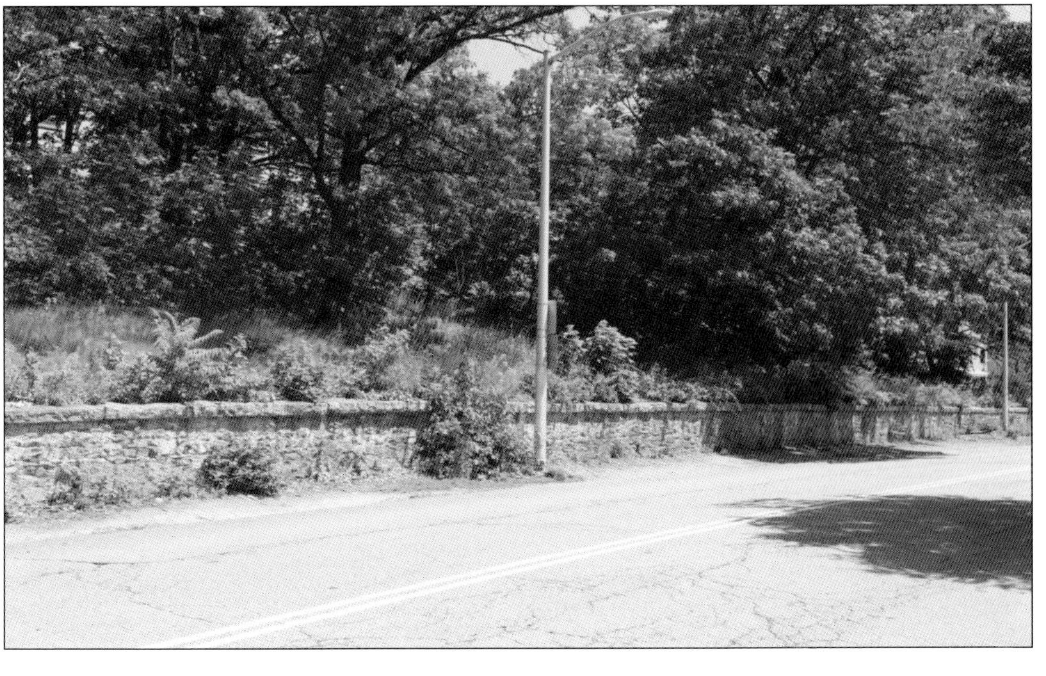

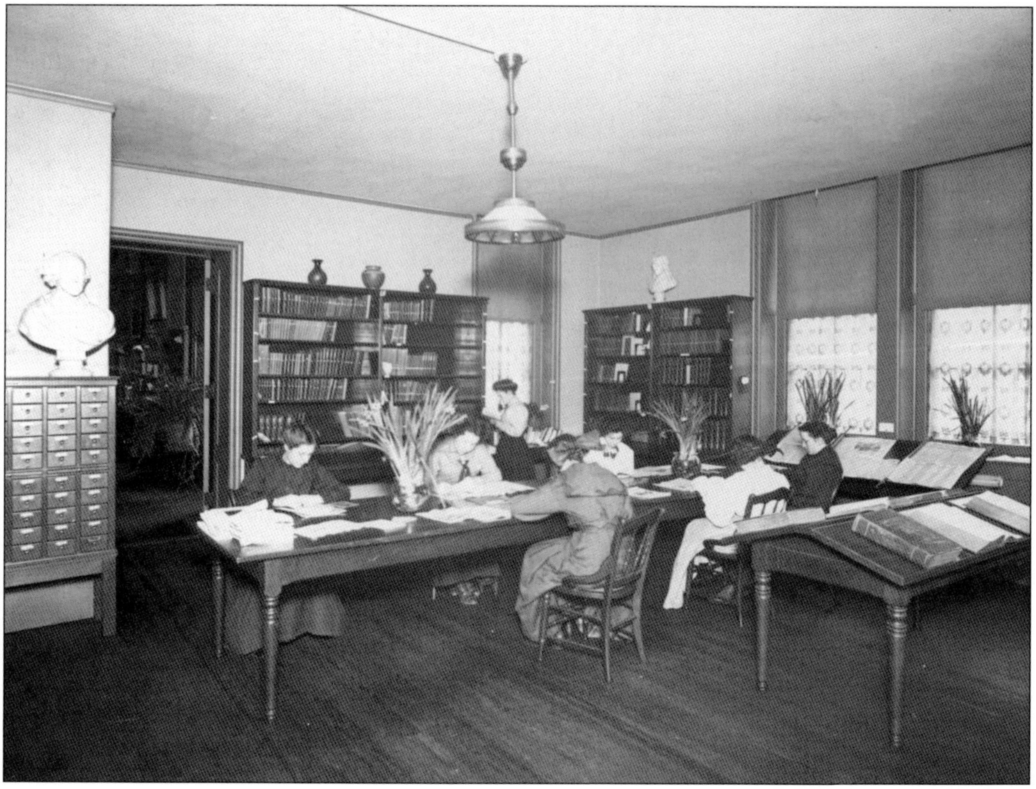

The university library has evolved significantly over time. The original library at the normal school (above) consisted of a few thousand volumes, but it quickly grew. When Worcester State Teachers College arrived on Chandler Street, the library occupied the fourth floor of the main building (below). (Below, WSU Office of University Advancement.)

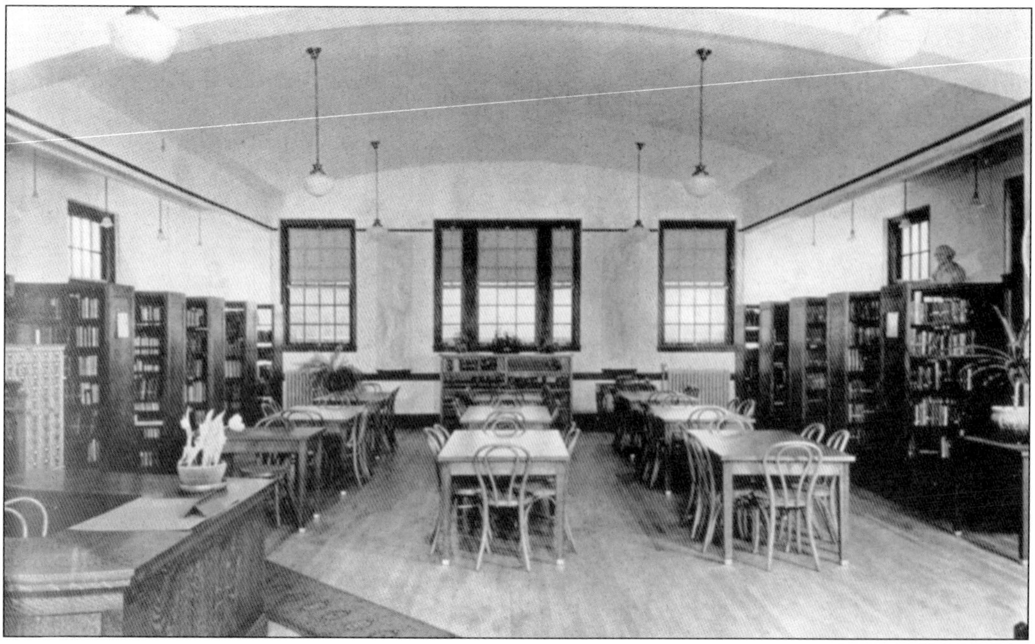

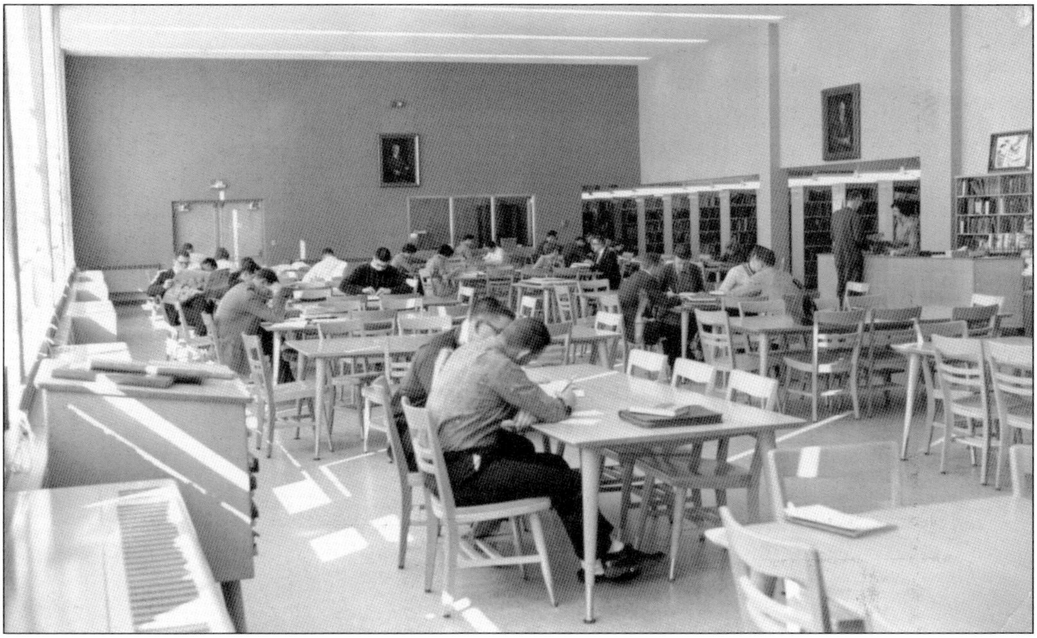

When the old gym was built, the library moved there (above), and it moved again to the Learning Resource Center when it opened (below). The library today contains over 200,000 items, including over 80,000 e-books and online articles. Further, the library has hired its first university archivist, who oversees a substantial growing collection of images, documents, written materials, and three-dimensional items spanning the university's history.

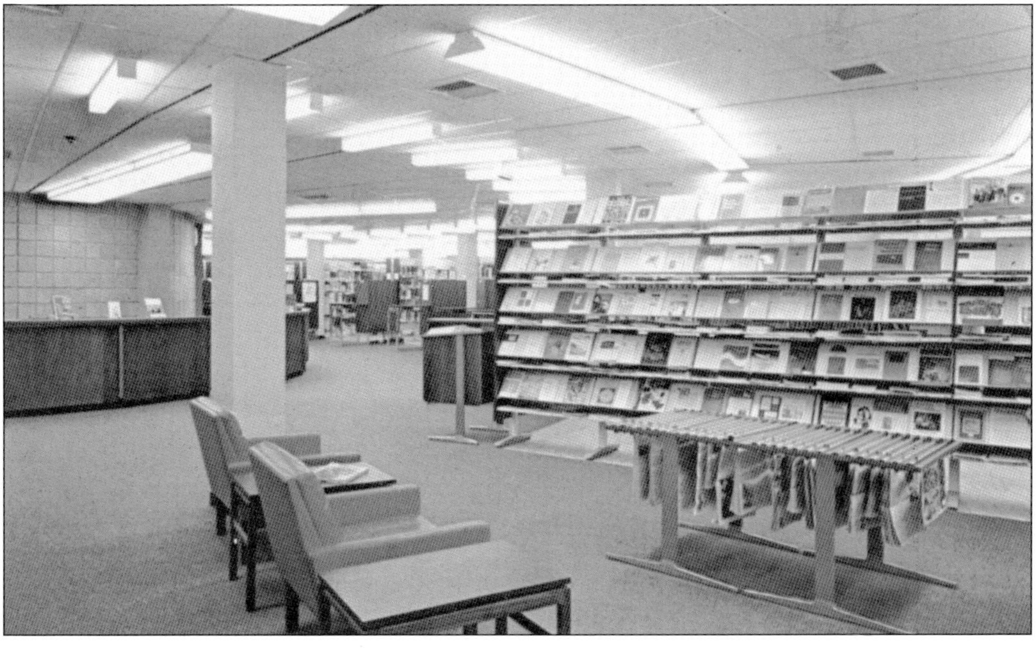

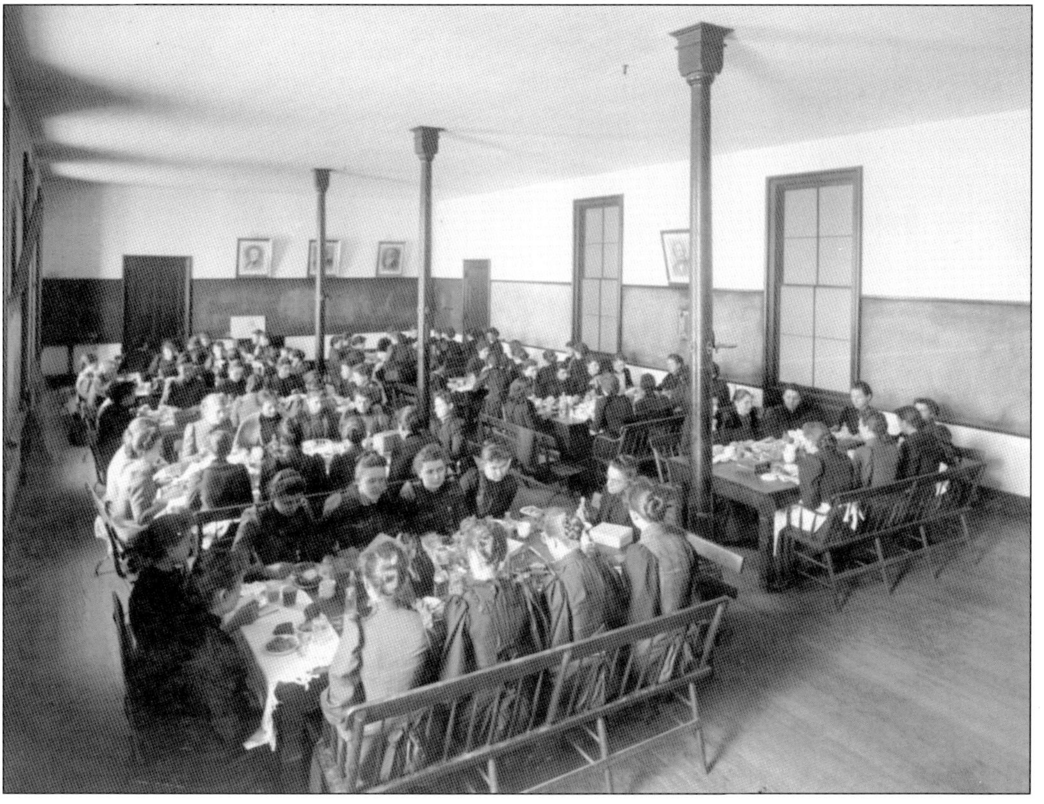

The lunchroom at the normal school (above) has come a particularly long way. Like the library, it moved to the administration building on the new campus and then became a cafeteria built into the old gym building (below). From there, two cafeterias were created in the Student Center; one is now a popular commuter café, and the other is occasionally used. The main cafeteria was significantly expanded after it was relocated to Sheehan Hall in 2014.

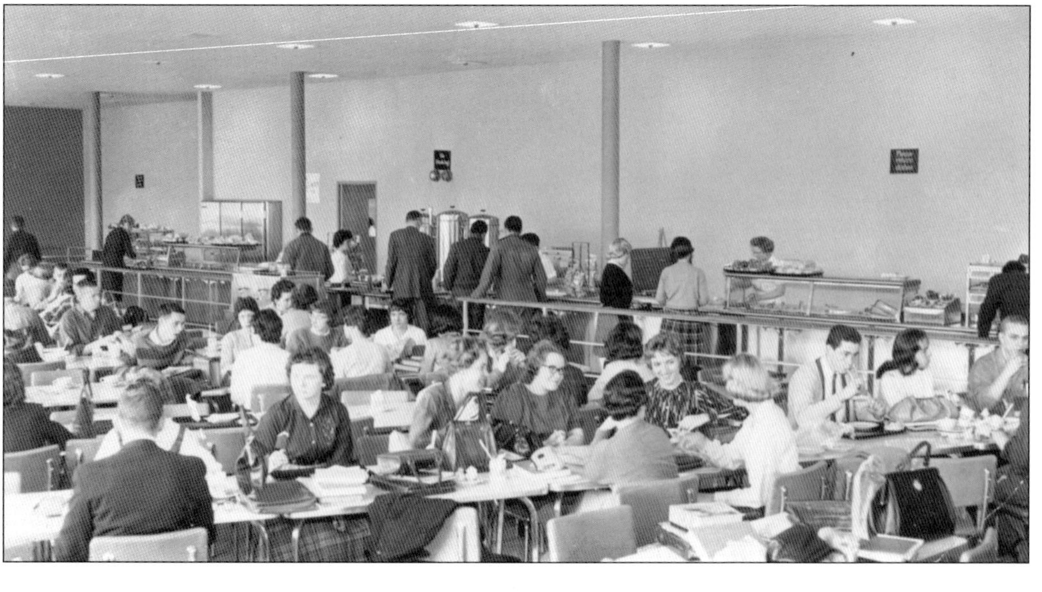

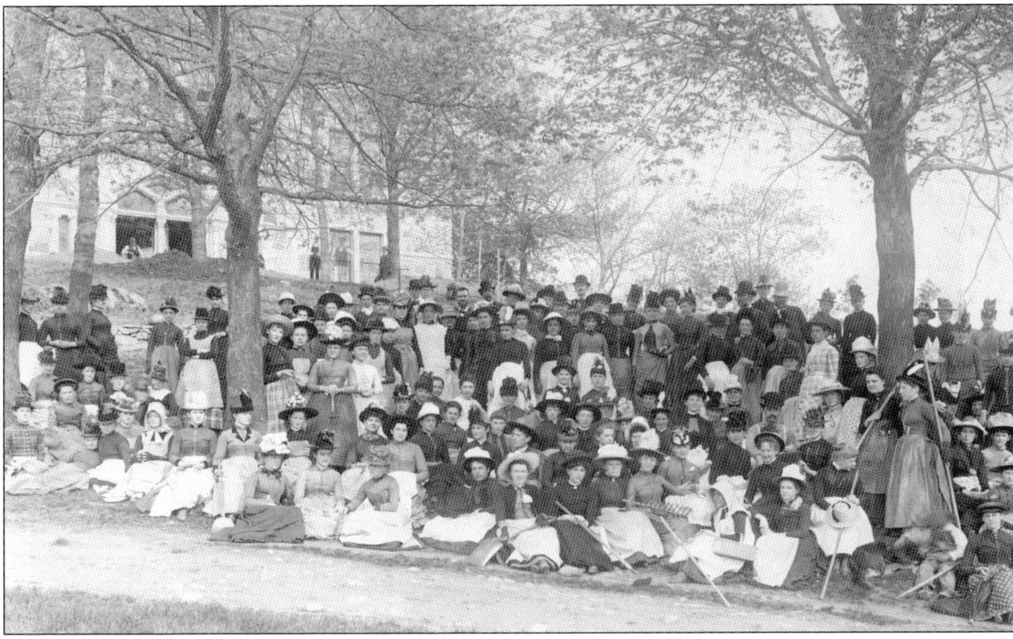

This image from 1887 shows one of the spring events at the normal school: a cleanup day that involved the whole school, with students and faculty alike. Armed with rakes, brooms, shovels, and other tools, the work crew spruced up the grounds and the interior spaces of the main building. (The gym was not yet built.)

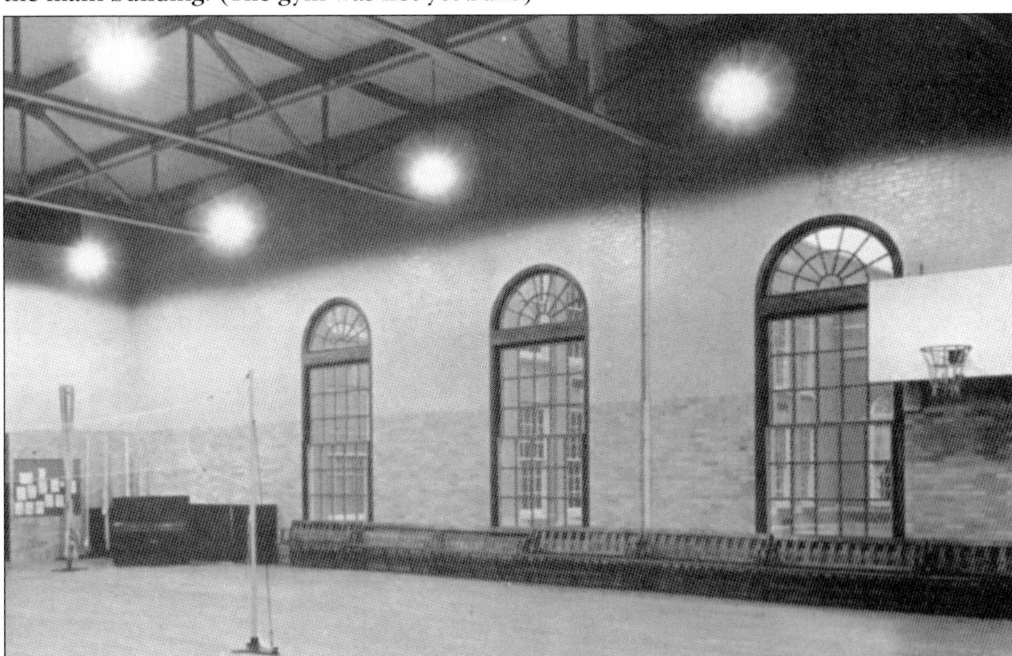

This 1940 interior view of the Worcester State Teachers College building shows the gym that once occupied that space. Today, this space has been cut into two floors and holds administrative offices such as university advancement and some administration and finance offices. (WSU Office of University Advancement.)

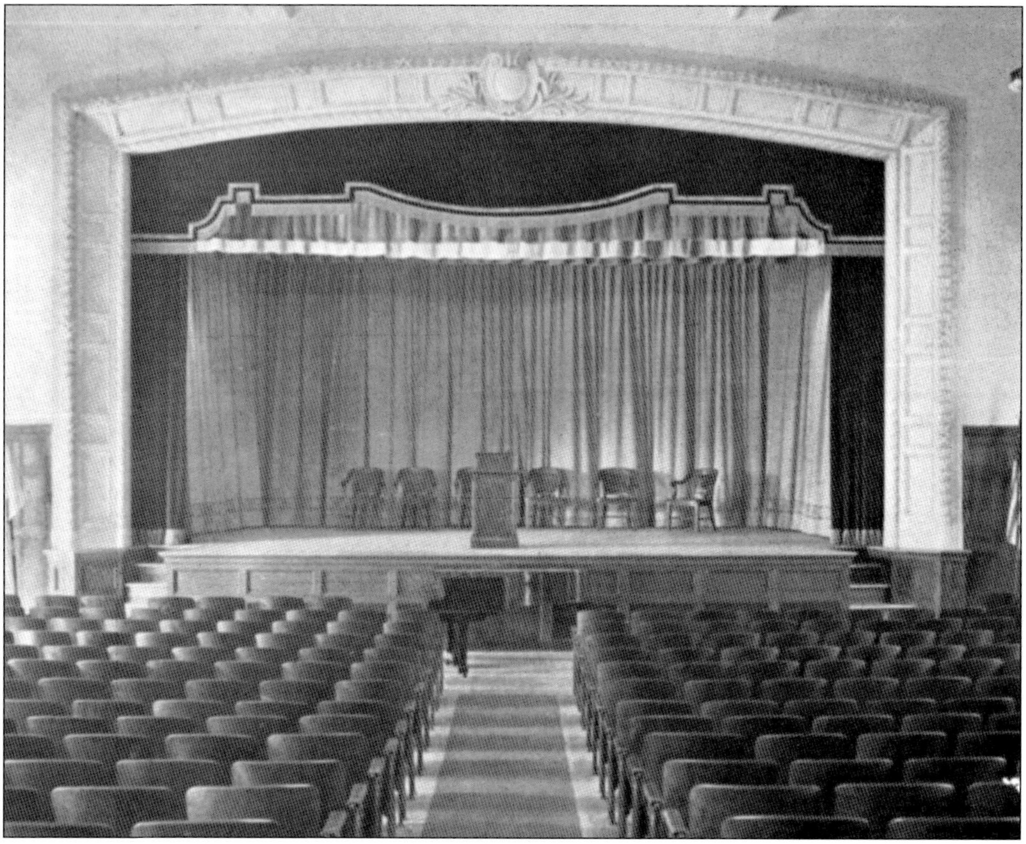

The main building of the teachers' college had an auditorium in the wing opposite the gym. Like the Great Hall at the original campus, it served a variety of assembly functions (above). A major renovation of the theater yielded a modern performance space in 2009, although the original proscenium arch remains (below). (Above, WSU Office of University Advancement; below, author's collection.)

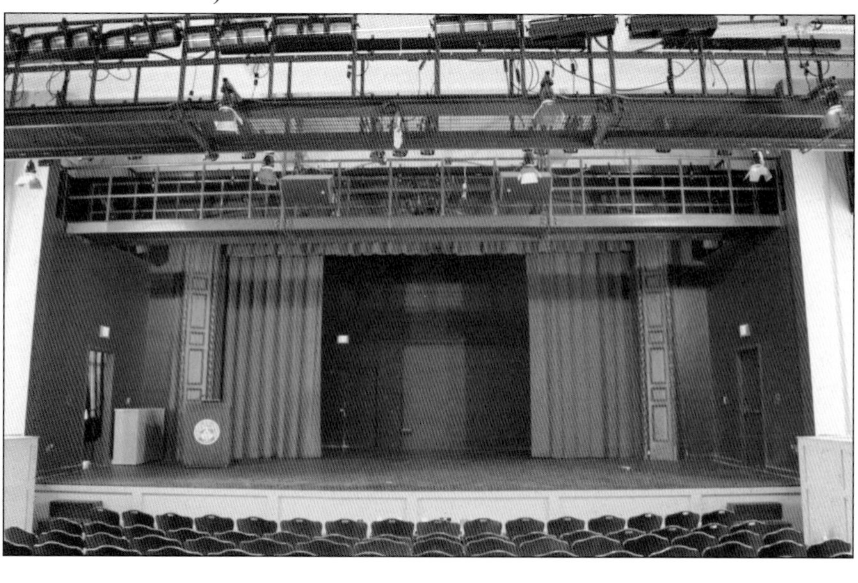

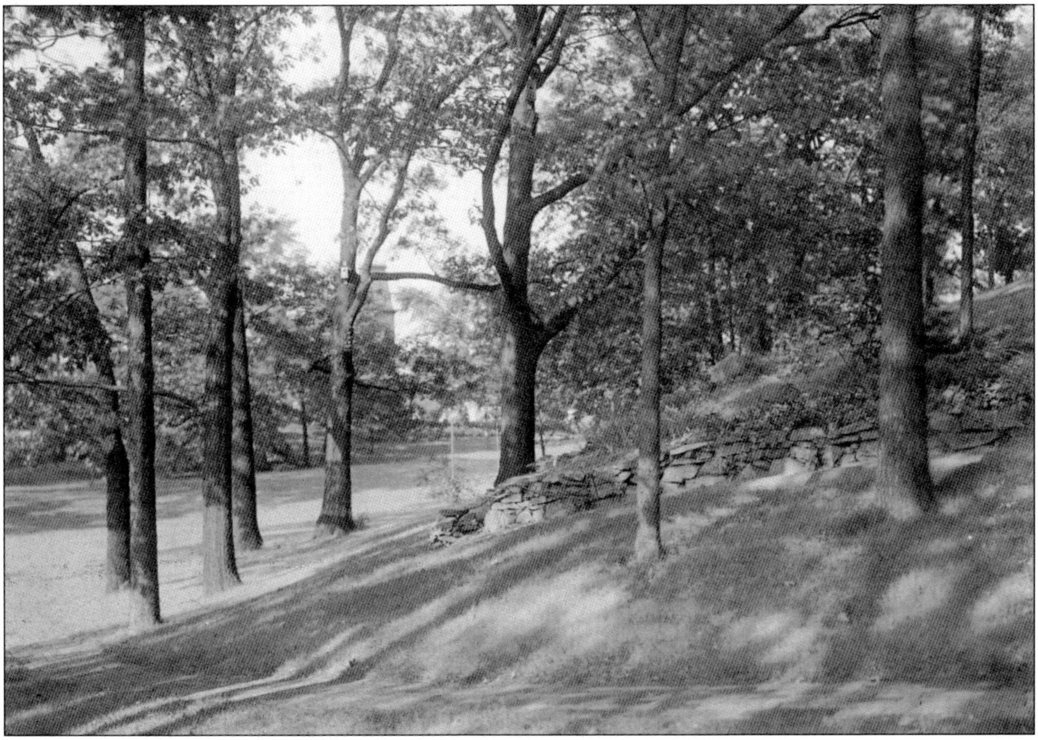

The grounds of the original campus were smaller than those at the Chandler Street campus, and its buildings were comparatively few (above). This left space for open vistas and brick pathways that students or faculty could walk. While there is certainly room on the current grounds to walk, there are also more structures and functions. This photograph with a view looking deep into campus, with Sheehan Hall dormitory at the center, was taken from across Chandler Street in the WSU Teaching Garden (below). (Below, author's collection.)

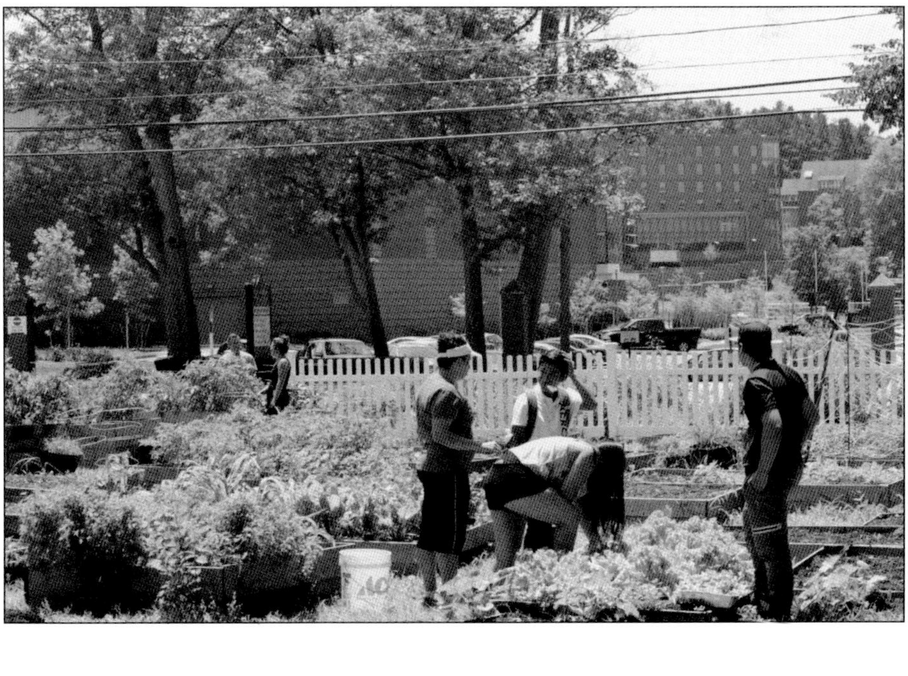

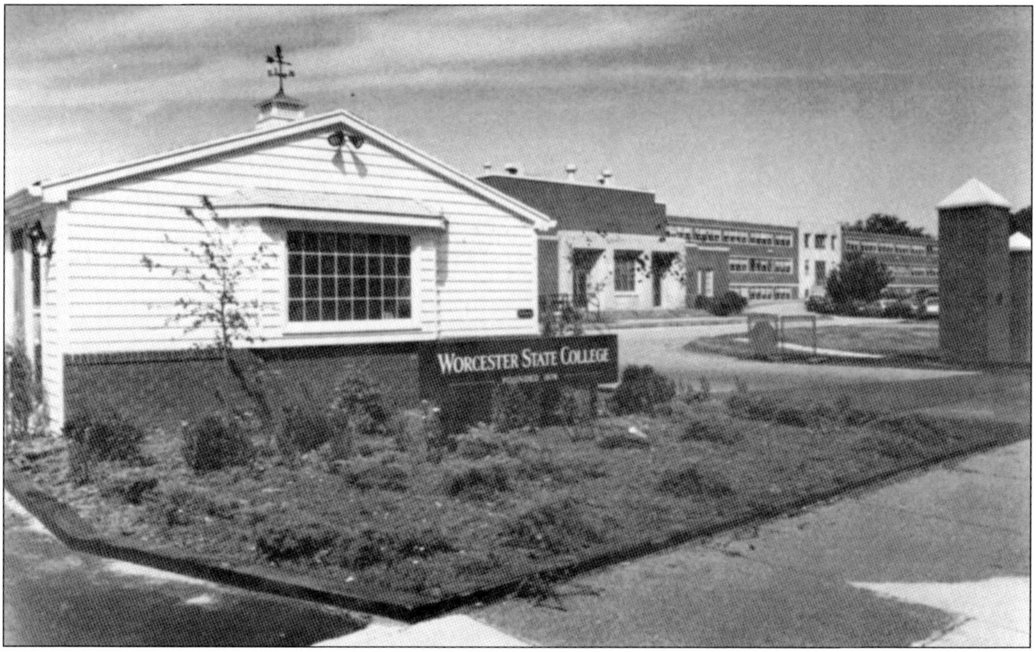

Not all that long ago, visitors to campus's south parking lot drove by this gatehouse. It was removed in the 2010s and the area landscaped to create a more welcoming entryway. (WSU Student Involvement and Leadership Development Collection.)

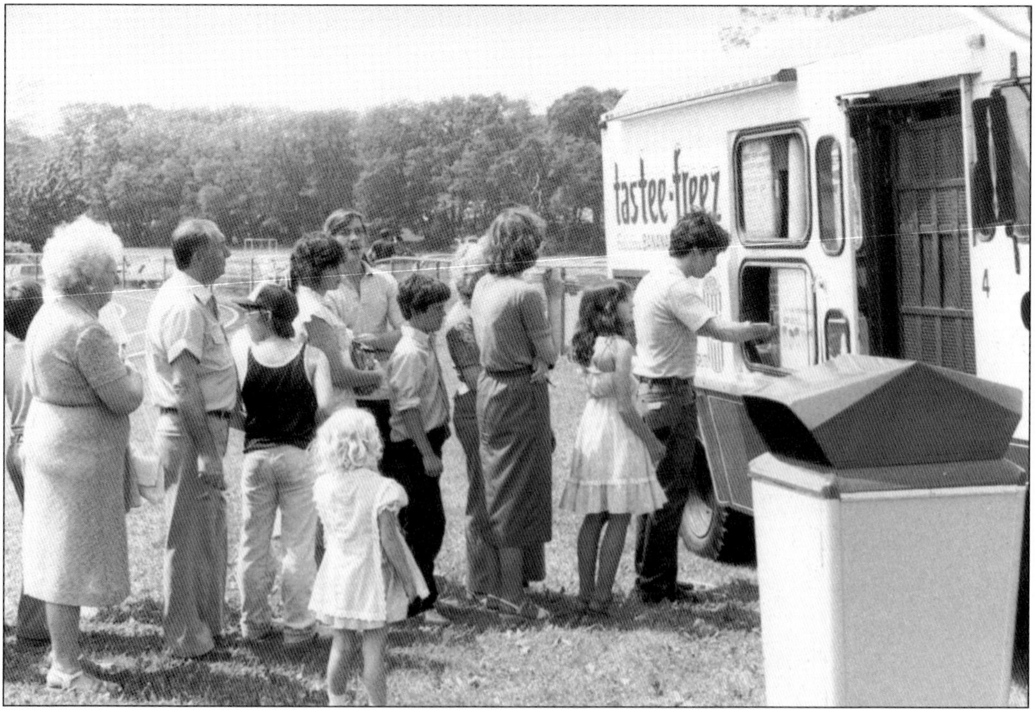

Before concession stands, or at games when they were not opened, ice-cream trucks provided snacks to spectators and fans. This picture from 1979 shows a Tastee-Freez truck, a far cry from today's food trucks but one that nevertheless fulfilled an important purpose.

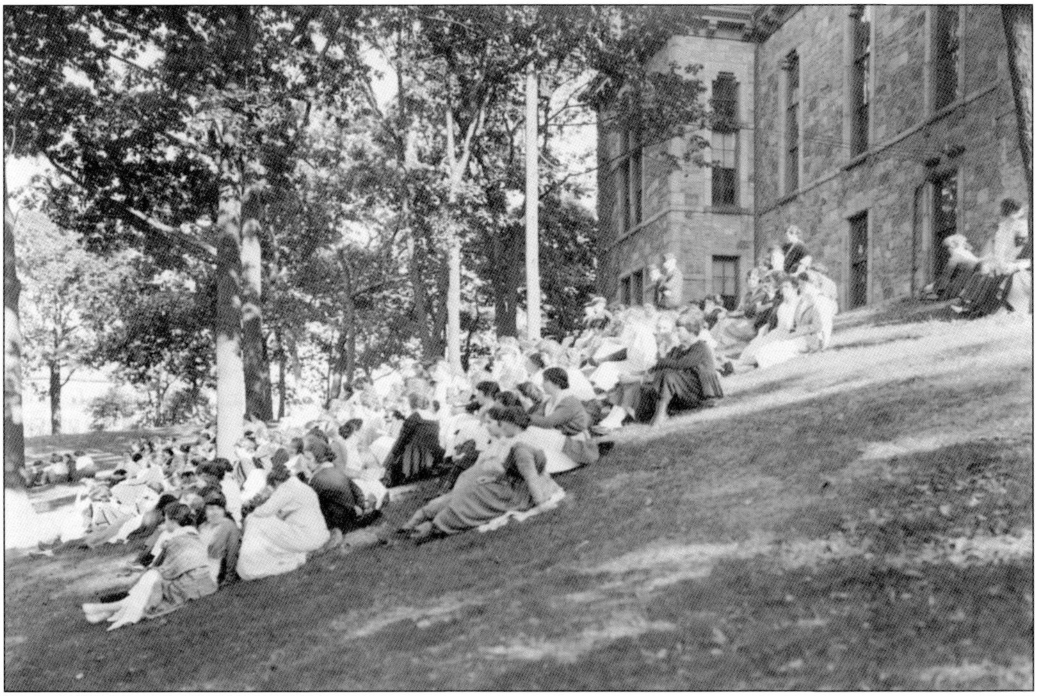

Above, students at the normal school relax on the grounds after classes outside the main building. About a century later, similar scenes could be glimpsed all over the campus. The c. 1979 image below shows students relaxing after sports practice.

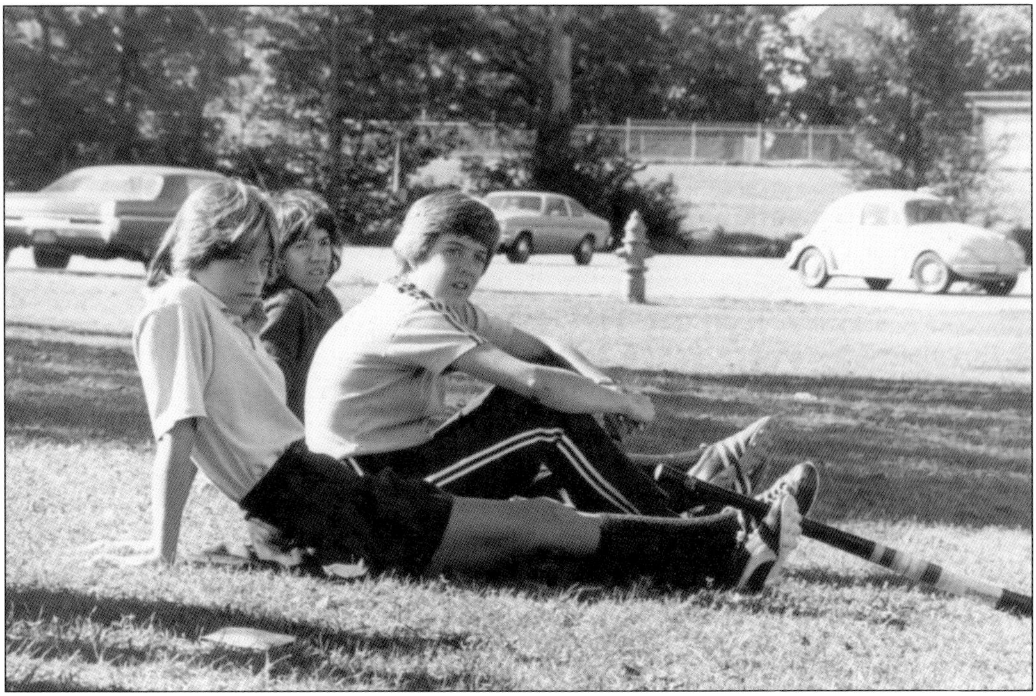

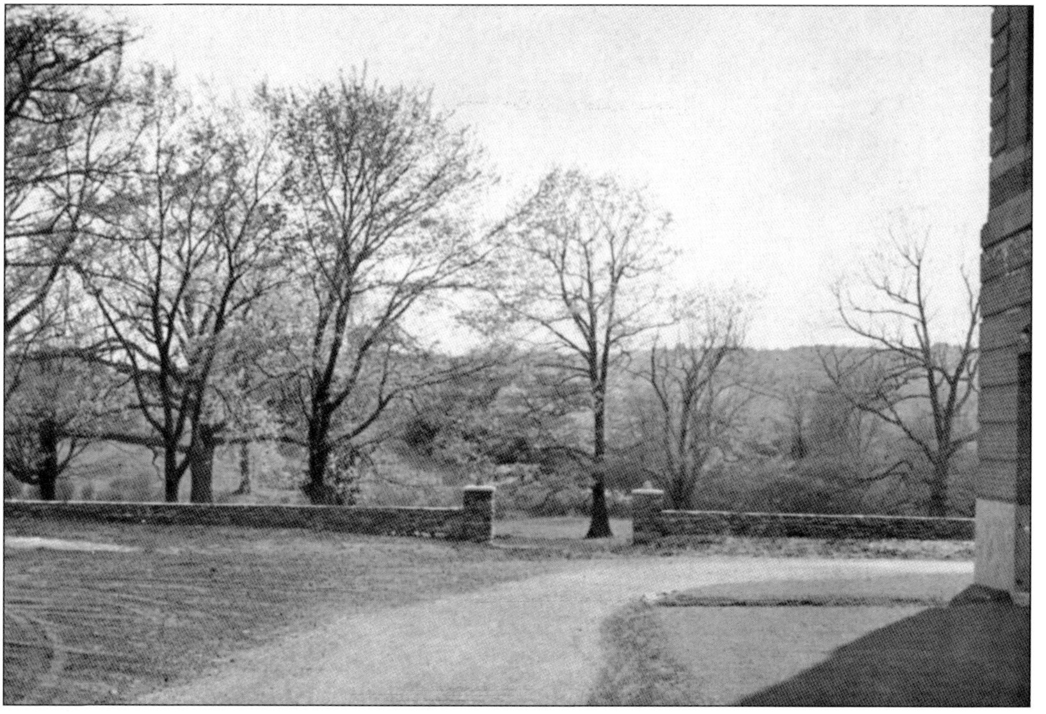

The picture above shows the area behind the administration building in 1937. The image is framed on the right side by the northwest corner of the building. As it had recently been a farm, the area was relatively undeveloped and cleared of thick tree and bush growth. Below, modern picture taken from the same vantage point shows how much the area has changed through building and development of the university. (Below, author's collection.)

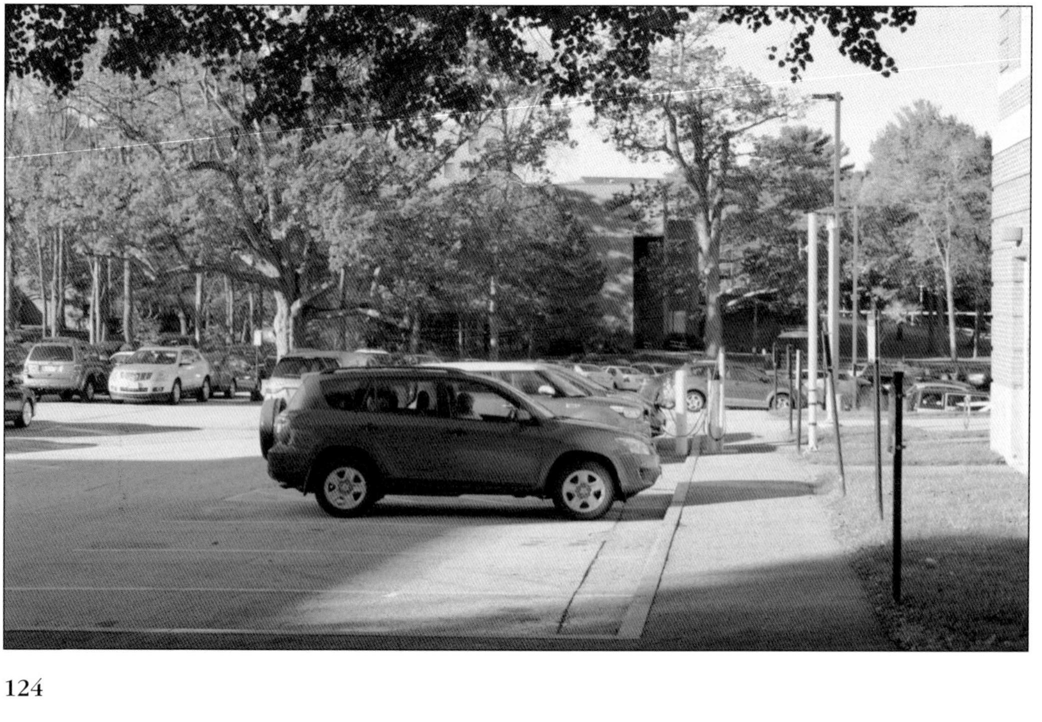

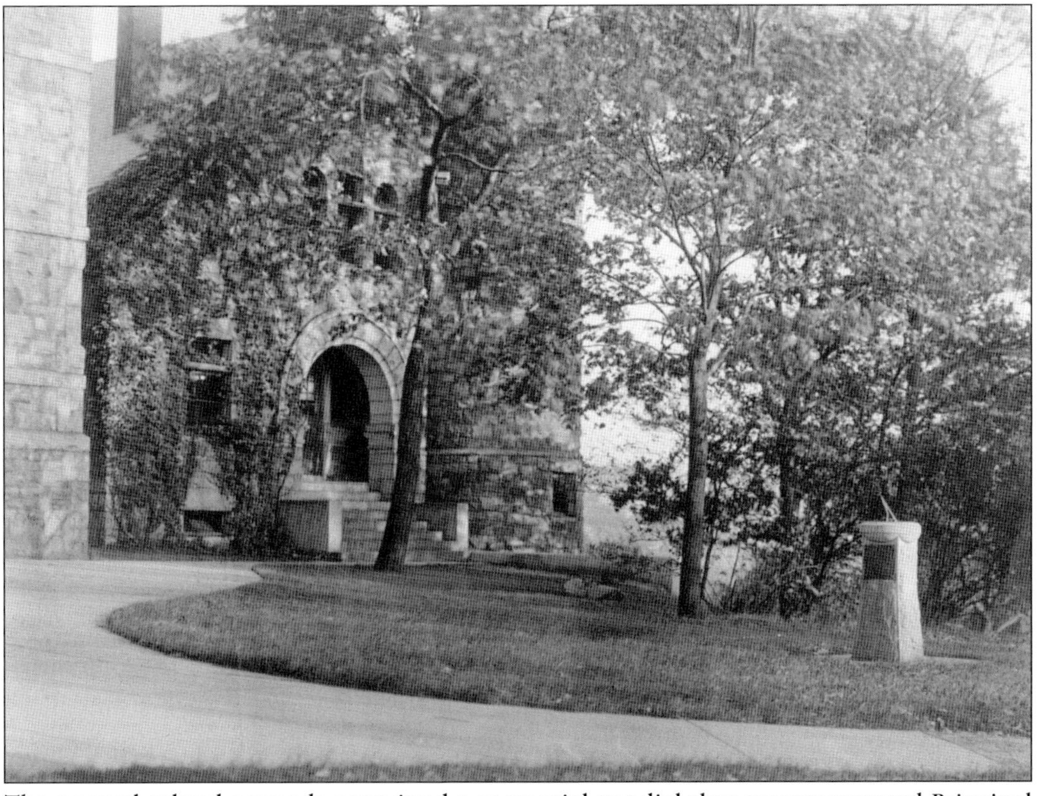

The normal school grounds contained a memorial sundial that commemorated Principal Russell's first 25 years. It is shown here in the space behind the main building, which was also the front side of the gym (above). The sundial made the move to the new campus and had a couple of homes there. It currently resides in the front of the administration building—the first building at the new campus (below). (Below, author's collection.)

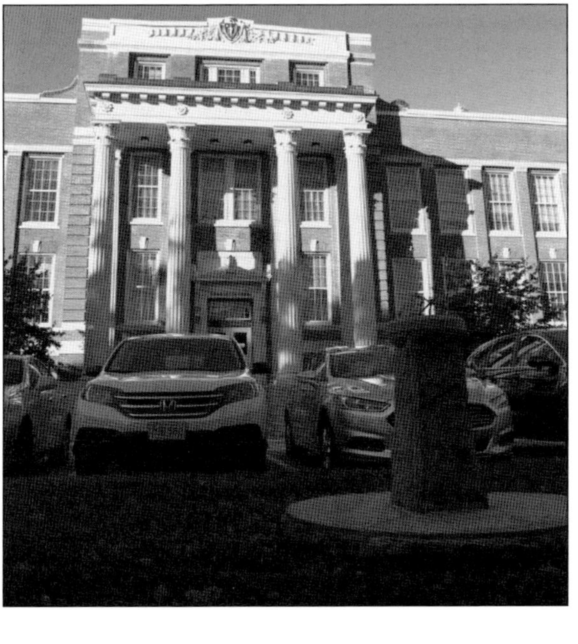

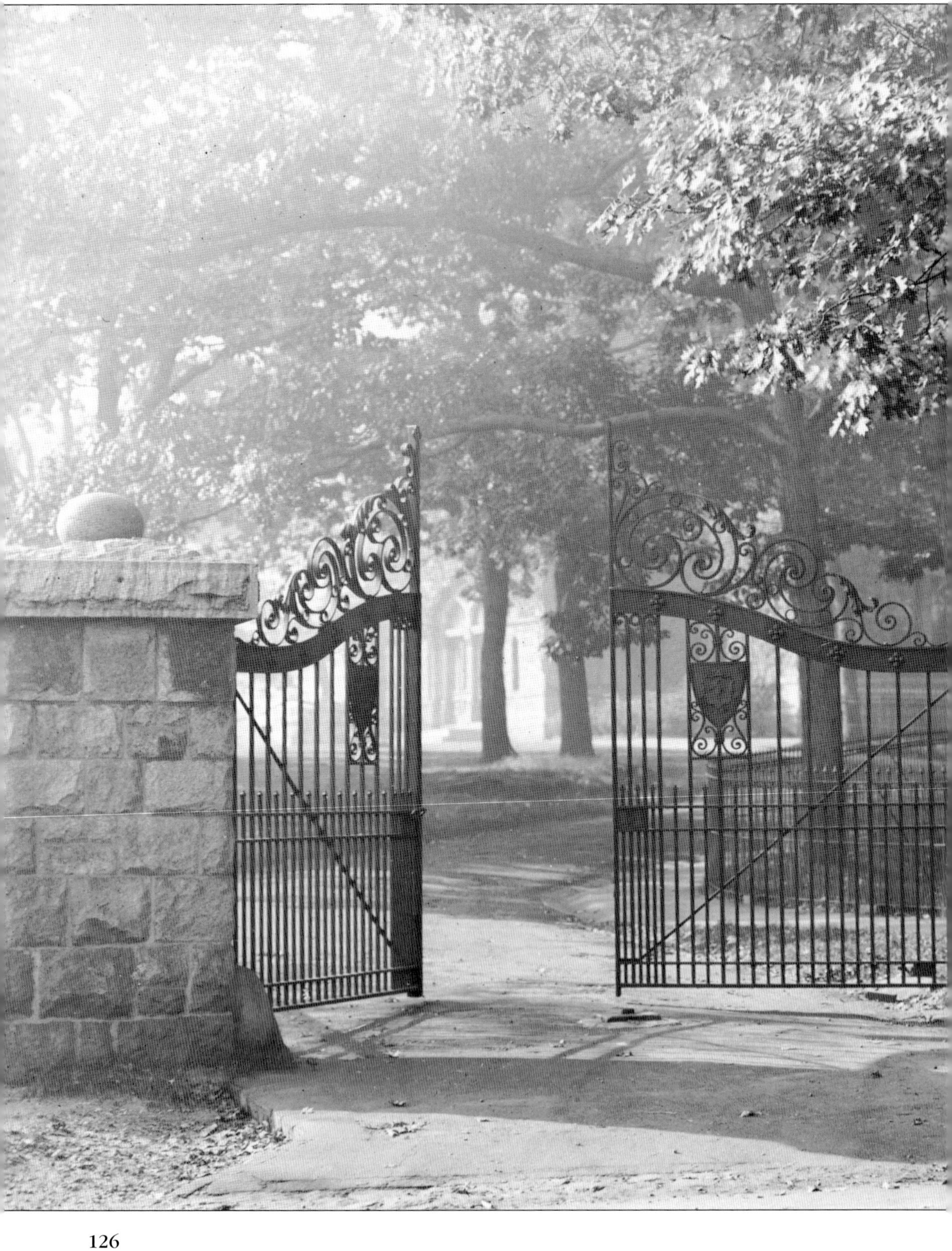

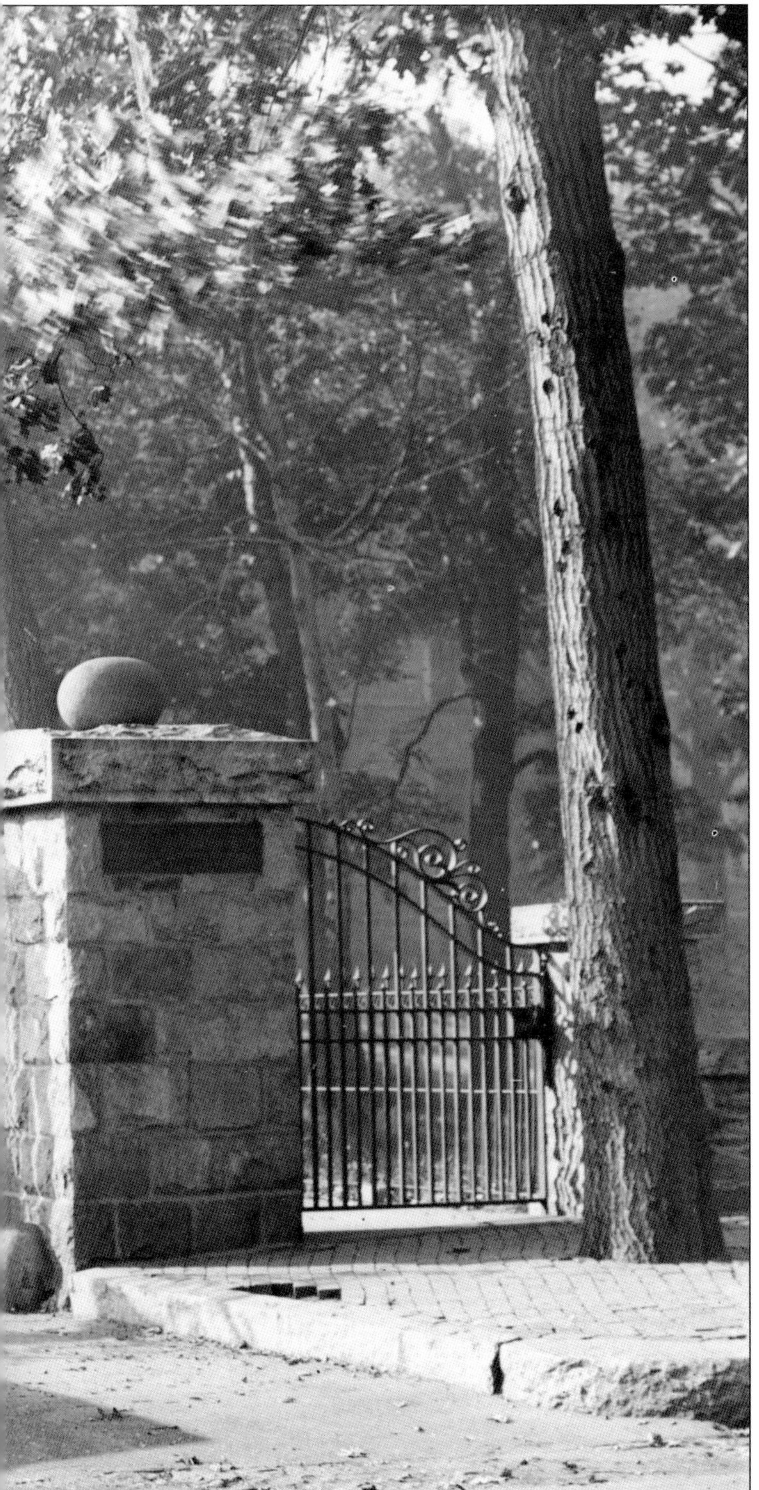

The alumni gates are located on Chandler Street in front of the Shaughnessy and Sullivan Buildings. Like the sundial, they were moved around on the current campus, but they had first stood at the original campus. The gates were a gift from the alumni association in 1914 and are shown here in their original aspect. To see them today requires a campus visit.